Constitutional Law

Fourth Edition

2015 Supplement

2015 Supplement

Constitutional Law

Fourth Edition

Erwin Chemerinsky
Dean and Distinguished Professor of Law
Raymond Pryke Professor of First Amendment Law
University of California, Irvine School of Law

To contact Customer Service, e-mail customer.service@wolterskluwer.com, call 1-800-234-1660, fax 1-800-901-9075, or mail correspondence to:

Wolters Kluwer
Attn: Order Department
PO Box 990
Frederick, MD 21705

Printed in the United States of America.

1 2 3 4 5 6 7 8 9 0

ISBN 978-1-4548-5931-4

About Wolters Kluwer Law & Business

Wolters Kluwer Law & Business is a leading global provider of intelligent information and digital solutions for legal and business professionals in key specialty areas, and respected educational resources for professors and law students. Wolters Kluwer Law & Business connects legal and business professionals as well as those in the education market with timely, specialized authoritative content and information-enabled solutions to support success through productivity, accuracy and mobility.

Serving customers worldwide, Wolters Kluwer Law & Business products include those under the Aspen Publishers, CCH, Kluwer Law International, Loislaw, ftwilliam.com and MediRegs family of products.

CCH products have been a trusted resource since 1913, and are highly regarded resources for legal, securities, antitrust and trade regulation, government contracting, banking, pension, payroll, employment and labor, and healthcare reimbursement and compliance professionals.

Aspen Publishers products provide essential information to attorneys, business professionals and law students. Written by preeminent authorities, the product line offers analytical and practical information in a range of specialty practice areas from securities law and intellectual property to mergers and acquisitions and pension/benefits. Aspen's trusted legal education resources provide professors and students with high-quality, up-to-date and effective resources for successful instruction and study in all areas of the law.

Kluwer Law International products provide the global business community with reliable international legal information in English. Legal practitioners, corporate counsel and business executives around the world rely on Kluwer Law journals, looseleafs, books, and electronic products for comprehensive information in many areas of international legal practice.

Loislaw is a comprehensive online legal research product providing legal content to law firm practitioners of various specializations. Loislaw provides attorneys with the ability to quickly and efficiently find the necessary legal information they need, when and where they need it, by facilitating access to primary law as well as state-specific law, records, forms and treatises.

ftwilliam.com offers employee benefits professionals the highest quality plan documents (retirement, welfare and non-qualified) and government forms (5500/PBGC, 1099 and IRS) software at highly competitive prices.

MediRegs products provide integrated health care compliance content and software solutions for professionals in healthcare, higher education and life sciences, including professionals in accounting, law and consulting.

Wolters Kluwer Law & Business, a division of Wolters Kluwer, is headquartered in New York. Wolters Kluwer is a market-leading global information services company focused on professionals.

Contents

Preface

The Fourth Edition of *Constitutional Law* was published in 2013 and covers Supreme Court cases through October Term 2011, which ended on June 28, 2012. This supplement presents the cases from October Terms 2012, 2013, and 2014.

As with past supplements to this casebook, this supplement is organized based on the casebook. The major cases included are:

—Chapter 1: *Clapper v. Amnesty International,* on the standing to challenge the National Security Agency's interception of communications; *Hollingsworth v. Perry*, on the standing of supporters of an initiative to appeal to defend it; and *United States v. Windsor*, on the Court's jurisdiction to decide the constitutionality of Section 3 of the Defense of Marriage Act.

—Chapter 2: *Shelby County, Alabama v. Holder,* on the constitutionality of key provisions of the Voting Rights Act of 1965 as an exercise of Congress's powers under the post–Civil War Amendments.

—Chapter 3: *NLRB v. Noel Canning,* on the President's power to make recess appointments, and *Zivotofsky v. Kerry*, declaring unconstitutional a federal statute requiring that the federal government allow parents to designate Jerusalem, Israel as the birthplace for their children born there.

—Chapter 4: *McBurney v. Young,* on whether a state law limiting access to information under a state's freedom of information law to in-state residents violates the Privileges and Immunities Clause of Article IV or the dormant Commerce Clause, and *Comptroller of the Treasury of Maryland v. Wynne,* declaring unconstitutional a state law taxing interstate commerce.

—Chapter 6: *Koontz v. St. Johns River Water Management District,* on when conditions are a taking when the government refuses to grant a permit for development, and *Horne v. Department of Agriculture,* declaring unconstitutional a federal law requiring that raisin growers must turn over a part of their crop to the federal government.

—Chapter 7: *Fisher v. University of Texas at Austin,* on the ability of colleges and universities to use race as a factor in making admissions decisions; and *United States v. Windsor,* on the constitutionality of Section 3 of the Defense of Marriage Act, and *Obergefell v. Hodges*, declaring unconstitutional state laws prohibiting same-sex marriage.

---Chapter 8: *Arizona State Legislature v. Arizona Independent Redistricting Commission*, upholding the constitutionality of states using independent commission to draw election districts.

—Chapter 9: *Reed v. Town of Gilbert*, declaring unconstitutional a municipal sign ordinance that was based on the content of the signs; *Williams-Yulee v. Florida State Bar*, which upheld a state law that prohibited candidates for elected judicial office from personally soliciting or receiving funds; *Walker v. Texas Division, Sons of Confederate Veterans*, allowing a state to refuse to put the confederate flag on its license plates on the ground that license plates are government speech; *McCutcheon v. Federal Election Commission* on whether aggregate contribution limits in election campaigns violate the First Amendment; *McCullen v. Coakley*, on the constitutionality of a Massachusetts law creating a 35-foot buffer zone around reproductive health care facilities.

—Chapter 10: *Burwell v. Hobby Lobby*, on whether the contraceptive mandate under the Affordable Care Act violates the federal Religious Freedom Restoration Act for businesses whose owners have religious objections to certain forms of contraceptives; and *Town of Greece v. Galloway*, on whether a town board violates the Establishment Clause when it invites almost exclusively Christian clergy members to deliver prayers before its meetings over a 10-year period and their prayers are often explicitly Christian in their content.

I will prepare annual supplements each summer and plan a new edition every four years. I welcome comments and suggestions from users of the supplement and casebook.

Erwin Chemerinsky
August 2015

Constitutional Law

Fourth Edition

2015 Supplement

Chapter 1

The Federal Judicial Power

B. Limits on the Federal Judicial Power

3. Justiciability Limits

b. Standing

i. Constitutional Standing Requirements (casebook, p. 45)

In October Term 2012, the Court decided three important cases concerning standing. In *Clapper v. Amnesty International USA*, the Court considered whether those who feared that their communications would be intercepted by the National Security Agency had standing to challenge its electronic eavesdropping.

CLAPPER v. AMNESTY INTERNATIONAL USA
133 S. Ct. 1138 (2013)

Justice ALITO delivered the opinion of the Court.

Section 702 of the Foreign Intelligence Surveillance Act of 1978 allows the Attorney General and the Director of National Intelligence to acquire foreign intelligence information by jointly authorizing the surveillance of individuals who are not "United States persons"[1] and are reasonably believed to be located outside the United States. Before doing so, the Attorney General and the Director of National Intelligence normally must obtain the Foreign Intelligence Surveillance Court's approval. Respondents are United States persons whose work, they allege, requires them to engage in sensitive international communications

---

1. The term "United States person" includes citizens of the United States, aliens admitted for permanent residence, and certain associations and corporations. (Footnote by the Court).

with individuals who they believe are likely targets of surveillance under § 1881a. Respondents seek a declaration that § 1881a is unconstitutional, as well as an injunction against § 1881a-authorized surveillance. The question before us is whether respondents have Article III standing to seek this prospective relief.

Respondents assert that they can establish injury in fact because there is an objectively reasonable likelihood that their communications will be acquired under § 1881a at some point in the future. But respondents' theory of *future* injury is too speculative to satisfy the well-established requirement that threatened injury must be "certainly impending." And even if respondents could demonstrate that the threatened injury is certainly impending, they still would not be able to establish that this injury is fairly traceable to § 1881a. As an alternative argument, respondents contend that they are suffering *present* injury because the risk of § 1881a-authorized surveillance already has forced them to take costly and burdensome measures to protect the confidentiality of their international communications. But respondents cannot manufacture standing by choosing to make expenditures based on hypothetical future harm that is not certainly impending. We therefore hold that respondents lack Article III standing.

I

A

In 1978, after years of debate, Congress enacted the Foreign Intelligence Surveillance Act (FISA) to authorize and regulate certain governmental electronic surveillance of communications for foreign intelligence purposes. In constructing such a framework for foreign intelligence surveillance, Congress created two specialized courts. In FISA, Congress authorized judges of the Foreign Intelligence Surveillance Court (FISC) to approve electronic surveillance for foreign intelligence purposes if there is probable cause to believe that "the target of the electronic surveillance is a foreign power or an agent of a foreign power," and that each of the specific "facilities or places at which the electronic surveillance is directed is being used, or is about to be used, by a foreign power or an agent of a foreign power." Additionally, Congress vested the Foreign Intelligence Surveillance Court of Review with jurisdiction to review any denials by the FISC of applications for electronic surveillance.

In the wake of the September 11th attacks, President George W. Bush authorized the National Security Agency (NSA) to conduct warrantless wiretapping of telephone and e-mail communications where one party to the communication was located outside the United States and a participant in "the call was reasonably believed to be a member or agent of al Qaeda or an affiliated terrorist organization." In January 2007, the FISC issued orders authorizing the Government to target international communications into or out of the United States where there was probable cause to believe that one participant to the communication was a member or agent of al Qaeda or an associated terrorist organization. These FISC orders subjected any electronic surveillance that was then occurring under the NSA's program to the approval of the FISC. After a FISC Judge subsequently narrowed the FISC's authorization of such surveillance, however, the Executive asked Congress to amend FISA so that it would provide the intelligence community with additional authority to meet the challenges of modern technology and international terrorism.

When Congress enacted the FISA Amendments Act of 2008 (FISA Amendments Act), it left much of FISA intact, but it "established a new and independent source of intelligence collection authority, beyond that granted in traditional FISA." As relevant here, § 702 of FISA, which was enacted as part of the FISA Amendments Act, supplements preexisting FISA authority by creating a new framework under which the Government may seek the FISC's authorization of certain foreign intelligence surveillance targeting the communications of non-U.S. persons located abroad. Unlike traditional FISA surveillance, § 1881a does not require the Government to demonstrate probable cause that the target of the electronic surveillance is a foreign power or agent of a foreign power. And, unlike traditional FISA, § 1881a does not require the Government to specify the nature and location of each of the particular facilities or places at which the electronic surveillance will occur.

The present case involves a constitutional challenge to § 1881a. Surveillance under § 1881a is subject to statutory conditions, judicial authorization, congressional supervision, and compliance with the Fourth Amendment. Section 1881a provides that, upon the issuance of an order from the Foreign Intelligence Surveillance Court, "the Attorney General and the Director of National Intelligence may authorize jointly, for a period of up to 1 year . . . , the targeting of persons reasonably believed to be located outside the United States to acquire foreign intelligence information." Surveillance under § 1881a may not be intentionally targeted at any person known to be in the United States or any U.S. person reasonably believed to be located abroad. § 1881a(b)(1)-(3); see also § 1801(i). Additionally, acquisitions under § 1881a must comport with the Fourth Amendment. Moreover, surveillance under § 1881a is subject to congressional oversight and several types of Executive Branch review.

B

Respondents are attorneys and human rights, labor, legal, and media organizations whose work allegedly requires them to engage in sensitive and sometimes privileged telephone and e-mail communications with colleagues, clients, sources, and other individuals located abroad. Respondents believe that some of the people with whom they exchange foreign intelligence information are likely targets of surveillance under § 1881a. Specifically, respondents claim that they communicate by telephone and e-mail with people the Government "believes or believed to be associated with terrorist organizations," "people located in geographic areas that are a special focus" of the Government's counterterrorism or diplomatic efforts, and activists who oppose governments that are supported by the United States Government.

Respondents claim that § 1881a compromises their ability to locate witnesses, cultivate sources, obtain information, and communicate confidential information to their clients. Respondents also assert that they "have ceased engaging" in certain telephone and e-mail conversations. According to respondents, the threat of surveillance will compel them to travel abroad in order to have in-person conversations. In addition, respondents declare that they have undertaken "costly and burdensome measures" to protect the confidentiality of sensitive communications.

C

On the day when the FISA Amendments Act was enacted, respondents filed this action seeking (1) a declaration that § 1881a, on its face, violates the Fourth Amendment, the First Amendment, Article III, and separation-of-powers principles and (2) a permanent injunction against the use of § 1881a. Respondents assert what they characterize as two separate theories of Article III standing. First, they claim that there is an objectively reasonable likelihood that their communications will be acquired under § 1881a at some point in the future, thus causing them injury. Second, respondents maintain that the risk of surveillance under § 1881a is so substantial that they have been forced to take costly and burdensome measures to protect the confidentiality of their international communications; in their view, the costs they have incurred constitute present injury that is fairly traceable to § 1881a.

II

Article III of the Constitution limits federal courts' jurisdiction to certain "Cases" and "Controversies." As we have explained, "[n]o principle is more fundamental to the judiciary's proper role in our system of government than the constitutional limitation of federal-court jurisdiction to actual cases or controversies." "One element of the case-or-controversy requirement" is that plaintiffs "must establish that they have standing to sue." The law of Article III standing, which is built on separation-of-powers principles, serves to prevent the judicial process from being used to usurp the powers of the political branches.

To establish Article III standing, an injury must be "concrete, particularized, and actual or imminent; fairly traceable to the challenged action; and redressable by a favorable ruling." "Although imminence is concededly a somewhat elastic concept, it cannot be stretched beyond its purpose, which is to ensure that the alleged injury is not too speculative for Article III purposes—that the injury is *certainly* impending." Thus, we have repeatedly reiterated that "threatened injury must be *certainly impending* to constitute injury in fact," and that "[a]llegations of *possible* future injury" are not sufficient.

III

A

Respondents assert that they can establish injury in fact that is fairly traceable to § 1881a because there is an objectively reasonable likelihood that their communications with their foreign contacts will be intercepted under § 1881a at some point in the future. This argument fails. As an initial matter, the Second Circuit's "objectively reasonable likelihood" standard is inconsistent with our requirement that "threatened injury must be certainly impending to constitute injury in fact." Furthermore, respondents' argument rests on their highly speculative fear that: (1) the Government will decide to target the communications of non-U.S. persons with whom they communicate; (2) in doing so, the Government will choose to invoke its authority under § 1881a rather than utilizing another method of surveillance; (3) the Article III judges who serve on the Foreign Intelligence Surveillance Court will conclude that the Government's proposed surveillance procedures satisfy § 1881a's many safeguards and are consistent with the Fourth Amendment; (4) the Government will succeed in intercepting the communications of respondents' contacts; and (5) respondents will be parties to the particular communications that the Government intercepts. Respondents' theory of standing, which relies on a highly attenuated chain of possibilities, does not satisfy the requirement that threatened injury must be certainly impending. Moreover, even if respondents could demonstrate injury in fact, the second link in the

above-described chain of contingencies — which amounts to mere specu-
lation about whether surveillance would be under § 1881a or some other
authority — shows that respondents cannot satisfy the requirement that
any injury in fact must be fairly traceable to § 1881a.

First, it is speculative whether the Government will imminently target communications to which respondents are parties. Section 1881a
expressly provides that respondents, who are U.S. persons, cannot be targeted for surveillance under § 1881a. Accordingly, it is no surprise that
respondents fail to offer any evidence that their communications have
been monitored under § 1881a, a failure that substantially undermines
their standing theory. Indeed, respondents do not even allege that the
Government has sought the FISC's approval for surveillance of their communications. Accordingly, respondents' theory necessarily rests on their
assertion that the Government will target *other individuals* — namely,
their foreign contacts.

Yet respondents have no actual knowledge of the Government's
§ 1881a targeting practices. Instead, respondents merely speculate and
make assumptions about whether their communications with their foreign contacts will be acquired under § 1881a.

Second, even if respondents could demonstrate that the targeting of
their foreign contacts is imminent, respondents can only speculate as to
whether the Government will seek to use § 1881a-authorized surveillance
(rather than other methods) to do so. The Government has numerous other
methods of conducting surveillance, none of which is challenged here.
[B]ecause respondents can only speculate as to whether any (asserted)
interception would be under § 1881a or some other authority, they cannot
satisfy the "fairly traceable" requirement.

Third, even if respondents could show that the Government will seek
the Foreign Intelligence Surveillance Court's authorization to acquire the
communications of respondents' foreign contacts under § 1881a, respondents can only speculate as to whether that court will authorize such surveillance. In the past, we have been reluctant to endorse standing theories
that require guesswork as to how independent decisionmakers will exercise their judgment.

Fourth, even if the Government were to obtain the Foreign Intelligence
Surveillance Court's approval to target respondents' foreign contacts under
§ 1881a, it is unclear whether the Government would succeed in acquir-
ing the communications of respondents' foreign contacts. And fifth, even
if the Government were to conduct surveillance of respondents' foreign
contacts, respondents can only speculate as to whether *their own communications* with their foreign contacts would be incidentally acquired.

In sum, respondents' speculative chain of possibilities does not establish that injury based on potential future surveillance is certainly impending or is fairly traceable to § 1881a.

B

Respondents' alternative argument — namely, that they can establish standing based on the measures that they have undertaken to avoid § 1881a-authorized surveillance — fares no better. Respondents assert that they are suffering ongoing injuries that are fairly traceable to § 1881a because the risk of surveillance under § 1881a requires them to take costly and burdensome measures to protect the confidentiality of their communications. Respondents claim, for instance, that the threat of surveillance sometimes compels them to avoid certain e-mail and phone conversations, to "tal[k] in generalities rather than specifics," or to travel so that they can have in-person conversations.

The Second Circuit's analysis improperly allowed respondents to establish standing by asserting that they suffer present costs and burdens that are based on a fear of surveillance, so long as that fear is not "fanciful, paranoid, or otherwise unreasonable." This improperly waters down the fundamental requirements of Article III. Respondents' contention that they have standing because they incurred certain costs as a reasonable reaction to a risk of harm is unavailing — because the harm respondents seek to avoid is not certainly impending. In other words, respondents cannot manufacture standing merely by inflicting harm on themselves based on their fears of hypothetical future harm that is not certainly impending. Any ongoing injuries that respondents are suffering are not fairly traceable to § 1881a.

If the law were otherwise, an enterprising plaintiff would be able to secure a lower standard for Article III standing simply by making an expenditure based on a nonparanoid fear. Thus, allowing respondents to bring this action based on costs they incurred in response to a speculative threat would be tantamount to accepting a repackaged version of respondents' first failed theory of standing.

Because respondents do not face a threat of certainly impending interception under § 1881a, the costs that they have incurred to avoid surveillance are simply the product of their fear of surveillance, and our decision in *Laird* [v. *Tatum*] makes it clear that such a fear is insufficient to create standing. The plaintiffs in *Laird* argued that their exercise of First Amendment rights was being "chilled by the mere existence, without more, of [the Army's] investigative and data-gathering activity."

While acknowledging that prior cases had held that constitutional violations may arise from the chilling effect of "regulations that fall short of a direct prohibition against the exercise of First Amendment rights," the Court declared that none of those cases involved a "chilling effect aris[ing] merely from the individual's knowledge that a governmental agency was engaged in certain activities or from the individual's concomitant fear that, armed with the fruits of those activities, the agency might in the future take some *other* and additional action detrimental to that individual." Because "[a]llegations of a subjective 'chill' are not an adequate substitute for a claim of specific present objective harm or a threat of specific future harm," the plaintiffs in *Laird*—and respondents here—lack standing.

IV

Respondents also suggest that they should be held to have standing because otherwise the constitutionality of § 1881a could not be challenged. It would be wrong, they maintain, to "insulate the government's surveillance activities from meaningful judicial review." Respondents' suggestion is both legally and factually incorrect. First, " '[t]he assumption that if respondents have no standing to sue, no one would have standing, is not a reason to find standing.' "

Second, our holding today by no means insulates § 1881a from judicial review. Any dissatisfaction that respondents may have about the Foreign Intelligence Surveillance Court's rulings—or the congressional delineation of that court's role—is irrelevant to our standing analysis.

Additionally, if the Government intends to use or disclose information obtained or derived from a § 1881a acquisition in judicial or administrative proceedings, it must provide advance notice of its intent, and the affected person may challenge the lawfulness of the acquisition. Thus, if the Government were to prosecute one of respondent-attorney's foreign clients using § 1881a-authorized surveillance, the Government would be required to make a disclosure. Although the foreign client might not have a viable Fourth Amendment claim, it is possible that the monitoring of the target's conversations with his or her attorney would provide grounds for a claim of standing on the part of the attorney. Such an attorney would certainly have a stronger evidentiary basis for establishing standing than do respondents in the present case. In such a situation, unlike in the present case, it would at least be clear that the Government had acquired the foreign client's communications using § 1881a-authorized surveillance.

Finally, any electronic communications service provider that the Government directs to assist in § 1881a surveillance may challenge the lawfulness of that directive before the FISC.

* * *

We hold that respondents lack Article III standing because they cannot demonstrate that the future injury they purportedly fear is certainly impending and because they cannot manufacture standing by incurring costs in anticipation of non-imminent harm.

Justice BREYER, with whom Justice GINSBURG, Justice SOTOMAYOR, and Justice KAGAN join, dissenting.

The plaintiffs' standing depends upon the likelihood that the Government, acting under the authority of 50 U.S.C. § 1881a, will harm them by intercepting at least some of their private, foreign, telephone, or e-mail conversations. In my view, this harm is not "speculative." Indeed it is as likely to take place as are most future events that commonsense inference and ordinary knowledge of human nature tell us will happen. This Court has often found the occurrence of similar future events sufficiently certain to support standing. I dissent from the Court's contrary conclusion.

I

No one here denies that the Government's interception of a private telephone or e-mail conversation amounts to an injury that is "concrete and particularized." Moreover, the plaintiffs, respondents here, seek as relief a judgment declaring unconstitutional (and enjoining enforcement of) a statutory provision authorizing those interceptions; and, such a judgment would redress the injury by preventing it. Thus, the basic question is whether the injury, *i.e.,* the interception, is "actual or imminent."

II

Since the plaintiffs fear interceptions of a kind authorized by § 1881a, it is important to understand just what kind of surveillance that section authorizes. The addition of § 1881a in 2008 changed this prior law in three important ways. First, it eliminated the requirement that the Government describe to the court each specific target and identify each facility at which its surveillance would be directed, thus permitting surveillance on a programmatic, not necessarily individualized, basis. Second, it eliminated the requirement that a target be a "foreign power or an agent of a foreign power." Third, it diminished the court's authority to insist upon, and eliminated its authority to supervise, instance-specific privacy-intrusion minimization procedures (though the Government still must use court-approved general minimization procedures). Thus, using the authority of § 1881a, the Government can obtain court approval for its surveillance of electronic communications between places within the United States and targets in foreign territories by showing the court (1) that "a significant purpose of the acquisition is to obtain foreign intelligence information," and (2) that it will use general targeting and privacy-intrusion minimization procedures of a kind that the court had previously approved.

III

Several considerations, based upon the record along with common-sense inferences, convince me that there is a very high likelihood that Government, *acting under the authority of § 1881a,* will intercept at least some of the communications just described. First, the plaintiffs have engaged, and continue to engage, in electronic communications of a kind that the 2008 amendment, but not the prior Act, authorizes the Government to intercept. These communications include discussions with family members of those detained at Guantanamo, friends and acquaintances of those persons, and investigators, experts and others with knowledge of circumstances related to terrorist activities. These persons are foreigners located outside the United States. They are not "foreign power[s]" or "agent[s] of . . . foreign power[s]." And the plaintiffs state that they exchange with these persons "foreign intelligence information," defined to include information that "relates to" "international terrorism" and "the national defense or the security of the United States."

Second, the plaintiffs have a strong *motive* to engage in, and the Government has a strong *motive* to listen to, conversations of the kind described. A lawyer representing a client normally seeks to learn the circumstances surrounding the crime (or the civil wrong) of which the client is accused. Journalists and human rights workers have strong similar motives to conduct conversations of this kind.

At the same time, the Government has a strong motive to conduct surveillance of conversations that contain material of this kind. The Government, after all, seeks to learn as much as it can reasonably learn about suspected terrorists (such as those detained at Guantanamo), as well as about their contacts and activities, along with those of friends and family members.

Third, the Government's *past behavior* shows that it has sought, and hence will in all likelihood continue to seek, information about alleged terrorists and detainees through means that include surveillance of electronic communications.

Fourth, the Government has the *capacity* to conduct electronic surveillance of the kind at issue. To some degree this capacity rests upon technology available to the Government.

Of course, to exercise this capacity the Government must have intelligence court authorization. But the Government rarely files requests that fail to meet the statutory criteria. In 2011, of the 1,676 applications to the intelligence court, two were withdrawn by the Government, and the remaining 1,674 were approved, 30 with some modification. As the intelligence court itself has stated, its review under § 1881a is "narrowly circumscribed."

The upshot is that (1) similarity of content, (2) strong motives, (3) prior behavior, and (4) capacity all point to a very strong likelihood that the Government will intercept at least some of the plaintiffs' communications, including some that the 2008 amendment, § 1881a, but not the pre–2008 Act, authorizes the Government to intercept.

Consequently, we need only assume that the Government is doing its job (to find out about, and combat, terrorism) in order to conclude that there is a high probability that the Government will intercept at least some electronic communication to which at least some of the plaintiffs are parties. The majority is wrong when it describes the harm threatened plaintiffs as "speculative."

IV

The majority more plausibly says that the plaintiffs have failed to show that the threatened harm is *"certainly impending."* But, as the majority appears to concede, *certainty* is not, and never has been, the touchstone of standing. The future is inherently uncertain. Yet federal courts frequently entertain actions for injunctions and for declaratory relief aimed at preventing future activities that are reasonably likely or highly likely, but not absolutely certain, to take place. And that degree of certainty is all that is needed to support standing here.

More important, the Court's holdings in standing cases show that standing exists here. The Court has often *found* standing where the occurrence of the relevant injury was far *less* certain than here.

How could the law be otherwise? Suppose that a federal court faced a claim by homeowners that (allegedly) unlawful dam-building practices created a high risk that their homes would be flooded. Would the court deny them standing on the ground that the risk of flood was only 60, rather than 90, percent? Would federal courts deny standing to a plaintiff in a diversity action who claims an anticipatory breach of contract where the future breach depends on probabilities? The defendant, say, has threatened to load wheat onto a ship bound for India despite a promise to send the wheat to the United States. No one can know for certain that this will happen. Perhaps the defendant will change his mind; perhaps the ship will turn and head for the United States. Yet, despite the uncertainty, the Constitution does not prohibit a federal court from hearing such a claim. Would federal courts deny standing to a plaintiff who seeks to enjoin as a nuisance the building of a nearby pond which, the plaintiff believes, will very likely, but not inevitably, overflow his land?

In sum, as the Court concedes, the word "certainly" in the phrase "certainly impending" does not refer to absolute certainty. As our case law demonstrates, what the Constitution requires is something more akin to "reasonable probability" or "high probability." The use of some such standard is all that is necessary here to ensure the actual concrete injury that the Constitution demands. [T]he standard is readily met in this case.

While I express no view on the merits of the plaintiffs' constitutional claims, I do believe that at least some of the plaintiffs have standing to make those claims. I dissent, with respect, from the majority's contrary conclusion.

The Court decided two cases concerning standing in the context of challenges to laws prohibiting marriage equality for gays and lesbians. In *Hollingsworth v. Perry*, the Court held that the supporters of an initiative, California's Proposition 8, lacked standing to appeal to defend it when the defendant government officials decided not to appeal. But in *United States v. Windsor,* the Court found that there was standing even though the United States chose not to defend Section 3 of the Defense of Marriage Act, which says that for purposes of federal law marriage must be between a man and a woman. As you read these two cases, it is worth considering whether there is a persuasive distinction that explains why standing was found in the latter, but not the former.

HOLLINGSWORTH v. PERRY
133 S. Ct. 2652 (2013)

Chief Justice ROBERTS delivered the opinion of the Court.

The public is currently engaged in an active political debate over whether same-sex couples should be allowed to marry. That question has also given rise to litigation. In this case, petitioners, who oppose same-sex marriage, ask us to decide whether the Equal Protection Clause "prohibits the State of California from defining marriage as the union of a man and a woman." Respondents, same-sex couples who wish to marry, view the issue in somewhat different terms: For them, it is whether California — having previously recognized the right of same-sex couples to marry — may reverse that decision through a referendum.

Federal courts have authority under the Constitution to answer such questions only if necessary to do so in the course of deciding an actual "case" or "controversy." As used in the Constitution, those words do not include every sort of dispute, but only those "historically viewed as capable of resolution through the judicial process." This is an essential limit on our power: It ensures that we act *as judges,* and do not engage in policymaking properly left to elected representatives.

For there to be such a case or controversy, it is not enough that the party invoking the power of the court have a keen interest in the issue. That party must also have "standing," which requires, among other things, that it have suffered a concrete and particularized injury. Because we find that petitioners do not have standing, we have no authority to decide this case on the merits, and neither did the Ninth Circuit.

I

In 2008, the California Supreme Court held that limiting the official designation of marriage to opposite-sex couples violated the equal protection clause of the California Constitution. Later that year, California voters passed the ballot initiative at the center of this dispute, known as Proposition 8. That proposition amended the California Constitution to provide that "[o]nly marriage between a man and a woman is valid or recognized in California."

Respondents, two same-sex couples who wish to marry, filed suit in federal court, challenging Proposition 8 under the Due Process and Equal Protection Clauses of the Fourteenth Amendment to the Federal Constitution. The complaint named as defendants California's Governor, attorney general, and various other state and local officials responsible for enforcing California's marriage laws. Those officials refused to defend the law, although they have continued to enforce it throughout this litigation. The District Court allowed petitioners — the official proponents of the initiative — to intervene to defend it. After a 12-day bench trial, the District Court declared Proposition 8 unconstitutional, permanently enjoining the California officials named as defendants from enforcing the law, and "directing the official defendants that all persons under their control or supervision" shall not enforce it.

Those officials elected not to appeal the District Court order. When petitioners did, the Ninth Circuit asked them to address "why this appeal should not be dismissed for lack of Article III standing." After briefing and argument, the Ninth Circuit certified a question to the California Supreme Court:

> "Whether under Article II, Section 8 of the California Constitution, or otherwise under California law, the official proponents of an initiative measure possess either a particularized interest in the initiative's validity or the authority to assert the State's interest in the initiative's validity, which would enable them to defend the constitutionality of the initiative upon its adoption or appeal a judgment invalidating the initiative, when the public officials charged with that duty refuse to do so."

The California Supreme Court agreed to decide the certified question, and answered in the affirmative. Without addressing whether the proponents have a particularized interest of their own in an initiative's validity, the court concluded that "[i]n a postelection challenge to a voter-approved initiative measure, the official proponents of the initiative are authorized under California law to appear and assert the state's interest in the initiative's validity and to appeal a judgment invalidating the measure when the public officials who ordinarily defend the measure or appeal such a judgment decline to do so."

Relying on that answer, the Ninth Circuit concluded that petitioners had standing under federal law to defend the constitutionality of Proposition 8. California, it reasoned, " 'has standing to defend the constitutionality of its [laws],' " and States have the "prerogative, as independent sovereigns, to decide for themselves who may assert their interests." On the merits, the Ninth Circuit affirmed the District Court.

II

Article III of the Constitution confines the judicial power of federal courts to deciding actual "Cases" or "Controversies." § 2. One essential aspect of this requirement is that any person invoking the power of a federal court must demonstrate standing to do so. This requires the litigant to prove that he has suffered a concrete and particularized injury that is fairly traceable to the challenged conduct, and is likely to be redressed by a favorable judicial decision. In other words, for a federal court to have authority under the Constitution to settle a dispute, the party before it must seek a remedy for a personal and tangible harm. "The presence of a disagreement, however sharp and acrimonious it may be, is insufficient by itself to meet Art. III's requirements."

Most standing cases consider whether a plaintiff has satisfied the requirement when filing suit, but Article III demands that an "actual controversy" persist throughout all stages of litigation. That means that standing "must be met by persons seeking appellate review, just as it must be met by persons appearing in courts of first instance."

Respondents initiated this case in the District Court against the California officials responsible for enforcing Proposition 8. The parties do not contest that respondents had Article III standing to do so. Each couple expressed a desire to marry and obtain "official sanction" from the State, which was unavailable to them given the declaration in Proposition 8 that "marriage" in California is solely between a man and a woman.

After the District Court declared Proposition 8 unconstitutional and enjoined the state officials named as defendants from enforcing it, however, the inquiry under Article III changed. Respondents no longer had any injury to redress — they had won — and the state officials chose not to appeal.

The only individuals who sought to appeal that order were petitioners, who had intervened in the District Court. But the District Court had not ordered them to do or refrain from doing anything. To have standing, a litigant must seek relief for an injury that affects him in a "personal and individual way." He must possess a "direct stake in the outcome" of the case. Here, however, petitioners had no "direct stake" in the outcome of their appeal. Their only interest in having the District Court order reversed was to vindicate the constitutional validity of a generally applicable California law.

We have repeatedly held that such a "generalized grievance," no matter how sincere, is insufficient to confer standing. A litigant "raising only a generally available grievance about government — claiming only harm to his and every citizen's interest in proper application of the Constitution and laws, and seeking relief that no more directly and tangibly benefits him than it does the public at large — does not state an Article III case or controversy."

Petitioners argue that the California Constitution and its election laws give them a " 'unique,' 'special,' and 'distinct' role in the initiative process — one 'involving both authority and responsibilities that differ from other supporters of the measure.' " True enough — but only when it comes to the process of enacting the law. But once Proposition 8 was approved by the voters, the measure became "a duly enacted constitutional amendment or statute." Petitioners have no role — special or otherwise — in the enforcement of Proposition 8. They therefore have no "personal stake" in defending its enforcement that is distinguishable from the general interest of every citizen of California.

Article III standing "is not to be placed in the hands of 'concerned bystanders,' who will use it simply as a 'vehicle for the vindication of value interests.'" No matter how deeply committed petitioners may be to upholding Proposition 8 or how "zealous [their] advocacy," that is not a "particularized" interest sufficient to create a case or controversy under Article III.

III

Without a judicially cognizable interest of their own, petitioners attempt to invoke that of someone else. They assert that even if *they* have no cognizable interest in appealing the District Court's judgment, the State of California does, and they may assert that interest on the State's behalf. It is, however, a "fundamental restriction on our authority" that "[i]n the ordinary course, a litigant must assert his or her own legal rights and interests, and cannot rest a claim to relief on the legal rights or interests of third parties." There are "certain, limited exceptions" to that rule. But even when we have allowed litigants to assert the interests of others, the litigants themselves still "must have suffered an injury in fact, thus giving [them] a sufficiently concrete interest in the outcome of the issue in dispute." For the reasons we have explained, petitioners have likewise not suffered an injury in fact, and therefore would ordinarily have no standing to assert the State's interests.

Petitioners contend that this case is different, because the California Supreme Court has determined that they are "authorized under California law to appear and assert the state's interest" in the validity of Proposition 8.

Petitioners argue that, by virtue of the California Supreme Court's decision, they *are* authorized to act "'as agents of the people' of California." But that Court never described petitioners as "agents of the people," or of anyone else. Nor did the Ninth Circuit. The Ninth Circuit asked—and the California Supreme Court answered—only whether petitioners had "the authority to assert the State's interest in the initiative's validity." All that the California Supreme Court decision stands for is that, so far as California is concerned, petitioners may argue in defense of Proposition 8. This "does not mean that the proponents become de facto public officials"; the authority they enjoy is "simply the authority to participate as parties in a court action and to assert legal arguments in defense of the state's interest in the validity of the initiative measure." That interest is by definition a generalized one, and it is precisely because proponents assert such an interest that they lack standing under our precedents.

Neither the California Supreme Court nor the Ninth Circuit ever described the proponents as agents of the State, and they plainly do not qualify as such.

We have never before upheld the standing of a private party to defend the constitutionality of a state statute when state officials have chosen not to. We decline to do so for the first time here.

Because petitioners have not satisfied their burden to demonstrate standing to appeal the judgment of the District Court, the Ninth Circuit was without jurisdiction to consider the appeal. The judgment of the Ninth Circuit is vacated, and the case is remanded with instructions to dismiss the appeal for lack of jurisdiction.

Justice KENNEDY, with whom Justice THOMAS, Justice ALITO, and Justice SOTOMAYOR join, dissenting.

The Court's opinion is correct to state, and the Supreme Court of California was careful to acknowledge, that a proponent's standing to defend an initiative in federal court is a question of federal law. Proper resolution of the justiciability question requires, in this case, a threshold determination of state law. The state-law question is how California defines and elaborates the status and authority of an initiative's proponents who seek to intervene in court to defend the initiative after its adoption by the electorate. Those state-law issues have been addressed in a meticulous and unanimous opinion by the Supreme Court of California.

Under California law, a proponent has the authority to appear in court and assert the State's interest in defending an enacted initiative when the public officials charged with that duty refuse to do so. The State deems such an appearance essential to the integrity of its initiative process. Yet the Court today concludes that this state-defined status and this state-conferred right fall short of meeting federal requirements because the proponents cannot point to a formal delegation of authority that tracks the requirements of the Restatement of Agency. But the State Supreme Court's definition of proponents' powers is binding on this Court. And that definition is fully sufficient to establish the standing and adversity that are requisites for justiciability under Article III of the United States Constitution.

In my view Article III does not require California, when deciding who may appear in court to defend an initiative on its behalf, to comply with the Restatement of Agency or with this Court's view of how a State should make its laws or structure its government. The Court's reasoning does not take into account the fundamental principles or the practical dynamics of the initiative system in California, which uses this mechanism to control and to bypass public officials—the same officials who would not defend the initiative, an injury the Court now leaves unremedied. The Court's decision also has implications for the 26 other States that use an initiative or popular referendum system and which, like California, may choose to have initiative proponents stand in for the State when public officials decline to defend an initiative in litigation. In my submission, the Article III requirement for a justiciable case or controversy does not prevent proponents from having their day in court.

There is much irony in the Court's approach to justiciability in this case. A prime purpose of justiciability is to ensure vigorous advocacy, yet the Court insists upon litigation conducted by state officials whose preference is to lose the case. The doctrine is meant to ensure that courts are responsible and constrained in their power, but the Court's opinion today means that a single district court can make a decision with far-reaching effects that cannot be reviewed. And rather than honor the principle that justiciability exists to allow disputes of public policy to be resolved by the political process rather than the courts, here the Court refuses to allow a State's authorized representatives to defend the outcome of a democratic election.

The Court's opinion disrespects and disparages both the political process in California and the well-stated opinion of the California Supreme Court in this case. The California Supreme Court, not this Court, expresses concern for vigorous representation; the California Supreme Court, not this Court, recognizes the necessity to avoid conflicts of interest; the California Supreme Court, not this Court, comprehends the real interest at stake in this litigation and identifies the most proper party to defend that interest. The California Supreme Court's opinion reflects a better understanding of the dynamics and principles of Article III than does this Court's opinion.

Of course, the Court must be cautious before entering a realm of controversy where the legal community and society at large are still formulating ideas and approaches to a most difficult subject. But it is shortsighted to misconstrue principles of justiciability to avoid that subject. As the California Supreme Court recognized, "the question before us involves a fundamental procedural issue that may arise with respect to *any* initiative measure, without regard to its subject matter." If a federal court must rule on a constitutional point that either confirms or rejects the will of the people expressed in an initiative, that is when it is most necessary, not least necessary, to insist on rules that ensure the most committed and vigorous adversary arguments to inform the rulings of the courts.

In the end, what the Court fails to grasp or accept is the basic premise of the initiative process. And it is this. The essence of democracy is that the right to make law rests in the people and flows to the government, not the other way around. Freedom resides first in the people without need of a grant from government. The California initiative process embodies these principles and has done so for over a century. "Through the structure of its government, and the character of those who exercise government authority, a State defines itself as sovereign." In California and the 26 other States that permit initiatives and popular referendums, the people have exercised their own inherent sovereign right to govern themselves. The Court today frustrates that choice by nullifying, for failure to comply with the Restatement of Agency, a State Supreme Court decision holding that state law authorizes an enacted initiative's proponents to defend the law if and when the State's usual legal advocates decline to do so. The Court's opinion fails to abide by precedent and misapplies basic principles of justiciability. Those errors necessitate this respectful dissent.

UNITED STATES v. WINDSOR[2]
133 S. Ct. 2675 (2013)

Justice KENNEDY delivered the opinion of the Court

Two women then resident in New York were married in a lawful ceremony in Ontario, Canada, in 2007. Edith Windsor and Thea Spyer returned to their home in New York City. When Spyer died in 2009, she left her entire estate to Windsor. Windsor sought to claim the estate tax exemption for surviving spouses. She was barred from doing so, however, by a federal law, the Defense of Marriage Act, which excludes a same-sex partner from the definition of "spouse" as that term is used in federal statutes. Windsor paid the taxes but filed suit to challenge the constitutionality of this provision. The United States District Court and the Court of Appeals ruled that this portion of the statute is unconstitutional and ordered the United States to pay Windsor a refund. This Court granted certiorari and now affirms the judgment in Windsor's favor.

I

In 1996, as some States were beginning to consider the concept of same-sex marriage, and before any State had acted to permit it, Congress enacted the Defense of Marriage Act (DOMA). DOMA contains two

---

2. Presented here is just the discussion of the standing issue. The discussion of the merits of the constitutionality of Section 3 of the Defense of Marriage Act is presented below in Chapter 7. [Footnote by casebook author.]

operative sections: Section 2, which has not been challenged here, allows States to refuse to recognize same-sex marriages performed under the laws of other States.

Section 3 is at issue here. It amends the Dictionary Act in Title 1, § 7, of the United States Code to provide a federal definition of "marriage" and "spouse." Section 3 of DOMA provides as follows:

> "In determining the meaning of any Act of Congress, or of any ruling, regulation, or interpretation of the various administrative bureaus and agencies of the United States, the word 'marriage' means only a legal union between one man and one woman as husband and wife, and the word 'spouse' refers only to a person of the opposite sex who is a husband or a wife."

The definitional provision does not by its terms forbid States from enacting laws permitting same-sex marriages or civil unions or providing state benefits to residents in that status. The enactment's comprehensive definition of marriage for purposes of all federal statutes and other regulations or directives covered by its terms, however, does control over 1,000 federal laws in which marital or spousal status is addressed as a matter of federal law.

Edith Windsor and Thea Spyer met in New York City in 1963 and began a long-term relationship. Windsor and Spyer registered as domestic partners when New York City gave that right to same-sex couples in 1993. Concerned about Spyer's health, the couple made the 2007 trip to Canada for their marriage, but they continued to reside in New York City. The State of New York deems their Ontario marriage to be a valid one.

Spyer died in February 2009, and left her entire estate to Windsor. Because DOMA denies federal recognition to same-sex spouses, Windsor did not qualify for the marital exemption from the federal estate tax, which excludes from taxation "any interest in property which passes or has passed from the decedent to his surviving spouse." Windsor paid $363,053 in estate taxes and sought a refund. The Internal Revenue Service denied the refund, concluding that, under DOMA, Windsor was not a "surviving spouse." Windsor commenced this refund suit in the United States District Court for the Southern District of New York. She contended that DOMA violates the guarantee of equal protection, as applied to the Federal Government through the Fifth Amendment.

While the tax refund suit was pending, the Attorney General of the United States notified the Speaker of the House of Representatives, pursuant to 28 U.S.C. § 530D, that the Department of Justice would no longer defend the constitutionality of DOMA's § 3. Noting that "the Department has previously defended DOMA against . . . challenges involving legally married same-sex couples," the Attorney General informed Congress that "the President has concluded that given a number of factors, including a documented history of discrimination, classifications based on sexual orientation should be subject to a heightened standard of scrutiny." The Department of Justice has submitted many § 530D letters over the years refusing to defend laws it deems unconstitutional, when, for instance, a federal court has rejected the Government's defense of a statute and has issued a judgment against it. This case is unusual, however, because the § 530D letter was not preceded by an adverse judgment. The letter instead reflected the Executive's own conclusion, relying on a definition still being debated and considered in the courts, that heightened equal protection scrutiny should apply to laws that classify on the basis of sexual orientation.

Although "the President . . . instructed the Department not to defend the statute in *Windsor,*" he also decided "that Section 3 will continue to be enforced by the Executive Branch" and that the United States had an "interest in providing Congress a full and fair opportunity to participate in the litigation of those cases." The stated rationale for this dual-track procedure (determination of unconstitutionality coupled with ongoing enforcement) was to "recogniz[e] the judiciary as the final arbiter of the constitutional claims raised."

In response to the notice from the Attorney General, the Bipartisan Legal Advisory Group (BLAG) of the House of Representatives voted to intervene in the litigation to defend the constitutionality of § 3 of DOMA.

On the merits of the tax refund suit, the District Court ruled against the United States. It held that § 3 of DOMA is unconstitutional and ordered the Treasury to refund the tax with interest.

II

It is appropriate to begin by addressing whether either the Government or BLAG, or both of them, were entitled to appeal to the Court of Appeals and later to seek certiorari and appear as parties here.

There is no dispute that when this case was in the District Court it presented a concrete disagreement between opposing parties, a dispute suitable for judicial resolution. "[A] taxpayer has standing to challenge the collection of a specific tax assessment as unconstitutional; being forced to pay such a tax causes a real and immediate economic injury to the individual taxpayer." Windsor suffered a redressable injury when she was required to pay estate taxes from which, in her view, she was exempt but for the alleged invalidity of § 3 of DOMA.

The decision of the Executive not to defend the constitutionality of § 3 in court while continuing to deny refunds and to assess deficiencies does introduce a complication. Even though the Executive's current position was announced before the District Court entered its judgment, the Government's agreement with Windsor's position would not have deprived the District Court of jurisdiction to entertain and resolve the refund suit; for her injury (failure to obtain a refund allegedly required by law) was concrete, persisting, and unredressed. The Government's position — agreeing with Windsor's legal contention but refusing to give it effect — meant that there was a justiciable controversy between the parties, despite what the claimant would find to be an inconsistency in that stance. Windsor, the Government, BLAG, and the *amicus* appear to agree upon that point. The disagreement is over the standing of the parties, or aspiring parties, to take an appeal in the Court of Appeals and to appear as parties in further proceedings in this Court.

The *amicus'* position is that, given the Government's concession that § 3 is unconstitutional, once the District Court ordered the refund the case should have ended; and the *amicus* argues the Court of Appeals should have dismissed the appeal. The *amicus* submits that once the President agreed with Windsor's legal position and the District Court issued its judgment, the parties were no longer adverse. From this standpoint the United States was a prevailing party below, just as Windsor was. Accordingly, the *amicus* reasons, it is inappropriate for this Court to grant certiorari and proceed to rule on the merits; for the United States seeks no redress from the judgment entered against it.

This position, however, elides the distinction between two principles: the jurisdictional requirements of Article III and the prudential limits on its exercise. The latter are "essentially matters of judicial self-governance." The Court has kept these two strands separate: "Article III standing, which enforces the Constitution's case-or-controversy requirement, and prudential standing, which embodies 'judicially self-imposed limits on the exercise of federal jurisdiction.'"

In this case the United States retains a stake sufficient to support Article III jurisdiction on appeal and in proceedings before this Court. The judgment in question orders the United States to pay Windsor the refund she seeks. An order directing the Treasury to pay money is "a real and immediate economic injury," indeed as real and immediate as an order directing an individual to pay a tax. That the Executive may welcome this order to pay the refund if it is accompanied by the constitutional ruling it wants does not eliminate the injury to the national Treasury if payment is made, or to the taxpayer if it is not. The judgment orders the United

States to pay money that it would not disburse but for the court's order. The Government of the United States has a valid legal argument that it is injured even if the Executive disagrees with § 3 of DOMA, which results in Windsor's liability for the tax. Windsor's ongoing claim for funds that the United States refuses to pay thus establishes a controversy sufficient for Article III jurisdiction. It would be a different case if the Executive had taken the further step of paying Windsor the refund to which she was entitled under the District Court's ruling.

While these principles suffice to show that this case presents a justiciable controversy under Article III, the prudential problems inherent in the Executive's unusual position require some further discussion. The Executive's agreement with Windsor's legal argument raises the risk that instead of a " 'real, earnest and vital controversy,' " the Court faces a "friendly, non-adversary, proceeding . . . [in which] 'a party beaten in the legislature [seeks to] transfer to the courts an inquiry as to the constitutionality of the legislative act.' " Even when Article III permits the exercise of federal jurisdiction, prudential considerations demand that the Court insist upon "that concrete adverseness which sharpens the presentation of issues upon which the court so largely depends for illumination of difficult constitutional questions."

In the case now before the Court the attorneys for BLAG present a substantial argument for the constitutionality of § 3 of DOMA. BLAG's sharp adversarial presentation of the issues satisfies the prudential concerns that otherwise might counsel against hearing an appeal from a decision with which the principal parties agree. Were this Court to hold that prudential rules require it to dismiss the case, and, in consequence, that the Court of Appeals erred in failing to dismiss it as well, extensive litigation would ensue. The district courts in 94 districts throughout the Nation would be without precedential guidance not only in tax refund suits but also in cases involving the whole of DOMA's sweep involving over 1,000 federal statutes and a myriad of federal regulations. Rights and privileges of hundreds of thousands of persons would be adversely affected, pending a case in which all prudential concerns about justiciability are absent. That numerical prediction may not be certain, but it is certain that the cost in judicial resources and expense of litigation for all persons adversely affected would be immense. True, the very extent of DOMA's mandate means that at some point a case likely would arise without the prudential concerns raised here; but the costs, uncertainties, and alleged harm and injuries likely would continue for a time measured in years before the issue is resolved. In these unusual and urgent circumstances, the very term "prudential" counsels that it is a proper exercise of the Court's responsibility to take jurisdiction.

For these reasons, the prudential and Article III requirements are met here; and, as a consequence, the Court need not decide whether BLAG would have standing to challenge the District Court's ruling and its affirmance in the Court of Appeals on BLAG's own authority.

The Court's jurisdictional holding, it must be underscored, does not mean the arguments for dismissing this dispute on prudential grounds lack substance. Yet the difficulty the Executive faces should be acknowledged. When the Executive makes a principled determination that a statute is unconstitutional, it faces a difficult choice. Still, there is no suggestion here that it is appropriate for the Executive as a matter of course to challenge statutes in the judicial forum rather than making the case to Congress for their amendment or repeal. The integrity of the political process would be at risk if difficult constitutional issues were simply referred to the Court as a routine exercise. But this case is not routine. And the capable defense of the law by BLAG ensures that these prudential issues do not cloud the merits question, which is one of immediate importance to the Federal Government and to hundreds of thousands of persons. These circumstances support the Court's decision to proceed to the merits.

[The Court then declared Section 3 unconstitutional.]

Justice SCALIA, with whom Justice THOMAS joins, and with whom THE CHIEF JUSTICE joins as to Part I, dissenting.

This case is about power in several respects. It is about the power of our people to govern themselves, and the power of this Court to pronounce the law. Today's opinion aggrandizes the latter, with the predictable consequence of diminishing the former. We have no power to decide this case. And even if we did, we have no power under the Constitution to invalidate this democratically adopted legislation. The Court's errors on both points spring forth from the same diseased root: an exalted conception of the role of this institution in America.

I

The Court is eager—*hungry*—to tell everyone its view of the legal question at the heart of this case. Standing in the way is an obstacle, a technicality of little interest to anyone but the people of We the People, who created it as a barrier against judges' intrusion into their lives. They gave judges, in Article III, only the "judicial Power," a power to decide not abstract questions but real, concrete "Cases" and "Controversies." Yet the plaintiff and the Government agree entirely on what should happen in this lawsuit. They agree that the court below got it right; and they agreed in the court below that the court below that one got it right as well. What, then, are we *doing* here?

The answer lies at the heart of the jurisdictional portion of today's opinion, where a single sentence lays bare the majority's vision of our role. The Court says that we have the power to decide this case because if we did not, then our "primary role in determining the constitutionality of a law" (at least one that "has inflicted real injury on a plaintiff") would "become only secondary to the President's." But wait, the reader wonders—Windsor won below, and so *cured* her injury, and the President was glad to see it. True, says the majority, but judicial review must march on regardless, lest we "undermine the clear dictate of the separation-of-powers principle that when an Act of Congress is alleged to conflict with the Constitution, it is emphatically the province and duty of the judicial department to say what the law is."

That is jaw-dropping. It is an assertion of judicial supremacy over the people's Representatives in Congress and the Executive. It envisions a Supreme Court standing (or rather enthroned) at the apex of government, empowered to decide all constitutional questions, always and everywhere "primary" in its role.

This image of the Court would have been unrecognizable to those who wrote and ratified our national charter. They knew well the dangers of "primary" power, and so created branches of government that would be "perfectly coordinate by the terms of their common commission," none of which branches could "pretend to an exclusive or superior right of settling the boundaries between their respective powers." The Federalist, No. 49, p. 314 (C. Rossiter ed. 1961) (J. Madison). The people did this to protect themselves. They did it to guard their right to self-rule against the black-robed supremacy that today's majority finds so attractive. So it was that Madison could confidently state, with no fear of contradiction, that there was nothing of "greater intrinsic value" or "stamped with the authority of more enlightened patrons of liberty" than a government of separate and coordinate powers.

For this reason we are quite forbidden to say what the law is whenever (as today's opinion asserts) " 'an Act of Congress is alleged to conflict with the Constitution.' " We can do so only when that allegation will determine the outcome of a lawsuit, and is contradicted by the other party. The "judicial Power" is not, as the majority believes, the power " 'to say what the law is,' " giving the Supreme Court the "primary role in determining the constitutionality of laws." The majority must have in mind one of the foreign constitutions that pronounces such primacy for its constitutional court and allows that primacy to be exercised in contexts other than a lawsuit. The judicial power as Americans have understood it (and their English ancestors before them) is the power to adjudicate, with conclusive effect, disputed government claims (civil or criminal) against private persons, and disputed claims by private persons against the government or other private persons. Sometimes (though not always) the parties before the court disagree not with regard to the facts of their case (or not *only* with regard to the facts) but with regard to the applicable law — in which event (and *only* in which event) it becomes the " 'province and duty of the judicial department to say what the law is.' "

Our authority begins and ends with the need to adjudge the rights of an injured party who stands before us seeking redress. That is completely absent here. Windsor's injury was cured by the judgment in her favor. And while, in ordinary circumstances, the United States is injured by a directive to pay a tax refund, this suit is far from ordinary. Whatever injury the United States has suffered will surely not be redressed by the action that it, as a litigant, asks us to take. The final sentence of the Solicitor General's brief on the merits reads: "For the foregoing reasons, the judgment of the court of appeals *should be affirmed.*" That will not cure the Government's injury, but carve it into stone. One could spend many fruitless afternoons ransacking our library for any other petitioner's brief seeking an affirmance of the judgment against it. What the petitioner United States asks us to do in the case before us is exactly what the respondent Windsor asks us to do: not to provide relief from the judgment below but to say that that judgment was correct. And the same was true in the Court of Appeals: Neither party sought to undo the judgment for Windsor, and so that court should have dismissed the appeal (just as we should dismiss) for lack of jurisdiction. Since both parties agreed with the judgment of the District Court for the Southern District of New York, the suit should have ended there.

I find it wryly amusing that the majority seeks to dismiss the requirement of party-adverseness as nothing more than a "prudential" aspect of the sole Article III requirement of standing. (Relegating a jurisdictional requirement to "prudential" status is a wondrous device, enabling courts to ignore the requirement whenever they believe it "prudent" — which is to say, a good idea.)

It may be argued that if what we say is true some Presidential determinations that statutes are unconstitutional will not be subject to our review. That is as it should be, when both the President and the plaintiff agree that the statute is unconstitutional. Where the Executive is enforcing an unconstitutional law, suit will of course lie; but if, in that suit, the Executive admits the unconstitutionality of the law, the litigation should end in an order or a consent decree enjoining enforcement. This suit saw the light of day only because the President enforced the Act (and thus gave Windsor standing to sue) even though he believed it unconstitutional. He could have equally chosen (more appropriately, some would say) neither to enforce nor to defend the statute he believed to be unconstitutional—in which event Windsor would not have been injured, the District Court could not have refereed this friendly scrimmage, and the Executive's determination of unconstitutionality would have escaped this Court's desire to blurt out its view of the law. The matter would have been left, as so many matters ought to be left, to a tug of war between the President and the Congress, which has innumerable means (up to and including impeachment) of compelling the President to enforce the laws it has written. Or the President could have evaded presentation of the constitutional issue to this Court simply by declining to appeal the District Court and Court of Appeals dispositions he agreed with. Be sure of this much: If a President wants to insulate his judgment of unconstitutionality from our review, he can. What the views urged in this dissent produce is not insulation from judicial review but insulation from Executive contrivance.

The majority brandishes the famous sentence from *Marbury v. Madison* (1803) that "[i]t is emphatically the province and duty of the judicial department to say what the law is." But that sentence neither says nor implies that it is *always* the province and duty of the Court to say what the law is—much less that its responsibility in that regard is a "primary" one. The very next sentence of Chief Justice Marshall's opinion makes the crucial qualification that today's majority ignores: "*Those who apply the rule to particular cases,* must of necessity expound and interpret that rule." Only when a "particular case" is before us—that is, a controversy that it is our business to resolve under Article III—do we have the province and duty to pronounce the law. . . . There is, in the words of *Marbury,* no "necessity [to] expound and interpret" the law in this case; just a desire to place this Court at the center of the Nation's life.

[Justice Scalia then dissented as to the Court's decision to declare Section 3 of DOMA unconstitutional.]

Justice ALITO, with whom Justice THOMAS joins as to Parts II and III, dissenting.

I turn first to the question of standing. In my view, the United States clearly is not a proper petitioner in this case. The United States does not ask us to overturn the judgment of the court below or to alter that judgment in any way. Quite to the contrary, the United States argues emphatically in favor of the correctness of that judgment. We have never before reviewed a decision at the sole behest of a party that took such a position, and to do so would be to render an advisory opinion, in violation of Article III's dictates.

Whether the Bipartisan Legal Advisory Group of the House of Representatives (BLAG) has standing to petition is a much more difficult question.

A party invoking the Court's authority has a sufficient stake to permit it to appeal when it has "'suffered an injury in fact' that is caused by 'the conduct complained of' and that 'will be redressed by a favorable decision.'" In the present case, the House of Representatives, which has authorized BLAG to represent its interests in this matter, suffered just such an injury.

I appreciate the argument that the Constitution confers on the President alone the authority to defend federal law in litigation, but in my view, "Congress is the proper party to defend the validity of a statute" when the Executive refuses to do so on constitutional grounds. Accordingly, in the narrow category of cases in which a court strikes down an Act of Congress and the Executive declines to defend the Act, Congress both has standing to defend the undefended statute and is a proper party to do so.

[Justice Alito then went on to dissent as to the Court's declaring Section 3 of DOMA unconstitutional.]

Finally, it is worth noting that in *Arizona State Legislature v. Arizona Independent Redistricting Commission* (2015), the Supreme Court ruled that members of the Arizona State Legislature had standing to sue to challenge the existence of an independent commission to draw election districts. The Court then upheld the constitutionality of the redistricting commission. This case is presented below in Chapter 8.

c. *Ripeness* (casebook, p. 85)

In *Susan B. Anthony List v. Driehaus,* 134 S. Ct. 2334 (2014), the Court considered whether a group had standing to challenge an Ohio statute that prohibits "false statements" during the course of a political campaign. The Court explained that the "question in this case is whether their preenforcement challenge to that law is justiciable—and in particular, whether they have alleged a sufficiently imminent injury for the purposes of Article III." A member of Congress initiated proceedings against the Susan B. Anthony List in the Ohio Elections Commission, which found probable cause to proceed, but the matter was dismissed after the Congressman lost his reelection bid. The Susan B. Anthony Fund had brought a challenge to the Ohio law in federal court, and the issue before the Supreme Court was whether its challenge to the Ohio law could continue after the Ohio Elections Commission proceedings were dismissed.

The Supreme Court ruled unanimously in favor of the Susan B. Anthony fund and found that the matter was justiciable. Justice Thomas, writing for a unanimous Court, noted that "[w]hen an individual is subject to such a threat, an actual arrest, prosecution, or other enforcement action is not a prerequisite to challenging the law." The Court found that the matter was ripe for review because the plaintiffs "have alleged a credible threat of enforcement." The Court stressed that "the threat of future enforcement of the false statement statute is substantial."

Chapter 2

The Federal Legislative Power

E. *Congress's Powers Under the Post–Civil War Amendments*

2. What Is the Scope of Congress's Powers? (casebook, p. 255)

The Voting Rights Act of 1965 is a landmark federal civil rights statute. Section 2 prohibits state and local governments from having election practices or systems that discriminate against minority voters. It authorizes litigation to enforce this prohibition. Congress believed that this was insufficient; voting rights litigation is expensive and time consuming. Also, Congress was aware that Southern states in particular kept changing their election systems to disenfranchise minority voters. Section 5 provides that jurisdictions with a history of race discrimination in voting must get "preclearance" before changing their election systems from the Attorney General or a three-judge federal district court. Section 4(B) defines those jurisdictions that must get preclearance.

In 2006, Congress extended these latter provisions for another 25 years. In Shelby County, *Alabama v. Holder*, the Court declared Section 4(B) unconstitutional on the grounds that it intruded on state sovereignty and did so based on data that was decades old.

SHELBY COUNTY, ALABAMA v. HOLDER
133 S. Ct. 2612 (2013)

Chief Justice ROBERTS delivered the opinion of the Court.

The Voting Rights Act of 1965 employed extraordinary measures to address an extraordinary problem. Section 5 of the Act required States to obtain federal permission before enacting any law related to voting—a drastic departure from basic principles of federalism. And § 4 of the Act applied that requirement only to some States—an equally dramatic departure from the principle that all States enjoy equal sovereignty. This was strong medicine, but Congress determined it was needed to address entrenched racial discrimination in voting, "an insidious and pervasive evil which had been perpetuated in certain parts of our country through unremitting and ingenious defiance of the Constitution." As we explained in upholding the law, "exceptional conditions can justify legislative measures not otherwise appropriate." Reflecting the unprecedented nature of these measures, they were scheduled to expire after five years.

Nearly 50 years later, they are still in effect; indeed, they have been made more stringent, and are now scheduled to last until 2031. There is no denying, however, that the conditions that originally justified these measures no longer characterize voting in the covered jurisdictions. By 2009, "the racial gap in voter registration and turnout [was] lower in the States originally covered by § 5 than it [was] nationwide." Since that time, Census Bureau data indicate that African-American voter turnout has come to exceed white voter turnout in five of the six States originally covered by § 5, with a gap in the sixth State of less than one half of one percent.

At the same time, voting discrimination still exists; no one doubts that. The question is whether the Act's extraordinary measures, including its disparate treatment of the States, continue to satisfy constitutional requirements. As we put it a short time ago, "the Act imposes current burdens and must be justified by current needs."

I

A

The Fifteenth Amendment was ratified in 1870, in the wake of the Civil War. It provides that "[t]he right of citizens of the United States to vote shall not be denied or abridged by the United States or by any State on account of race, color, or previous condition of servitude," and it gives Congress the "power to enforce this article by appropriate legislation."

"The first century of congressional enforcement of the Amendment, however, can only be regarded as a failure." Inspired to action by the civil rights movement, Congress responded in 1965 with the Voting Rights Act. Section 2 was enacted to forbid, in all 50 States, any "standard, practice, or procedure . . . imposed or applied . . . to deny or abridge the right of any citizen of the United States to vote on account of race or color." The current version forbids any "standard, practice, or procedure" that "results in a denial or abridgement of the right of any citizen of the United States to vote on account of race or color." Both the Federal Government and individuals have sued to enforce § 2, and injunctive relief is available in appropriate cases to block voting laws from going into effect. Section 2 is permanent, applies nationwide, and is not at issue in this case.

Other sections targeted only some parts of the country. At the time of the Act's passage, these "covered" jurisdictions were those States or political subdivisions that had maintained a test or device as a prerequisite to voting as of November 1, 1964, and had less than 50 percent voter registration or turnout in the 1964 Presidential election. § 4(b). Such tests or devices included literacy and knowledge tests, good moral character requirements, the need for vouchers from registered voters, and the like. A covered jurisdiction could "bail out" of coverage if it had not used a test or device in the preceding five years "for the purpose or with the effect of denying or abridging the right to vote on account of race or color." In 1965, the covered States included Alabama, Georgia, Louisiana, Mississippi, South Carolina, and Virginia. The additional covered subdivisions included 39 counties in North Carolina and one in Arizona.

In those jurisdictions, § 4 of the Act banned all such tests or devices. Section 5 provided that no change in voting procedures could take effect until it was approved by federal authorities in Washington, D.C. — either the Attorney General or a court of three judges. A jurisdiction could obtain such "preclearance" only by proving that the change had neither "the purpose [nor] the effect of denying or abridging the right to vote on account of race or color."

Sections 4 and 5 were intended to be temporary; they were set to expire after five years. In 1970, Congress reauthorized the Act for another five years, and extended the coverage formula in § 4(b) to jurisdictions that had a voting test and less than 50 percent voter registration or turnout as of 1968. That swept in several counties in California, New Hampshire, and New York. Congress also extended the ban in § 4(a) on tests and devices nationwide.

In 1975, Congress reauthorized the Act for seven more years, and extended its coverage to jurisdictions that had a voting test and less than 50 percent voter registration or turnout as of 1972. As a result of these amendments, the States of Alaska, Arizona, and Texas, as well as several counties in California, Florida, Michigan, New York, North Carolina, and South Dakota, became covered jurisdictions.

In 1982, Congress reauthorized the Act for 25 years, but did not alter its coverage formula. Congress did, however, amend the bailout provisions, allowing political subdivisions of covered jurisdictions to bail out. Among other prerequisites for bailout, jurisdictions and their subdivisions must not have used a forbidden test or device, failed to receive preclearance, or lost a § 2 suit, in the ten years prior to seeking bailout.

We upheld each of these reauthorizations against constitutional challenge. See *Georgia v. United States* (1973); *City of Rome v. United States* (1980); *Lopez v. Monterey County* (1999).

In 2006, Congress again reauthorized the Voting Rights Act for 25 years, again without change to its coverage formula. Fannie Lou Hamer, Rosa Parks, and Coretta Scott King Voting Rights Act Reauthorization and Amendments Act. Congress also amended § 5 to prohibit more conduct than before. Section 5 now forbids voting changes with "any discriminatory purpose" as well as voting changes that diminish the ability of citizens, on account of race, color, or language minority status, "to elect their preferred candidates of choice."

B

Shelby County is located in Alabama, a covered jurisdiction. It has not sought bailout, as the Attorney General has recently objected to voting changes proposed from within the county. Instead, in 2010, the county sued the Attorney General in Federal District Court in Washington, D.C., seeking a declaratory judgment that sections 4(b) and 5 of the Voting Rights Act are facially unconstitutional, as well as a permanent injunction against their enforcement.

II

In *Northwest Austin Municipal District v. Holder* (2009), we stated that "the Act imposes current burdens and must be justified by current needs." And we concluded that "a departure from the fundamental principle of equal sovereignty requires a showing that a statute's disparate geographic coverage is sufficiently related to the problem that it targets." These basic principles guide our review of the question before us.

A

The Constitution and laws of the United States are "the supreme Law of the Land." U.S. Const., Art. VI, cl. 2. State legislation may not contravene federal law. The Federal Government does not, however, have a general right to review and veto state enactments before they go into effect. A proposal to grant such authority to "negative" state laws was considered at the Constitutional Convention, but rejected in favor of allowing state laws to take effect, subject to later challenge under the Supremacy Clause.

Outside the strictures of the Supremacy Clause, States retain broad autonomy in structuring their governments and pursuing legislative objectives. Indeed, the Constitution provides that all powers not specifically granted to the Federal Government are reserved to the States or citizens. Amdt. 10. This "allocation of powers in our federal system preserves the integrity, dignity, and residual sovereignty of the States." But the federal balance "is not just an end in itself: Rather, federalism secures to citizens the liberties that derive from the diffusion of sovereign power."

More specifically, " 'the Framers of the Constitution intended the States to keep for themselves, as provided in the Tenth Amendment, the power to regulate elections."

Not only do States retain sovereignty under the Constitution, there is also a "fundamental principle of equal sovereignty" among the States. Over a hundred years ago, this Court explained that our Nation "was and is a union of States, equal in power, dignity and authority." *Coyle v. Smith* (1911). Indeed, "the constitutional equality of the States is essential to the harmonious operation of the scheme upon which the Republic was organized."

The Voting Rights Act sharply departs from these basic principles. It suspends "all changes to state election law — however innocuous — until they have been precleared by federal authorities in Washington, D.C." States must beseech the Federal Government for permission to implement laws that they would otherwise have the right to enact and execute on their own, subject of course to any injunction in a § 2 action. The Attorney General has 60 days to object to a preclearance request, longer if he requests more information. If a State seeks preclearance from a three-judge court, the process can take years.

And despite the tradition of equal sovereignty, the Act applies to only nine States (and several additional counties). While one State waits months or years and expends funds to implement a validly enacted law, its neighbor can typically put the same law into effect immediately, through the normal legislative process. Even if a noncovered jurisdiction is sued, there are important differences between those proceedings and preclearance proceedings; the preclearance proceeding "not only switches the burden of proof to the supplicant jurisdiction, but also applies substantive standards quite different from those governing the rest of the nation."

All this explains why, when we first upheld the Act in 1966, we described it as "stringent" and "potent." We recognized that it "may have been an uncommon exercise of congressional power," but concluded that "legislative measures not otherwise appropriate" could be justified by "exceptional conditions." We have since noted that the Act "authorizes federal intrusion into sensitive areas of state and local policymaking," and represents an "extraordinary departure from the traditional course of relations between the States and the Federal Government." As we reiterated in Northwest Austin, the Act constitutes "extraordinary legislation otherwise unfamiliar to our federal system."

B

In 1966, we found these departures from the basic features of our system of government justified. The "blight of racial discrimination in voting" had "infected the electoral process in parts of our country for nearly a century." Several States had enacted a variety of requirements and tests "specifically designed to prevent" African-Americans from voting. Case-by-case litigation had proved inadequate to prevent such racial discrimination in voting, in part because States "merely switched to discriminatory devices not covered by the federal decrees," "enacted difficult new tests," or simply "defied and evaded court orders." Shortly before enactment of the Voting Rights Act, only 19.4 percent of African-Americans of voting age were registered to vote in Alabama, only 31.8 percent in Louisiana, and only 6.4 percent in Mississippi. Those figures were roughly 50 percentage points or more below the figures for whites.

In short, we concluded that "[u]nder the compulsion of these unique circumstances, Congress responded in a permissibly decisive manner." We also noted then and have emphasized since that this extraordinary legislation was intended to be temporary, set to expire after five years.

At the time, the coverage formula—the means of linking the exercise of the unprecedented authority with the problem that warranted it—made sense. We found that "Congress chose to limit its attention to the geographic areas where immediate action seemed necessary."

C

Nearly 50 years later, things have changed dramatically. Shelby County contends that the preclearance requirement, even without regard to its disparate coverage, is now unconstitutional. Its arguments have a good deal of force. In the covered jurisdictions, "[v]oter turnout and registration rates now approach parity. Blatantly discriminatory evasions of federal decrees are rare. And minority candidates hold office at unprecedented levels." The tests and devices that blocked access to the ballot have been forbidden nationwide for over 40 years.

Those conclusions are not ours alone. Congress said the same when it reauthorized the Act in 2006, writing that "[s]ignificant progress has been made in eliminating first generation barriers experienced by minority voters, including increased numbers of registered minority voters, minority voter turnout, and minority representation in Congress, State legislatures, and local elected offices."

Yet the Act has not eased the restrictions in § 5 or narrowed the scope of the coverage formula in § 4(b) along the way. Those extraordinary and unprecedented features were reauthorized—as if nothing had changed. In fact, the Act's unusual remedies have grown even stronger. When Congress reauthorized the Act in 2006, it did so for another 25 years on top of the previous 40—a far cry from the initial five-year period. Congress also expanded the prohibitions in § 5.

Respondents do not deny that there have been improvements on the ground, but argue that much of this can be attributed to the deterrent effect of § 5, which dissuades covered jurisdictions from engaging in discrimination that they would resume should § 5 be struck down. Under this theory, however, § 5 would be effectively immune from scrutiny; no matter how "clean" the record of covered jurisdictions, the argument could always be made that it was deterrence that accounted for the good behavior.

The provisions of § 5 apply only to those jurisdictions singled out by § 4. We now consider whether that coverage formula is constitutional in light of current conditions.

III

A

When upholding the constitutionality of the coverage formula in 1966, we concluded that it was "rational in both practice and theory." The formula looked to cause (discriminatory tests) and effect (low voter registration and turnout), and tailored the remedy (preclearance) to those jurisdictions exhibiting both.

By 2009, however, we concluded that the "coverage formula raise[d] serious constitutional questions." As we explained, a statute's "current burdens" must be justified by "current needs," and any "disparate geographic coverage" must be "sufficiently related to the problem that it targets." The coverage formula met that test in 1965, but no longer does so.

Coverage today is based on decades-old data and eradicated practices. The formula captures States by reference to literacy tests and low voter registration and turnout in the 1960s and early 1970s. But such tests have been banned nationwide for over 40 years. And voter registration and turnout numbers in the covered States have risen dramatically in the years since.

In 1965, the States could be divided into two groups: those with a recent history of voting tests and low voter registration and turnout, and those without those characteristics. Congress based its coverage formula on that distinction. Today the Nation is no longer divided along those lines, yet the Voting Rights Act continues to treat it as if it were.

B

But history did not end in 1965. By the time the Act was reauthorized in 2006, there had been 40 more years of it. In assessing the "current need[ ]" for a preclearance system that treats States differently from one another today, that history cannot be ignored. During that time, largely because of the Voting Rights Act, voting tests were abolished, disparities in voter registration and turnout due to race were erased, and African-Americans attained political office in record numbers. And yet the coverage formula that Congress reauthorized in 2006 ignores these developments, keeping the focus on decades-old data relevant to decades-old problems, rather than current data reflecting current needs.

The Fifteenth Amendment commands that the right to vote shall not be denied or abridged on account of race or color, and it gives Congress the power to enforce that command. The Amendment is not designed to punish for the past; its purpose is to ensure a better future. To serve that purpose, Congress—if it is to divide the States—must identify those jurisdictions to be singled out on a basis that makes sense in light of current conditions. It cannot rely simply on the past. We made that clear in Northwest Austin, and we make it clear again today.

C

In defending the coverage formula, the Government, the intervenors, and the dissent also rely heavily on data from the record that they claim justify disparate coverage. Congress compiled thousands of pages of evidence before reauthorizing the Voting Rights Act.

But a more fundamental problem remains: Congress did not use the record it compiled to shape a coverage formula grounded in current conditions. It instead reenacted a formula based on 40-year-old facts having no logical relation to the present day. Contrary to the dissent's contention, we are not ignoring the record; we are simply recognizing that it played no role in shaping the statutory formula before us today.

There is no valid reason to insulate the coverage formula from review merely because it was previously enacted 40 years ago. If Congress had started from scratch in 2006, it plainly could not have enacted the present coverage formula. It would have been irrational for Congress to distinguish between States in such a fundamental way based on 40-year-old data, when today's statistics tell an entirely different story. And it would have been irrational to base coverage on the use of voting tests 40 years ago, when such tests have been illegal since that time. But that is exactly what Congress has done.

Our decision in no way affects the permanent, nationwide ban on racial discrimination in voting found in § 2. We issue no holding on § 5 itself, only on the coverage formula. Congress may draft another formula based on current conditions. Such a formula is an initial prerequisite to a determination that exceptional conditions still exist justifying such an "extraordinary departure from the traditional course of relations between the States and the Federal Government." Our country has changed, and while any racial discrimination in voting is too much, Congress must ensure that the legislation it passes to remedy that problem speaks to current conditions.

Justice THOMAS, concurring.

I join the Court's opinion in full but write separately to explain that I would find § 5 of the Voting Rights Act unconstitutional as well. The Court's opinion sets forth the reasons. . . .

Today, our Nation has changed. "[T]he conditions that originally justified [§ 5] no longer characterize voting in the covered jurisdictions."

While the Court claims to "issue no holding on § 5 itself," its own opinion compellingly demonstrates that Congress has failed to justify " current burdens " with a record demonstrating " current needs. " By leaving the inevitable conclusion unstated, the Court needlessly prolongs the demise of that provision. For the reasons stated in the Court's opinion, I would find § 5 unconstitutional.

Justice GINSBURG, with whom Justice BREYER, Justice SOTOMAYOR, and Justice KAGAN join, dissenting.

In the Court's view, the very success of § 5 of the Voting Rights Act demands its dormancy. Congress was of another mind. Recognizing that large progress has been made, Congress determined, based on a voluminous record, that the scourge of discrimination was not yet extirpated. The question this case presents is who decides whether, as currently operative, § 5 remains justifiable, this Court, or a Congress charged with the obligation to enforce the post-Civil War Amendments "by appropriate legislation." With overwhelming support in both Houses, Congress concluded that, for two prime reasons, § 5 should continue in force, unabated. First, continuance would facilitate completion of the impressive gains thus far made; and second, continuance would guard against backsliding. Those assessments were well within Congress' province to make and should elicit this Court's unstinting approbation.

I

"[V]oting discrimination still exists; no one doubts that." But the Court today terminates the remedy that proved to be best suited to block that discrimination. The Voting Rights Act of 1965 (VRA) has worked to combat voting discrimination where other remedies had been tried and failed. Particularly effective is the VRA's requirement of federal preclearance for all changes to voting laws in the regions of the country with the most aggravated records of rank discrimination against minority voting rights.

Congress learned from experience that laws targeting particular electoral practices or enabling case-by-case litigation were inadequate to the task. Answering that need, the Voting Rights Act became one of the most consequential, efficacious, and amply justified exercises of federal legislative power in our Nation's history. Requiring federal preclearance of changes in voting laws in the covered jurisdictions — those States and localities where opposition to the Constitution's commands were most virulent — the VRA provided a fit solution for minority voters as well as for States.

After a century's failure to fulfill the promise of the Fourteenth and Fifteenth Amendments, passage of the VRA finally led to signal improvement on this front.

Although the VRA wrought dramatic changes in the realization of minority voting rights, the Act, to date, surely has not eliminated all vestiges of discrimination against the exercise of the franchise by minority citizens. Jurisdictions covered by the preclearance requirement continued to submit, in large numbers, proposed changes to voting laws that the Attorney General declined to approve, auguring that barriers to minority voting would quickly resurface were the preclearance remedy eliminated. Congress also found that as "registration and voting of minority citizens increas[ed], other measures may be resorted to which would dilute increasing minority voting strength." Efforts to reduce the impact of minority votes, in contrast to direct attempts to block access to the ballot, are aptly described as "second-generation barriers" to minority voting.

Second-generation barriers come in various forms. One of the blockages is racial gerrymandering, the redrawing of legislative districts in an "effort to segregate the races for purposes of voting." Another is adoption of a system of at-large voting in lieu of district-by-district voting in a city with a sizable black minority. By switching to at-large voting, the overall majority could control the election of each city council member, effectively eliminating the potency of the minority's votes. A similar effect could be achieved if the city engaged in discriminatory annexation by incorporating majority-white areas into city limits, thereby decreasing the effect of VRA-occasioned increases in black voting. Whatever the device employed, this Court has long recognized that vote dilution, when adopted with a discriminatory purpose, cuts down the right to vote as certainly as denial of access to the ballot.

In response to evidence of these substituted barriers, Congress reauthorized the VRA for five years in 1970, for seven years in 1975, and for 25 years in 1982. Each time, this Court upheld the reauthorization as a valid exercise of congressional power. As the 1982 reauthorization approached its 2007 expiration date, Congress again considered whether the VRA's preclearance mechanism remained an appropriate response to the problem of voting discrimination in covered jurisdictions.

Congress did not take this task lightly. Quite the opposite. The 109th Congress that took responsibility for the renewal started early and conscientiously. In October 2005, the House began extensive hearings, which continued into November and resumed in March 2006. In April 2006, the Senate followed suit, with hearings of its own. In May 2006, the bills that became the VRA's reauthorization were introduced in both Houses. The House held further hearings of considerable length, as did the Senate, which continued to hold hearings into June and July. In mid-July, the House considered and rejected four amendments, then passed the reauthorization by a vote of 390 yeas to 33 nays. The bill was read and debated in the Senate, where it passed by a vote of 98 to 0. President Bush signed it a week later.

In the long course of the legislative process, Congress "amassed a sizable record." The House and Senate Judiciary Committees held 21 hearings, heard from scores of witnesses, received a number of investigative reports and other written documentation of continuing discrimination in covered jurisdictions. In all, the legislative record Congress compiled filled more than 15,000 pages. The compilation presents countless "examples of flagrant racial discrimination" since the last reauthorization; Congress also brought to light systematic evidence that "intentional racial discrimination in voting remains so serious and widespread in covered jurisdictions that section 5 preclearance is still needed."

II

In answering this question, the Court does not write on a clean slate. It is well established that Congress' judgment regarding exercise of its power to enforce the Fourteenth and Fifteenth Amendments warrants substantial deference. The VRA addresses the combination of race discrimination and the right to vote, which is "preservative of all rights." When confronting the most constitutionally invidious form of discrimination, and the most fundamental right in our democratic system, Congress' power to act is at its height.

The basis for this deference is firmly rooted in both constitutional text and precedent. The Fifteenth Amendment, which targets precisely and only racial discrimination in voting rights, states that, in this domain, "Congress shall have power to enforce this article by appropriate legislation." In choosing this language, the Amendment's framers invoked Chief Justice Marshall's formulation of the scope of Congress' powers under the Necessary and Proper Clause: "Let the end be legitimate, let it be within the scope of the constitution, and all means which are appropriate, which are plainly adapted to that end, which are not prohibited, but consist with the letter and spirit of the constitution, are constitutional." *McCulloch v. Maryland* (1819).

It cannot tenably be maintained that the VRA, an Act of Congress adopted to shield the right to vote from racial discrimination, is inconsistent with the letter or spirit of the Fifteenth Amendment, or any provision of the Constitution read in light of the Civil War Amendments. Nowhere in today's opinion, or in Northwest Austin, is there clear recognition of the transformative effect the Fifteenth Amendment aimed to achieve.

Until today, in considering the constitutionality of the VRA, the Court has accorded Congress the full measure of respect its judgments in this domain should garner.

For three reasons, legislation reauthorizing an existing statute is especially likely to satisfy the minimal requirements of the rational-basis test. First, when reauthorization is at issue, Congress has already assembled a legislative record justifying the initial legislation. Congress is entitled to consider that preexisting record as well as the record before it at the time of the vote on reauthorization. This is especially true where, as here, the Court has repeatedly affirmed the statute's constitutionality and Congress has adhered to the very model the Court has upheld.

Second, the very fact that reauthorization is necessary arises because Congress has built a temporal limitation into the Act. It has pledged to review, after a span of years (first 15, then 25) and in light of contemporary evidence, the continued need for the VRA.

Third, a reviewing court should expect the record supporting reauthorization to be less stark than the record originally made. Demand for a record of violations equivalent to the one earlier made would expose Congress to a catch-22. If the statute was working, there would be less evidence of discrimination, so opponents might argue that Congress should not be allowed to renew the statute. In contrast, if the statute was not working, there would be plenty of evidence of discrimination, but scant reason to renew a failed regulatory regime.

This is not to suggest that congressional power in this area is limitless. It is this Court's responsibility to ensure that Congress has used appropriate means. The question meet for judicial review is whether the chosen means are "adapted to carry out the objects the amendments have in view." The Court's role, then, is not to substitute its judgment for that of Congress, but to determine whether the legislative record sufficed to show that "Congress could rationally have determined that [its chosen] provisions were appropriate methods."

In summary, the Constitution vests broad power in Congress to protect the right to vote, and in particular to combat racial discrimination in voting. This Court has repeatedly reaffirmed Congress' prerogative to use any rational means in exercise of its power in this area. And both precedent and logic dictate that the rational-means test should be easier to satisfy, and the burden on the statute's challenger should be higher, when what is at issue is the reauthorization of a remedy that the Court has previously affirmed, and that Congress found, from contemporary evidence, to be working to advance the legislature's legitimate objective.

III

The 2006 reauthorization of the Voting Rights Act fully satisfies the standard stated in McCulloch: Congress may choose any means "appropriate" and "plainly adapted to" a legitimate constitutional end. As we shall see, it is implausible to suggest otherwise.

I begin with the evidence on which Congress based its decision to continue the preclearance remedy. The surest way to evaluate whether that remedy remains in order is to see if preclearance is still effectively preventing discriminatory changes to voting laws. On that score, the record before Congress was huge. In fact, Congress found there were more DOJ objections between 1982 and 2004 (626) than there were between 1965 and the 1982 reauthorization (490). All told, between 1982 and 2006, DOJ objections blocked over 700 voting changes based on a determination that the changes were discriminatory.

Congress also received evidence that litigation under § 2 of the VRA was an inadequate substitute for preclearance in the covered jurisdictions. Litigation occurs only after the fact, when the illegal voting scheme has already been put in place and individuals have been elected pursuant to it, thereby gaining the advantages of incumbency.

Conditions in the South have impressively improved since passage of the Voting Rights Act. Congress noted this improvement and found that the VRA was the driving force behind it. But Congress also found that voting discrimination had evolved into subtler second-generation barriers, and that eliminating preclearance would risk loss of the gains that had been made.

There is no question, moreover, that the covered jurisdictions have a unique history of problems with racial discrimination in voting. Consideration of this long history, still in living memory, was altogether appropriate. The Court criticizes Congress for failing to recognize that "history did not end in 1965." But the Court ignores that "what's past is prologue." W. Shakespeare, The Tempest, act 2, sc. 1. And "[t]hose who cannot remember the past are condemned to repeat it." 1 G. Santayana, The Life of Reason 284 (1905). Congress was especially mindful of the need to reinforce the gains already made and to prevent backsliding.

Of particular importance, even after 40 years and thousands of discriminatory changes blocked by preclearance, conditions in the covered jurisdictions demonstrated that the formula was still justified by "current needs."

IV

Congress approached the 2006 reauthorization of the VRA with great care and seriousness. The same cannot be said of the Court's opinion today. The Court makes no genuine attempt to engage with the massive legislative record that Congress assembled. Instead, it relies on increases in voter registration and turnout as if that were the whole story. Without even identifying a standard of review, the Court dismissively brushes off arguments based on "data from the record," and declines to enter the "debat[e about] what [the] record shows." One would expect more from an opinion striking at the heart of the Nation's signal piece of civil-rights legislation.

I note the most disturbing lapses. First, by what right, given its usual restraint, does the Court even address Shelby County's facial challenge to the VRA? Second, the Court veers away from controlling precedent regarding the "equal sovereignty" doctrine without even acknowledging that it is doing so. Third, hardly showing the respect ordinarily paid when Congress acts to implement the Civil War Amendments, and as just stressed, the Court does not even deign to grapple with the legislative record.

Beyond question, the VRA is no ordinary legislation. It is extraordinary because Congress embarked on a mission long delayed and of extraordinary importance: to realize the purpose and promise of the Fifteenth Amendment. For a half century, a concerted effort has been made to end racial discrimination in voting. Thanks to the Voting Rights Act, progress once the subject of a dream has been achieved and continues to be made.

The record supporting the 2006 reauthorization of the VRA is also extraordinary. It was described by the Chairman of the House Judiciary Committee as "one of the most extensive considerations of any piece of legislation that the United States Congress has dealt with in the 27 [and a half] years" he had served in the House. After exhaustive evidence-gathering and deliberative process, Congress reauthorized the VRA, including the coverage provision, with overwhelming bipartisan support. It was the judgment of Congress that "40 years has not been a sufficient amount of time to eliminate the vestiges of discrimination following nearly 100 years of disregard for the dictates of the 15th amendment and to ensure that the right of all citizens to vote is protected as guaranteed by the Constitution." That determination of the body empowered to enforce the Civil War Amendments "by appropriate legislation" merits this Court's utmost respect. In my judgment, the Court errs egregiously by overriding Congress' decision.

Chapter 3

The Federal Executive Power

C. The Constitutional Problem of the Administrative State

3. Checking Administrative Power

The Appointment Power (casebook, p. 353)

In *NLRB v. Noel Canning,* the Supreme Court considered an aspect of the presidential appointment power, and a constitutional provision, that it had never before examined: the President's power to make recess appointments.

NLRB v. NOEL CANNING
134 S. Ct. 2550 (2014)

Justice BREYER delivered the opinion of the Court.

Ordinarily the President must obtain "the Advice and Consent of the Senate" before appointing an "Office[r] of the United States." But the Recess Appointments Clause creates an exception. It gives the President alone the power "to fill up all Vacancies that may happen during the Recess of the Senate, by granting Commissions which shall expire at the End of their next Session." Art. II, §2, cl. 3. We here consider three questions about the application of this Clause.

The first concerns the scope of the words "recess of the Senate." Does that phrase refer only to an inter-session recess (*i.e.,* a break between formal sessions of Congress), or does it also include an intra-session recess, such as a summer recess in the midst of a session? We conclude that the Clause applies to both kinds of recess.

The second question concerns the scope of the words "vacancies that may happen." Does that phrase refer only to vacancies that first come into existence during a recess, or does it also include vacancies that arise prior to a recess but continue to exist during the recess? We conclude that the Clause applies to both kinds of vacancy.

The third question concerns calculation of the length of a "recess." The President made the appointments here at issue on January 4, 2012. At that time the Senate was in recess pursuant to a December 17, 2011, resolution providing for a series of brief recesses punctuated by "*pro forma* session[s]," with "no business . . . transacted," every Tuesday and Friday through January 20, 2012. In calculating the length of a recess are we to ignore the *pro forma* sessions, thereby treating the series of brief recesses as a single, month-long recess? We conclude that we cannot ignore these *pro forma* sessions.

Our answer to the third question means that, when the appointments before us took place, the Senate was in the midst of a 3-day recess. Three days is too short a time to bring a recess within the scope of the Clause. Thus we conclude that the President lacked the power to make the recess appointments here at issue.

I

The case before us arises out of a labor dispute. The National Labor Relations Board (NLRB) found that a Pepsi-Cola distributor, Noel Canning, had unlawfully refused to reduce to writing and execute a collective-bargaining agreement with a labor union. The Board ordered the distributor to execute the agreement and to make employees whole for any losses.

The Pepsi-Cola distributor subsequently asked the Court of Appeals for the District of Columbia Circuit to set the Board's order aside. It claimed that three of the five Board members had been invalidly appointed, leaving the Board without the three lawfully appointed members necessary for it to act.

The three members in question were Sharon Block, Richard Griffin, and Terence Flynn. In 2011 the President had nominated each of them to the Board. As of January 2012, Flynn's nomination had been pending in the Senate awaiting confirmation for approximately a year. The nominations of each of the other two had been pending for a few weeks. On January 4, 2012, the President, invoking the Recess Appointments Clause, appointed all three to the Board.

II

Before turning to the specific questions presented, we shall mention two background considerations that we find relevant to all three. First, *the Recess Appointments Clause sets forth a subsidiary, not a primary, method for appointing officers of the United States.* The immediately preceding Clause — Article II, Section 2, Clause 2 — provides the primary method of appointment. It says that the President "shall nominate, *and by and with the Advice and Consent of the Senate,* shall appoint Ambassadors, other public Ministers and Consuls, Judges of the supreme Court, and all other Officers of the United States." The Federalist Papers make clear that the Founders intended this method of appointment, requiring Senate approval, to be the norm (at least for principal officers).

Thus the Recess Appointments Clause reflects the tension between, on the one hand, the President's continuous need for "the assistance of subordinates," and, on the other, the Senate's practice, particularly during the Republic's early years, of meeting for a single brief session each year.

Second, *in interpreting the Clause, we put significant weight upon historical practice.* For one thing, the interpretive questions before us concern the allocation of power between two elected branches of Government. We recognize, of course, that the separation of powers can serve to safeguard individual liberty, and that it is the "duty of the judicial department" — in a separation-of-powers case as in any other — "to say what the law is." But it is equally true that the longstanding "practice of the government," can inform our determination of "what the law is." That principle is neither new nor controversial.

There is a great deal of history to consider here. Presidents have made recess appointments since the beginning of the Republic. Their frequency suggests that the Senate and President have recognized that recess appointments can be both necessary and appropriate in certain circumstances. We have not previously interpreted the Clause, and, when doing so for the first time in more than 200 years, we must hesitate to upset the compromises and working arrangements that the elected branches of Government themselves have reached.

III

The first question concerns the scope of the phrase "*the recess* of the Senate." The Constitution provides for congressional elections every two years. And the 2-year life of each elected Congress typically consists of two formal 1-year sessions, each separated from the next by an "intersession recess." The Senate or the House of Representatives announces an inter-session recess by approving a resolution stating that it will "adjourn *sine die,*" *i.e.,* without specifying a date to return (in which case Congress will reconvene when the next formal session is scheduled to begin).

The Senate and the House also take breaks in the midst of a session. The Senate or the House announces any such "intra-session recess" by adopting a resolution stating that it will "adjourn" to a fixed date, a few days or weeks or even months later. All agree that the phrase "the recess of the Senate" covers inter-session recesses. The question is whether it includes intra-session recesses as well.

In our view, the phrase "the recess" includes an intra-session recess of substantial length. Its words taken literally can refer to both types of recess. Founding-era dictionaries define the word "recess," much as we do today, simply as "a period of cessation from usual work."

We recognize that the word "the" in "*the* recess" might suggest that the phrase refers to the single break separating formal sessions of Congress. That is because the word "the" frequently (but not always) indicates "a particular thing." But the word can also refer "to a term used generically or universally." Reading "the" generically in this way, there is no linguistic problem applying the Clause's phrase to both kinds of recess. And, in fact, the phrase "the recess" was used to refer to intra-session recesses at the time of the founding.

The constitutional text is thus ambiguous. And we believe the Clause's purpose demands the broader interpretation. The Clause gives the President authority to make appointments during "the recess of the Senate" so that the President can ensure the continued functioning of the Federal Government when the Senate is away. The Senate is equally away during both an inter-session and an intra-session recess, and its capacity to participate in the appointments process has nothing to do with the words it uses to signal its departure.

History also offers strong support for the broad interpretation. We concede that pre-Civil War history is not helpful. But it shows only that Congress generally took long breaks between sessions, while taking no significant intra-session breaks at all (five times it took a break of a week or so at Christmas). Obviously, if there are no significant intra-session recesses, there will be no intra-session recess appointments. In 1867 and 1868, Congress for the first time took substantial, nonholiday intra-session breaks, and President Andrew Johnson made dozens of recess appointments.

In all, between the founding and the Great Depression, Congress took substantial intra-session breaks (other than holiday breaks) in four years: 1867, 1868, 1921, and 1929. And in each of those years the President made intra-session recess appointments.

Since 1929, and particularly since the end of World War II, Congress has shortened its inter-session breaks as it has taken longer and more frequent intra-session breaks; Presidents have correspondingly made more intra-session recess appointments. Indeed, if we include military appointments, Presidents have made thousands of intra-session recess appointments.

The upshot is that restricting the Clause to inter-session recesses would frustrate its purpose. It would make the President's recess-appointment power dependent on a formalistic distinction of Senate procedure. Moreover, the President has consistently and frequently interpreted the word "recess" to apply to intra-session recesses, and has acted on that interpretation. The Senate as a body has done nothing to deny the validity of this practice for at least three-quarters of a century. And three-quarters of a century of settled practice is long enough to entitle a practice to "great weight in a proper interpretation" of the constitutional provision.

The greater interpretive problem is determining how long a recess must be in order to fall within the Clause. Is a break of a week, or a day, or an hour too short to count as a "recess"? The Clause itself does not say. And Justice Scalia claims that this silence itself shows that the Framers intended the Clause to apply only to an inter-session recess.

We disagree. For one thing, the most likely reason the Framers did not place a textual floor underneath the word "recess" is that they did not foresee the *need* for one. They might have expected that the Senate would meet for a single session lasting at most half a year. Moreover, the lack of a textual floor raises a problem that plagues *both* interpretations — Justice Scalia's and ours. Today a brief inter-session recess is just as possible as a brief intra-session recess.

Even the Solicitor General, arguing for a broader interpretation, acknowledges that there is a lower limit applicable to both kinds of recess. He argues that the lower limit should be three days by analogy to the Adjournments Clause of the Constitution.

We agree with the Solicitor General that a 3-day recess would be too short. A Senate recess that is so short that it does not require the consent of the House is not long enough to trigger the President's recess-appointment power.

That is not to say that the President may make recess appointments during any recess that is "more than three days." The Recess Appointments Clause seeks to permit the Executive Branch to function smoothly when Congress is unavailable. And though Congress has taken short breaks for almost 200 years, and there have been many thousands of recess appointments in that time, we have not found a single example of a recess appointment made during an intra-session recess that was shorter than 10 days.

In sum, we conclude that the phrase "the recess" applies to both intra-session and inter-session recesses. If a Senate recess is so short that it does not require the consent of the House, it is too short to trigger the Recess Appointments Clause. And a recess lasting less than 10 days is presumptively too short as well.

IV

The second question concerns the scope of the phrase "vacancies *that may happen* during the recess of the Senate." All agree that the phrase applies to vacancies that initially occur during a recess. But does it also apply to vacancies that initially occur before a recess and continue to exist during the recess? In our view the phrase applies to both kinds of vacancy.

We believe that the Clause's language, read literally, permits, though it does not naturally favor, our broader interpretation. We concede that the most natural meaning of "happens" as applied to a "vacancy" (at least to a modern ear) is that the vacancy "happens" when it initially occurs. But that is not the only possible way to use the word.

In any event, the linguistic question here is not whether the phrase can be, but whether it must be, read more narrowly. The question is whether the Clause is ambiguous. And the broader reading, we believe, is at least a permissible reading of a " 'doubtful' " phrase. We consequently go on to consider the Clause's purpose and historical practice.

The Clause's purpose strongly supports the broader interpretation. That purpose is to permit the President to obtain the assistance of subordinate officers when the Senate, due to its recess, cannot confirm them.

At the same time, we recognize one important purpose-related consideration that argues in the opposite direction. A broad interpretation might permit a President to avoid Senate confirmations as a matter of course. If the Clause gives the President the power to "fill up all vacancies" that occur before, and continue to exist during, the Senate's recess, a President might not submit any nominations to the Senate. He might simply wait for a recess and then provide all potential nominees with recess appointments. He might thereby routinely avoid the constitutional need to obtain the Senate's "advice and consent."

A recess appointee only serves a limited term. That, combined with the lack of Senate approval, may diminish the recess appointee's ability, as a practical matter, to get a controversial job done. And even where the President and Senate are at odds over politically sensitive appointments, compromise is normally possible. In an unusual instance, where a matter is important enough to the Senate, that body can remain in session, preventing recess appointments by refusing to take a recess. In any event, the Executive Branch has adhered to the broader interpretation for two centuries, and Senate confirmation has always remained the norm for officers that require it.

While we concede that both interpretations carry with them some risk of undesirable consequences, we believe the narrower interpretation risks undermining constitutionally conferred powers more seriously and more often. It would prevent the President from making any recess appointment that arose before a recess, no matter who the official, no matter how dire the need, no matter how uncontroversial the appointment, and no matter how late in the session the office fell vacant.

Historical practice over the past 200 years strongly favors the broader interpretation. The tradition of applying the Clause to pre-recess vacancies dates at least to President James Madison.

The upshot is that the President has consistently and frequently interpreted the Recess Appointments Clause to apply to vacancies that initially occur before, but continue to exist during, a recess of the Senate. The Senate as a body has not countered this practice for nearly three-quarters of a century, perhaps longer. The tradition is long enough to entitle the practice "to great regard in determining the true construction" of the constitutional provision. And we are reluctant to upset this traditional practice where doing so would seriously shrink the authority that Presidents have believed existed and have exercised for so long.

In light of some linguistic ambiguity, the basic purpose of the Clause, and the historical practice we have described, we conclude that the phrase "all vacancies" includes vacancies that come into existence while the Senate is in session.

V

The third question concerns the calculation of the length of the Senate's "recess." On December 17, 2011, the Senate by unanimous consent adopted a resolution to convene "*pro forma* session[s]" only, with "no business . . . transacted," on every Tuesday and Friday from December 20, 2011, through January 20, 2012. At the end of each *pro forma* session, the Senate would "adjourn until" the following *pro forma* session. During that period, the Senate convened and adjourned as agreed. It held *pro forma* sessions on December 20, 23, 27, and 30, and on January 3, 6, 10, 13, 17, and 20; and at the end of each *pro forma* session, it adjourned until the time and date of the next.

The President made the recess appointments before us on January 4, 2012, in between the January 3 and the January 6 *pro forma* sessions. We must determine the significance of these sessions—that is, whether, for purposes of the Clause, we should treat them as periods when the Senate was in session or as periods when it was in recess. If the former, the period between January 3 and January 6 was a 3-day recess, which is too short to trigger the President's recess-appointment power. If the latter, however, then the 3-day period was part of a much longer recess during which the President did have the power to make recess appointments.

The Solicitor General argues that we must treat the *pro forma* sessions as periods of recess. He says that these "sessions" were sessions in name only because the Senate was in recess as a *functional* matter. The Senate, he contends, remained in a single, unbroken recess from January 3, when the second session of the 112th Congress began by operation of the Twentieth Amendment, until January 23, when the Senate reconvened to do regular business.

In our view, however, the *pro forma* sessions count as sessions, not as periods of recess. We hold that, for purposes of the Recess Appointments Clause, the Senate is in session when it says it is, provided that, under its own rules, it retains the capacity to transact Senate business. The Senate met that standard here.

The standard we apply is consistent with the Constitution's broad delegation of authority to the Senate to determine how and when to conduct its business. The Constitution explicitly empowers the Senate to "determine the Rules of its Proceedings." Art. I, §5, cl. 2.

For these reasons, we conclude that we must give great weight to the Senate's own determination of when it is and when it is not in session. But our deference to the Senate cannot be absolute. When the Senate is without the *capacity* to act, under its own rules, it is not in session even if it so declares. In that circumstance, the Senate is not simply unlikely or unwilling to act upon nominations of the President. It is *unable* to do so. The purpose of the Clause is to ensure the continued functioning of the Federal Government while the Senate is unavailable. This purpose would count for little were we to treat the Senate as though it were in session even when it lacks the ability to provide its "advice and consent." Accordingly, we conclude that when the Senate declares that it is in session and possesses the capacity, under its own rules, to conduct business, it is in session for purposes of the Clause.

Applying this standard, we find that the *pro forma* sessions were sessions for purposes of the Clause. First, the Senate said it was in session. The Journal of the Senate and the Congressional Record indicate that the

Senate convened for a series of twice-weekly "sessions" from December 20 through January 20. And these reports of the Senate "must be assumed to speak the truth."

Second, the Senate's rules make clear that during its *pro forma* sessions, despite its resolution that it would conduct no business, the Senate retained the power to conduct business. During any *pro forma* session, the Senate could have conducted business simply by passing a unanimous consent agreement. The Senate in fact conducts much of its business through unanimous consent. Senate rules presume that a quorum is present unless a present Senator questions it. And when the Senate has a quorum, an agreement is unanimously passed if, upon its proposal, no present Senator objects. It is consequently unsurprising that the Senate *has* enacted legislation during *pro forma* sessions even when it has said that no business will be transacted.

By way of contrast, we do not see how the Senate could conduct business during a recess. It could terminate the recess and then, when in session, pass a bill. But in that case, of course, the Senate would no longer be in recess. It would be in session. And that is the crucial point. Senate rules make clear that, once in session, the Senate can act even if it has earlier said that it would not.

VI

The Recess Appointments Clause responds to a structural difference between the Executive and Legislative Branches: The Executive Branch is perpetually in operation, while the Legislature only acts in intervals separated by recesses. The purpose of the Clause is to allow the Executive to continue operating while the Senate is unavailable. We believe that the Clause's text, standing alone, is ambiguous. It does not resolve whether the President may make appointments during intra-session recesses, or whether he may fill pre-recess vacancies. But the broader reading better serves the Clause's structural function. Moreover, that broader reading is reinforced by centuries of history, which we are hesitant to disturb. We thus hold that the Constitution empowers the President to fill any existing vacancy during any recess — intra-session or inter-session — of sufficient length.

Justice Scalia would render illegitimate thousands of recess appointments reaching all the way back to the founding era. More than that: Calling the Clause an "anachronism," he would basically read it out of the Constitution. He performs this act of judicial excision in the name of liberty. We fail to see how excising the Recess Appointments Clause preserves freedom.

Given our answer to the last question before us, we conclude that the Recess Appointments Clause does not give the President the constitutional authority to make the appointments here at issue. Because the Court of Appeals reached the same ultimate conclusion (though for reasons we reject), its judgment is affirmed.

Justice SCALIA, with whom THE CHIEF JUSTICE, Justice THOMAS, and Justice ALITO join, concurring in the judgment.

To prevent the President's recess-appointment power from nullifying the Senate's role in the appointment process, the Constitution cabins that power in two significant ways. First, it may be exercised only in "the Recess of the Senate," that is, the intermission between two formal legislative sessions. Second, it may be used to fill only those vacancies that "happen during the Recess," that is, offices that become vacant during that intermission. Both conditions are clear from the Constitution's text and structure, and both were well understood at the founding. The Court of Appeals correctly held that the appointments here at issue are invalid because they did not meet either condition.

Today's Court agrees that the appointments were in-valid, but for the far narrower reason that they were made during a 3-day break in the Senate's session. On its way to that result, the majority sweeps away the key textual limitations on the recess-appointment power. It holds, first, that the President can make appointments without the Senate's participation even during short breaks in the middle of the Senate's session, and second, that those appointments can fill offices that became vacant long before the break in which they were filled. The majority justifies those atextual results on an adverse-possession theory of executive authority: Presidents have long claimed the powers in question, and the Senate has not disputed those claims with sufficient vigor, so the Court should not "upset the compromises and working arrangements that the elected branches of Government themselves have reached."

The Court's decision transforms the recess-appointment power from a tool carefully designed to fill a narrow and specific need into a weapon to be wielded by future Presidents against future Senates. To reach that result, the majority casts aside the plain, original meaning of the constitutional text in deference to late-arising historical practices that are ambiguous at best. The majority's insistence on deferring to the Executive's untenably broad interpretation of the power is in clear conflict with our precedent and forebodes a diminution of this Court's role in controversies involving the separation of powers and the structure of government. I concur in the judgment only.

I. OUR RESPONSIBILITY

Today's majority disregards two overarching principles that ought to guide our consideration of the questions presented here.

First, the Constitution's core, government-structuring provisions are no less critical to preserving liberty than are the later adopted provisions of the Bill of Rights. Indeed, "[s]o convinced were the Framers that liberty of the person inheres in structure that at first they did not consider a Bill of Rights necessary."

Second and relatedly, when questions involving the Constitution's government-structuring provisions are presented in a justiciable case, it is the solemn responsibility of the Judicial Branch "to say what the law is." This Court does not defer to the other branches' resolution of such controversies; our role is in no way "lessened" because it might be said that "the two political branches are adjusting their own powers between themselves." Since the separation of powers exists for the protection of individual liberty, its vitality "does not depend" on "whether 'the encroached-upon branch approves the encroachment.'" Rather, policing the "enduring structure" of constitutional government when the political branches fail to do so is "one of the most vital functions of this Court."

II. INTRA-SESSION BREAKS

The first question presented is whether "the Recess of the Senate," during which the President's recess-appointment power is active, is (a) the period between two of the Senate's formal sessions, or (b) any break in the Senate's proceedings. I would hold that "the Recess" is the gap between sessions and that the appointments at issue here are invalid because they undisputedly were made *during* the Senate's session. The Court's contrary conclusion—that "the Recess" includes "breaks in the midst of a session,"—is inconsistent with the Constitution's text and structure, and it requires judicial fabrication of vague, unadministrable limits on the recess-appointment power (thus defined) that overstep the judicial role. And although the majority relies heavily on "historical practice," no practice worthy of our deference supports the majority's conclusion on this issue.

A. PLAIN MEANING

A sensible interpretation of the Recess Appointments Clause should start by recognizing that the Clause uses the term "Recess" in contradistinction to the term "Session." In the founding era, the terms "recess" and "session" had well-understood meanings in the marking-out of legislative time. The life of each elected Congress typically consisted (as it still does) of two or more formal sessions separated by adjournments "*sine die*," that is, without a specified return date.

To be sure, in colloquial usage both words, "recess" and "session," could take on alternative, less precise meanings. A session could include any short period when a legislature's members were "assembled for business," and a recess could refer to any brief "suspension" of legislative "business." But as even the majority acknowledges, the Constitution's use of "the word 'the' in '*the* [R]ecess'" tends to suggest "that the phrase refers to the single break separating formal sessions."

Besides being linguistically unsound, the majority's reading yields the strange result that an appointment made during a short break near the beginning of one official session will not terminate until the end of the *following* official session, enabling the appointment to last for up to two years.

To avoid the absurd results that follow from its colloquial reading of "the Recess," the majority is forced to declare that some intra-session breaks-though undisputedly within the phrase's colloquial meaning-are simply "too short to trigger the Recess Appointments Clause." But it identifies no textual basis whatsoever for limiting the length of "the Recess," nor does it point to any clear standard for determining how short is too short. It is inconceivable that the Framers would have left the circumstances in which the President could exercise such a significant and potentially dangerous power so utterly indeterminate.

And what about breaks longer than three days? The majority says that a break of four to nine days is "presumptively too short" but that the presumption may be rebutted in an "unusual circumstance," such as a "national catastrophe . . . that renders the Senate unavailable but calls for an urgent response." The majority must hope that the *in terrorem* effect of its "presumptively too short" pronouncement will deter future Presidents from making any recess appointments during 4-to-9-day breaks and thus save us from the absurd spectacle of unelected judges evaluating (after an evidentiary hearing?) whether an alleged "catastrophe" was sufficiently "urgent" to trigger the recess-appointment power.

As for breaks of 10 or more days: We are presumably to infer that such breaks do not trigger any "presumpt[ion]" against recess appointments, but does that mean the President has an utterly free hand? Or can litigants seek invalidation of an appointment made during a 10-day break by pointing to an absence of "unusual" or "urgent" circumstances necessitating an immediate appointment, albeit without the aid of a "presumpt[ion]" in their favor? Or, to put the question as it will present itself to lawyers in the Executive Branch: Can the President make an appointment during a 10-day break simply to overcome "political opposition in the Senate" despite the absence of any "national catastrophe," even though it "go[es] without saying" that he cannot do so during a 9-day break? Who knows? The majority does not say, and neither does the Constitution.

Even if the many questions raised by the majority's failure to articulate a standard could be answered, a larger question would remain: If the Constitution's text empowers the President to make appointments during any break in the Senate's proceedings, by what right does the majority subject the President's exercise of that power to vague, court-crafted limitations with no textual basis? The majority claims its temporal guideposts are informed by executive practice, but a President's self-restraint cannot "bind his successors by diminishing their powers."

B. HISTORICAL PRACTICE

For the foregoing reasons, the Constitution's text and structure unambiguously refute the majority's freewheeling interpretation of "the Recess." It is not plausible that the Constitution uses that term in a sense that authorizes the President to make unilateral appointments during *any* break in Senate proceedings, subject only to hazy, atextual limits crafted by this Court centuries after ratification. The majority, however, insists that history "offers strong support" for its interpretation. The historical practice of the political branches is, of course, irrelevant when the Constitution is clear. But even if the Constitution were thought ambiguous on this point, history does not support the majority's interpretation.

What does all this amount to? In short: Intra-session recess appointments were virtually unheard of for the first 130 years of the Republic, were deemed unconstitutional by the first Attorney General to address them, were not openly defended by the Executive until 1921, were not made in significant numbers until after World War II, and have been repeatedly criticized as unconstitutional by Senators of both parties. It is astonishing for the majority to assert that this history lends "strong support," to its interpretation of the Recess Appointments Clause. And the majority's contention that recent executive practice in this area merits deference because the Senate has not done more to oppose it is utterly divorced from our precedent. "The structural interests protected by the Appointments Clause are not those of any one branch of Government but of the entire Republic," and the Senate could not give away those protections even if it wanted to.

III. PRE-RECESS VACANCIES

The second question presented is whether vacancies that "happen during the Recess of the Senate," which the President is empowered to fill with recess appointments, are (a) vacancies that *arise* during the recess, or (b) all vacancies that *exist* during the recess, regardless of when they arose. I would hold that the recess-appointment power is limited to vacancies that arise during the recess in which they are filled, and I would hold that the appointments at issue here—which undisputedly filled pre-recess vacancies—are invalid for that reason as well as for the reason that they were made during the session. The Court's contrary conclusion is inconsistent with the Constitution's text and structure, and it further undermines the balance the Framers struck between Presidential and Senatorial power. Historical practice also fails to support the majority's conclusion on this issue.

A. PLAIN MEANING

As the majority concedes, "the most natural meaning of 'happens' as applied to a 'vacancy' . . . is that the vacancy 'happens' when it initially occurs." The majority adds that this meaning is most natural "to a modern ear," but it fails to show that founding-era ears heard it differently. "Happen" meant then, as it does now, "[t]o fall out; to chance; to come to pass." Thus, a vacancy that *happened* during the Recess was most reasonably understood as one that *arose* during the recess. It was, of course, possible in certain contexts for the word "happen" to mean "happen to be" rather than "happen to occur," as in the idiom "it so happens." But that meaning is not at all natural when the subject is a vacancy, a state of affairs that comes into existence at a particular moment in time.

In any event, no reasonable reader would have understood the Recess Appointments Clause to use the word "happen" in the majority's "happen to be" sense, and thus to empower the President to fill all vacancies that might *exist* during a recess, regardless of when they arose. For one thing, the Clause's language would have been a surpassingly odd way of giving the President that power. The Clause easily could have been written to convey that meaning clearly: It could have referred to "all Vacancies that may exist during the Recess," or it could have omitted the qualifying phrase entirely and simply authorized the President to "fill up all Vacancies during the Recess." Given those readily available alternative phrasings, the reasonable reader might have wondered, why would any intelligent drafter intending the majority's reading have inserted the words "that may happen"—words that, as the majority admits, make the majority's desired reading awkward and unnatural, and that must be effectively read out of the Clause to achieve that reading?

For another thing, the majority's reading not only strains the Clause's language but distorts its constitutional role, which was meant to be subordinate. As Hamilton explained, appointment with the advice and consent of the Senate was to be "the general mode of appointing officers of the United States."

If, however, the Clause had allowed the President to fill *all* preexisting vacancies during the recess by granting commissions that would last throughout the following session, it would have been impossible to regard it—as the Framers plainly did—as a mere codicil to the Constitution's principal, power-sharing scheme for filling federal offices. On the majority's reading, the President would have had no need *ever* to seek the Senate's advice and consent for his appointments: Whenever there was a fair prospect of the Senate's rejecting his preferred nominee, the President could have appointed that individual unilaterally during the recess, allowed the appointment to expire at the end of the next session, renewed the appointment the following day, and so on *ad infinitum*. (Circumvention would have been especially easy if, as the majority also concludes, the President was authorized to make such appointments during any intra-session break of more than a few days.) It is unthinkable that such an obvious means for the Executive to expand its power would have been overlooked during the ratification debates.

B. HISTORICAL PRACTICE

For the reasons just given, it is clear that the Constitution authorizes the President to fill unilaterally only those vacancies that arise during a recess, not every vacancy that happens to exist during a recess. Again, however, the majority says "[h]istorical practice" requires the broader interpretation. And again the majority is mistaken. Even if the Constitution were wrongly thought to be ambiguous on this point, a fair recounting of the relevant history does not support the majority's interpretation.

In sum: Washington's and Adams' Attorneys General read the Constitution to restrict recess appointments to vacancies arising during the recess, and there is no evidence that any of the first four Presidents consciously departed from that reading. The contrary reading was first defended by an executive official in 1823, was vehemently rejected by the Senate in 1863, was vigorously resisted by legislation in place from 1863 until 1940, and is arguably inconsistent with legislation in place from 1940 to the present. The Solicitor General has identified only about 100 appointments that have ever been made under the broader reading, and while it seems likely that a good deal more have been made in the last few decades, there is good reason to doubt that many were made before 1940 (since the appointees could not have been compensated). I can conceive of no sane constitutional theory under which this evidence of "historical practice" -which is actually evidence of a long-simmering inter-branch conflict-would require us to defer to the views of the Executive Branch.

IV. CONCLUSION

What the majority needs to sustain its judgment is an ambiguous text and a clear historical practice. What it has is a clear text and an at-best-ambiguous historical practice. Even if the Executive could accumulate power through adverse possession by engaging in a *consistent* and *unchallenged* practice over a long period of time, the oft-disputed practices at issue here would not meet that standard. Nor have those practices created any justifiable expectations that could be disappointed by enforcing the Constitution's original meaning. There is thus no ground for the majority's deference to the unconstitutional recess-appointment practices of the Executive Branch.

The majority replaces the Constitution's text with a new set of judge-made rules to govern recess appointments. Henceforth, the Senate can avoid triggering the President's now-vast recess-appointment power by the odd contrivance of never adjourning for more than three days without holding a *pro forma* session at which it is understood that no business will be conducted. How this new regime will work in practice remains to be seen. Perhaps it will reduce the prevalence of recess appointments. But perhaps not: Members of the President's party in Congress may be able to prevent the Senate from holding *pro forma* sessions with the necessary frequency, and if the House and Senate disagree, the President may be able to adjourn both "to such Time as he shall think proper." U.S. Const., Art. II, § 3. In any event, the limitation upon the President's appointment power is there not for the benefit of the Senate, but for the protection of the people; it should not be dependent on Senate action for its existence.

The real tragedy of today's decision is not simply the abolition of the Constitution's limits on the recess-appointment power and the substitution of a novel framework invented by this Court. It is the damage done to our separation-of-powers jurisprudence more generally. It is not every day that we encounter a proper case or controversy requiring interpretation of the Constitution's structural provisions. Most of the time, the interpretation of those provisions is left to the political branches-which, in deciding how much respect to afford the constitutional text, often take their cues from this Court. We should therefore take every opportunity to affirm the primacy of the Constitution's enduring principles over the politics of the moment. Our failure to do so today will resonate well beyond the particular dispute at hand. Sad, but true: The Court's embrace of the adverse-possession theory of executive power (a characterization the majority resists but does not refute) will be cited in diverse contexts, including those presently unimagined, and will have the effect of aggrandizing the Presidency beyond its constitutional bounds and undermining respect for the separation of powers.

D. Separation of Powers and Foreign Policy (casebook, p. 369)

4. Recognition Power (new)

In *Zivotofsky v. Kerry*, the Court considered the constitutionality of a federal law that allowed American citizens who had a child born in Jerusalem to have the child's passport say, "Jerusalem, Israel" as the place of birth. The Court declared the law unconstitutional. The decision is thus important for its consideration of the recognition power and also for being the first time that the Court has declared unconstitutional a federal law limiting presidential power in foreign affairs.

ZIVOTOFSKY v. KERRY
135 S. Ct. 2076 (2015)

Justice KENNEDY delivered the opinion of the Court.

A delicate subject lies in the background of this case. That subject is Jerusalem. Questions touching upon the history of the ancient city and its present legal and international status are among the most difficult and complex in international affairs. In our constitutional system these matters are committed to the Legislature and the Executive, not the Judiciary. As a result, in this opinion the Court does no more, and must do no more, than note the existence of international debate and tensions respecting Jerusalem. Those matters are for Congress and the President to discuss and consider as they seek to shape the Nation's foreign policies.

The Court addresses two questions to resolve the interbranch dispute now before it. First, it must determine whether the President has the exclusive power to grant formal recognition to a foreign sovereign. Second, if he has that power, the Court must determine whether Congress can command the President and his Secretary of State to issue a formal statement that contradicts the earlier recognition. The statement in question here is a congressional mandate that allows a United States citizen born in Jerusalem to direct the President and Secretary of State, when issuing his passport, to state that his place of birth is "Israel."

I

Jerusalem's political standing has long been, and remains, one of the most sensitive issues in American foreign policy, and indeed it is one of the most delicate issues in current international affairs. In 1948, President Truman formally recognized Israel in a signed statement of "recognition." That statement did not recognize Israeli sovereignty over Jerusalem. Over the last 60 years, various actors have sought to assert full or partial sovereignty over the city, including Israel, Jordan, and the Palestinians. Yet, in contrast to a consistent policy of formal recognition of Israel, neither President Truman nor any later United States President has issued an official statement or declaration acknowledging any country's sovereignty over Jerusalem. Instead, the Executive Branch has maintained that "'the status of Jerusalem . . . should be decided not unilaterally but in consultation with all concerned.'"

The President's position on Jerusalem is reflected in State Department policy regarding passports and consular reports of birth abroad. Understanding that passports will be construed as reflections of American policy, the State Department's Foreign Affairs Manual instructs its employees, in general, to record the place of birth on a passport as the "country [having] present sovereignty over the actual area of birth." Dept. of State, 7 Foreign Affairs Manual (FAM) § 1383.4 (1987). If a citizen objects to the country listed as sovereign by the State Department, he or she may list the city or town of birth rather than the country. The FAM, however, does not allow citizens to list a sovereign that conflicts with Executive Branch policy. See generally id., § 1383. Because the United States does not recognize any country as having sovereignty over Jerusalem, the FAM instructs employees to record the place of birth for citizens born there as "Jerusalem."

In 2002, Congress passed the Act at issue here, the Foreign Relations Authorization Act, Fiscal Year 2003. Section 214 of the Act is titled "United States Policy with Respect to Jerusalem as the Capital of Israel." The subsection that lies at the heart of this case, § 214(d), addresses passports. That subsection seeks to override the FAM by allowing citizens born in Jerusalem to list their place of birth as "Israel." Titled "Record of Place of Birth as Israel for Passport Purposes," § 214(d) states "[f]or purposes of the registration of birth, certification of nationality, or issuance of a passport of a United States citizen born in the city of Jerusalem, the Secretary shall, upon the request of the citizen or the citizen's legal guardian, record the place of birth as Israel."

When he signed the Act into law, President George W. Bush issued a statement declaring his position that § 214 would, "if construed as mandatory rather than advisory, impermissibly interfere with the President's constitutional authority to formulate the position of the United States, speak for the Nation in international affairs, and determine the terms on which recognition is given to foreign states." The President concluded, "U.S. policy regarding Jerusalem has not changed."

In 2002, petitioner Menachem Binyamin Zivotofsky was born to United States citizens living in Jerusalem. In December 2002, Zivotofsky's mother visited the American Embassy in Tel Aviv to request both a passport and a consular report of birth abroad for her son. She asked that his place of birth be listed as " 'Jerusalem, Israel.' " The Embassy clerks explained that, pursuant to State Department policy, the passport would list only "Jerusalem." Zivotofsky's parents objected and, as his guardians, brought suit on his behalf in the United States District Court for the District of Columbia, seeking to enforce § 214(d).

II

In considering claims of Presidential power this Court refers to Justice Jackson's familiar tripartite framework from *Youngstown Sheet & Tube Co. v. Sawyer* (1952) (concurring opinion). The framework divides exercises of Presidential power into three categories: First, when "the President acts pursuant to an express or implied authorization of Congress, his authority is at its maximum, for it includes all that he possesses in his own right plus all that Congress can delegate." Second, "in absence of either a congressional grant or denial of authority" there is a "zone of twilight in which he and Congress may have concurrent authority," and where "congressional inertia, indifference or quiescence may" invite the exercise of executive power. Finally, when "the President takes measures incompatible with the expressed or implied will of Congress . . . he can rely only upon his own constitutional powers minus any constitutional powers of Congress over the matter." To succeed in this third category, the President's asserted power must be both "exclusive" and "conclusive" on the issue.

In this case the Secretary contends that § 214(d) infringes on the President's exclusive recognition power by "requiring the President to contradict his recognition position regarding Jerusalem in official communications with foreign sovereigns." In so doing the Secretary acknowledges the President's power is "at its lowest ebb." Because the President's refusal to implement § 214(d) falls into Justice Jackson's third category, his claim must be "scrutinized with caution," and he may rely solely on powers the Constitution grants to him alone. To determine whether the President possesses the exclusive power of recognition the Court examines the Constitution's text and structure, as well as precedent and history bearing on the question.

Recognition is a "formal acknowledgement" that a particular "entity possesses the qualifications for statehood" or "that a particular regime is the effective government of a state." It may also involve the determination of a state's territorial bounds. Recognition is often effected by an express "written or oral declaration." It may also be implied — for example, by concluding a bilateral treaty or by sending or receiving diplomatic agents.

Legal consequences follow formal recognition. Recognized sovereigns may sue in United States courts, and may benefit from sovereign immunity when they are sued. The actions of a recognized sovereign committed within its own territory also receive deference in domestic courts under the act of state doctrine. Recognition at international law, furthermore, is a precondition of regular diplomatic relations. Recognition is thus "useful, even necessary," to the existence of a state.

Despite the importance of the recognition power in foreign relations, the Constitution does not use the term "recognition," either in Article II or elsewhere. The Secretary asserts that the President exercises the recognition power based on the Reception Clause, which directs that the President "shall receive Ambassadors and other public Ministers." Art. II, § 3. As Zivotofsky notes, the Reception Clause received little attention at the Constitutional Convention. In fact, during the ratification debates, Alexander Hamilton claimed that the power to receive ambassadors was "more a matter of dignity than of authority," a ministerial duty largely "without consequence." The Federalist No. 69, p. 420 (C. Rossiter ed. 1961).

At the time of the founding, however, prominent international scholars suggested that receiving an ambassador was tantamount to recognizing the sovereignty of the sending state. It is a logical and proper inference, then, that a Clause directing the President alone to receive ambassadors would be understood to acknowledge his power to recognize other nations.

As a result, the Reception Clause provides support, although not the sole authority, for the President's power to recognize other nations.

The inference that the President exercises the recognition power is further supported by his additional Article II powers. It is for the President, "by and with the Advice and Consent of the Senate," to "make Treaties, provided two thirds of the Senators present concur." Art. II, § 2, cl. 2. In addition, "he shall nominate, and by and with the Advice and Consent of the Senate, shall appoint Ambassadors" as well as "other public Ministers and Consuls."

As a matter of constitutional structure, these additional powers give the President control over recognition decisions. At international law, recognition may be effected by different means, but each means is dependent upon Presidential power. In addition to receiving an ambassador, recognition may occur on "the conclusion of a bilateral treaty," or the "formal initiation of diplomatic relations," including the dispatch of an ambassador. The President has the sole power to negotiate treaties, and the Senate may not conclude or ratify a treaty without Presidential action. The President, too, nominates the Nation's ambassadors and dispatches other diplomatic agents. Congress may not send an ambassador without his involvement. Beyond that, the President himself has the power to open diplomatic channels simply by engaging in direct diplomacy with foreign heads of state and their ministers. The Constitution thus assigns the President means to effect recognition on his own initiative. Congress, by contrast, has no constitutional power that would enable it to initiate diplomatic relations with a foreign nation. Because these specific Clauses confer the recognition power on the President, the Court need not consider whether or to what extent the Vesting Clause, which provides that the "executive Power" shall be vested in the President, provides further support for the President's action here. Art. II, § 1, cl. 1.

The text and structure of the Constitution grant the President the power to recognize foreign nations and governments. The question then becomes whether that power is exclusive. The various ways in which the President may unilaterally effect recognition — and the lack of any similar power vested in Congress — suggest that it is. So, too, do functional considerations. Put simply, the Nation must have a single policy regarding which governments are legitimate in the eyes of the United States and which are not. Foreign countries need to know, before entering into diplomatic relations or commerce with the United States, whether their ambassadors will be received; whether their officials will be immune from suit in federal court; and whether they may initiate lawsuits here to vindicate their rights. These assurances cannot be equivocal.

Recognition is a topic on which the Nation must "'speak . . . with one voice.'" That voice must be the President's. Between the two political branches, only the Executive has the characteristic of unity at all times. And with unity comes the ability to exercise, to a greater degree, "[d]ecision, activity, secrecy, and dispatch." The Federalist No. 70, p. 424 (A. Hamilton). The President is capable, in ways Congress is not, of engaging in the delicate and often secret diplomatic contacts that may lead to a decision on recognition. These qualities explain why the Framers listed the traditional avenues of recognition—receiving ambassadors, making treaties, and sending ambassadors—as among the President's Article II powers.

As described in more detail below, the President since the founding has exercised this unilateral power to recognize new states—and the Court has endorsed the practice. Texts and treatises on international law treat the President's word as the final word on recognition.

In foreign affairs, as in the domestic realm, the Constitution "enjoins upon its branches separateness but interdependence, autonomy but reciprocity." Although the President alone effects the formal act of recognition, Congress' powers, and its central role in making laws, give it substantial authority regarding many of the policy determinations that precede and follow the act of recognition itself. If Congress disagrees with the President's recognition policy, there may be consequences. Formal recognition may seem a hollow act if it is not accompanied by the dispatch of an ambassador, the easing of trade restrictions, and the conclusion of treaties. And those decisions require action by the Senate or the whole Congress.

In practice, then, the President's recognition determination is just one part of a political process that may require Congress to make laws. The President's exclusive recognition power encompasses the authority to acknowledge, in a formal sense, the legitimacy of other states and governments, including their territorial bounds. Albeit limited, the exclusive recognition power is essential to the conduct of Presidential duties. The formal act of recognition is an executive power that Congress may not qualify. If the President is to be effective in negotiations over a formal recognition determination, it must be evident to his counterparts abroad that he speaks for the Nation on that precise question.

B

No single precedent resolves the question whether the President has exclusive recognition authority and, if so, how far that power extends. In part that is because, until today, the political branches have resolved their disputes over questions of recognition. The relevant cases, though providing important instruction, address the division of recognition power between the Federal Government and the States, or between the courts and the political branches, not between the President and Congress. As the parties acknowledge, some isolated statements in those cases lend support to the position that Congress has a role in the recognition process. In the end, however, a fair reading of the cases shows that the President's role in the recognition process is both central and exclusive.

Having examined the Constitution's text and this Court's precedent, it is appropriate to turn to accepted understandings and practice. In separation-of-powers cases this Court has often "put significant weight upon historical practice." Here, history is not all on one side, but on balance it provides strong support for the conclusion that the recognition power is the President's alone. As Zivotofsky argues, certain historical incidents can be interpreted to support the position that recognition is a shared power. But the weight of historical evidence supports the opposite view, which is that the formal determination of recognition is a power to be exercised only by the President.

But even a brief survey of the major historical examples, with an emphasis on those said to favor Zivotofsky, establishes no more than that some Presidents have chosen to cooperate with Congress, not that Congress itself has exercised the recognition power.

From the first Administration forward, the President has claimed unilateral authority to recognize foreign sovereigns. For the most part, Congress has acquiesced in the Executive's exercise of the recognition power. On occasion, the President has chosen, as may often be prudent, to consult and coordinate with Congress. As Judge Tatel noted in this case, however, "the most striking thing" about the history of recognition "is what is absent from it: a situation like this one," where Congress has enacted a statute contrary to the President's formal and considered statement concerning recognition.

For the most part, Congress has respected the Executive's policies and positions as to formal recognition. At times, Congress itself has defended the President's constitutional prerogative. Over the last 100 years, there has been scarcely any debate over the President's power to recognize foreign states. In this respect the Legislature, in the narrow context of recognition, on balance has acknowledged the importance of speaking "with one voice." The weight of historical evidence indicates Congress has accepted that the power to recognize foreign states and governments and their territorial bounds is exclusive to the Presidency.

III

As the power to recognize foreign states resides in the President alone, the question becomes whether § 214(d) infringes on the Executive's consistent decision to withhold recognition with respect to Jerusalem.

Section 214(d) requires that, in a passport or consular report of birth abroad, "the Secretary shall, upon the request of the citizen or the citizen's legal guardian, record the place of birth as Israel" for a "United States citizen born in the city of Jerusalem." That is, § 214(d) requires the President, through the Secretary, to identify citizens born in Jerusalem who so request as being born in Israel. But according to the President, those citizens were not born in Israel. As a matter of United States policy, neither Israel nor any other country is acknowledged as having sovereignty over Jerusalem. In this way, § 214(d) "directly contradicts" the "carefully calibrated and longstanding Executive branch policy of neutrality toward Jerusalem."

If the power over recognition is to mean anything, it must mean that the President not only makes the initial, formal recognition determination but also that he may maintain that determination in his and his agent's statements. This conclusion is a matter of both common sense and necessity. If Congress could command the President to state a recognition position inconsistent with his own, Congress could override the President's recognition determination. Under international law, recognition may be effected by "written or oral declaration of the recognizing state." In addition an act of recognition must "leave no doubt as to the intention to grant it." Thus, if Congress could alter the President's statements on matters of recognition or force him to contradict them, Congress in effect would exercise the recognition power.

As Justice Jackson wrote in *Youngstown,* when a Presidential power is "exclusive," it "disabl[es] the Congress from acting upon the subject." Here, the subject is quite narrow: The Executive's exclusive power extends no further than his formal recognition determination. But as to that determination, Congress may not enact a law that directly contradicts it. This is not to say Congress may not express its disagreement with the President in myriad ways. For example, it may enact an embargo, decline to confirm an ambassador, or even declare war. But none of these acts would alter the President's recognition decision.

If Congress may not pass a law, speaking in its own voice, that effects formal recognition, then it follows that it may not force the President himself to contradict his earlier statement. That congressional command would not only prevent the Nation from speaking with one voice but also prevent the Executive itself from doing so in conducting foreign relations.

Although the statement required by § 214(d) would not itself constitute a formal act of recognition, it is a mandate that the Executive contradict his prior recognition determination in an official document issued by the Secretary of State. As a result, it is unconstitutional. This is all the more clear in light of the longstanding treatment of a passport's place-of-birth section as an official executive statement implicating recognition.

From the face of § 214, from the legislative history, and from its reception, it is clear that Congress wanted to express its displeasure with the President's policy by, among other things, commanding the Executive to contradict his own, earlier stated position on Jerusalem. This Congress may not do.

It is true, as Zivotofsky notes, that Congress has substantial authority over passports. The Court does not question the power of Congress to enact passport legislation of wide scope.

The problem with § 214(d), however, lies in how Congress exercised its authority over passports. It was an improper act for Congress to "aggrandiz[e] its power at the expense of another branch" by requiring the President to contradict an earlier recognition determination in an official document issued by the Executive Branch. To allow Congress to control the President's communication in the context of a formal recognition determination is to allow Congress to exercise that exclusive power itself. As a result, the statute is unconstitutional.

In holding § 214(d) invalid the Court does not question the substantial powers of Congress over foreign affairs in general or passports in particular. This case is confined solely to the exclusive power of the President to control recognition determinations, including formal statements by the Executive Branch acknowledging the legitimacy of a state or government and its territorial bounds. Congress cannot command the President to contradict an earlier recognition determination in the issuance of passports.

Justice THOMAS, concurring in the judgment in part and dissenting in part.

Our Constitution allocates the powers of the Federal Government over foreign affairs in two ways. First, it expressly identifies certain foreign affairs powers and vests them in particular branches, either individually or jointly. Second, it vests the residual foreign affairs powers of the Federal Government — i.e., those not specifically enumerated in the Constitution — in the President by way of Article II's Vesting Clause.

Section 214(d) of the Foreign Relations Authorization Act, Fiscal Year 2003, ignores that constitutional allocation of power insofar as it directs the President, contrary to his wishes, to list "Israel" as the place of birth of Jerusalem-born citizens on their passports. The President has long regulated passports under his residual foreign affairs power, and this portion of § 214(d) does not fall within any of Congress' enumerated powers.

By contrast, § 214(d) poses no such problem insofar as it regulates consular reports of birth abroad. Unlike passports, these reports were developed to effectuate the naturalization laws, and they continue to serve the role of identifying persons who need not be naturalized to obtain U.S. citizenship. The regulation of these reports does not fall within the President's foreign affairs powers, but within Congress' enumerated powers under the Naturalization and Necessary and Proper Clauses.

Rather than adhere to the Constitution's division of powers, the Court relies on a distortion of the President's recognition power to hold both of these parts of § 214(d) unconstitutional. Because I cannot join this faulty analysis, I concur only in the portion of the Court's judgment holding § 214(d) unconstitutional as applied to passports.

I

The President's longstanding practice of exercising unenumerated foreign affairs powers reflects a constitutional directive that "the President ha[s] primary responsibility — along with the necessary power — to protect the national security and to conduct the Nation's foreign relations." Specifically, the Vesting Clause of Article II provides that "[t]he executive Power shall be vested in a President of the United States." Art. II, § 1. This Clause is notably different from the Vesting Clause of Article I, which provides only that "[a]ll legislative Powers *herein granted* shall be vested in a Congress of the United States," Art. I, § 1. By omitting the words "herein granted" in Article II, the Constitution indicates that the "executive Power" vested in the President is not confined to those powers expressly identified in the document. Instead, it includes all powers originally understood as falling within the "executive Power" of the Federal Government.

Founding-era evidence reveals that the "executive Power" included the foreign affairs powers of a sovereign State. Given this pervasive view of executive power, it is unsurprising that those who ratified the Constitution understood the "executive Power" vested by Article II to include those foreign affairs powers not otherwise allocated in the Constitution.

II

The President is not constitutionally compelled to implement § 214(d) as it applies to passports because passport regulation falls squarely within his residual foreign affairs power and Zivotofsky has identified no source of congressional power to require the President to list Israel as the place of birth for a citizen born in Jerusalem on that citizen's passport. Section 214(d) can, however, be constitutionally applied to consular reports of birth abroad because those documents do not fall within the President's foreign affairs authority but do fall within Congress' enumerated powers over naturalization.

Because the President has residual foreign affairs authority to regulate passports and because there appears to be no congressional power that justifies § 214(d)'s application to passports, Zivotofsky's challenge to the Executive's designation of his place of birth on his passport must fail.

Although the consular report of birth abroad shares some features with a passport, it is historically associated with naturalization, not foreign affairs. In order to establish a "uniform Rule of Naturalization," Congress must be able to identify the categories of persons who are eligible for naturalization, along with the rules for that process. Congress thus has always regulated the "acquisition of citizenship by being born abroad of American parents . . . in the exercise of the power conferred by the Constitution to establish a uniform rule of naturalization."

The consular report of birth abroad is well suited to carrying into execution the power conferred on Congress in the Naturalization Clause. The report developed in response to Congress' requirement that children born abroad to U.S. citizens register with the consulate or lose their citizenship. And it continues to certify the acquisition of U.S. citizenship at birth by a person born abroad to a U.S. citizen.

Because regulation of the consular report of birth abroad is justified as an exercise of Congress' powers under the Naturalization and Necessary and Proper Clauses and does not fall within the President's foreign affairs powers, § 214(d)'s treatment of that document is constitutional.

Adhering to the Constitution's allocation of powers leads me to reach a different conclusion in this case from my colleagues: Section 214(d) can be constitutionally applied to consular reports of birth abroad, but not passports. I therefore respectfully concur in the judgment in part and dissent in part.

Chief Justice ROBERTS, with whom Justice ALITO joins, dissenting.

Today's decision is a first: Never before has this Court accepted a President's direct defiance of an Act of Congress in the field of foreign affairs. We have instead stressed that the President's power reaches "its lowest ebb" when he contravenes the express will of Congress, "for what is at stake is the equilibrium established by our constitutional system." *Youngstown Sheet & Tube Co. v. Sawyer* (1952) (Jackson, J., concurring).

In this case, the President claims the exclusive and preclusive power to recognize foreign sovereigns. The Court devotes much of its analysis to accepting the Executive's contention. I have serious doubts about that position. The majority places great weight on the Reception Clause, which directs that the Executive "shall receive Ambassadors and other public Ministers." But that provision, framed as an obligation rather than an authorization, appears alongside the *duties* imposed on the President by Article II, Section 3, not the *powers* granted to him by Article II, Section 2. Indeed, the People ratified the Constitution with Alexander Hamilton's assurance that executive reception of ambassadors "is more a matter of dignity than of authority" and "will be without consequence in the administration of the government." In short, at the time of the founding, "there was no reason to view the reception clause as a source of discretionary authority for the president." Adler, The President's Recognition Power: Ministerial or Discretionary?

The majority's other asserted textual bases are even more tenuous. The President does have power to make treaties and appoint ambassadors. Art. II, § 2. But those authorities are *shared* with Congress, so they hardly support an inference that the recognition power is *exclusive*.

Precedent and history lend no more weight to the Court's position. The majority cites dicta suggesting an exclusive executive recognition power, but acknowledges contrary dicta suggesting that the power is shared. When the best you can muster is conflicting dicta, precedent can hardly be said to support your side.

As for history, the majority admits that it too points in both directions. Some Presidents have claimed an exclusive recognition power, but others have expressed uncertainty about whether such preclusive authority exists. Those in the skeptical camp include Andrew Jackson and Abraham Lincoln, leaders not generally known for their cramped conceptions of Presidential power. Congress has also asserted its authority over recognition determinations at numerous points in history. The majority therefore falls short of demonstrating that "Congress has accepted" the President's exclusive recognition power. In any event, we have held that congressional acquiescence is only "pertinent" when the President acts in the absence of express congressional authorization, not when he asserts power to disregard a statute, as the Executive does here.

In sum, although the President has authority over recognition, I am not convinced that the Constitution provides the "conclusive and preclusive" power required to justify defiance of an express legislative mandate.

But even if the President does have exclusive recognition power, he still cannot prevail in this case, because the statute at issue *does not implicate recognition*. The relevant provision, § 214(d), simply gives an American citizen born in Jerusalem the option to designate his place of birth as Israel "[f]or purposes of" passports and other documents. The State Department itself has explained that "identification"—not recognition—"is the principal reason that U.S. passports require 'place of birth.'" Congress has not disputed the Executive's assurances that § 214(d) does not alter the longstanding United States position on Jerusalem. And the annals of diplomatic history record no examples of official recognition accomplished via optional passport designation.

The majority acknowledges both that the "Executive's exclusive power extends no further than his formal recognition determination" and that § 214(d) does "not itself constitute a formal act of recognition." Taken together, these statements come close to a confession of error. The majority attempts to reconcile its position by reconceiving § 214(d) as a "mandate that the Executive contradict his prior recognition determination in an official document issued by the Secretary of State." But as just noted, neither Congress nor the Executive Branch regards § 214(d) as a recognition determination, so it is hard to see how the statute could contradict any such determination.

At most, the majority worries that there may be a *perceived* contradiction based on a *mistaken* understanding of the effect of § 214(d), insisting that some "observers interpreted § 214 as altering United States policy regarding Jerusalem." To afford controlling weight to such impressions, however, is essentially to subject a duly enacted statute to an international heckler's veto.

The expansive language in *Curtiss–Wright* casting the President as the "sole organ" of the Nation in foreign affairs certainly has attraction for members of the Executive Branch. The Solicitor General invokes the case no fewer than ten times in his brief. But our precedents have never accepted such a sweeping understanding of executive power.

Resolving the status of Jerusalem may be vexing, but resolving this case is not. Whatever recognition power the President may have, exclusive or otherwise, is not implicated by § 214(d). It has not been necessary over the past 225 years to definitively resolve a dispute between Congress and the President over the recognition power. Perhaps we could have waited another 225 years. But instead the majority strains to reach the question based on the mere possibility that observers overseas might misperceive the significance of the birthplace designation at issue in this case. And in the process, the Court takes the perilous step—for the first time in our history — of allowing the President to defy an Act of Congress in the field of foreign affairs.

Justice SCALIA, with whom THE CHIEF JUSTICE and Justice ALITO join, dissenting.

Before this country declared independence, the law of England entrusted the King with the exclusive care of his kingdom's foreign affairs. The royal prerogative included the "sole power of sending ambassadors to foreign states, and receiving them at home," the sole authority to "make treaties, leagues, and alliances with foreign states and princes," "the sole prerogative of making war and peace," and the "sole power of raising and regulating fleets and armies." The People of the United States had other ideas when they organized our Government. They considered a sound structure of balanced powers essential to the preservation of just government, and international relations formed no exception to that principle.

The People therefore adopted a Constitution that divides responsibility for the Nation's foreign concerns between the legislative and executive departments. The Constitution gave the President the "executive Power," authority to send and responsibility to receive ambassadors, power to make treaties, and command of the Army and Navy — though they qualified some of these powers by requiring consent of the Senate. Art. II, §§ 1-3. At the same time, they gave Congress powers over war, foreign commerce, naturalization, and more. Art. I, § 8. "Fully eleven of the powers that Article I, § 8 grants Congress deal in some way with foreign affairs."

This case arises out of a dispute between the Executive and Legislative Branches about whether the United States should treat Jerusalem as a part of Israel. The Constitution contemplates that the political branches will make policy about the territorial claims of foreign nations the same way they make policy about other international matters: The President will exercise his powers on the basis of his views, Congress its powers on the basis of its views. That is just what has happened here.

Before turning to Presidential power under Article II, I think it well to establish the statute's basis in congressional power under Article I. Congress's power to "establish an uniform Rule of Naturalization," Art. I, § 8, cl. 4, enables it to grant American citizenship to someone born abroad. The naturalization power also enables Congress to furnish the people it makes citizens with papers verifying their citizenship — say a consular report of birth abroad (which certifies citizenship of an American born outside the United States) or a passport (which certifies citizenship for purposes of international travel). As the Necessary and Proper Clause confirms, every congressional power "carries with it all those incidental powers which are necessary to its complete and effectual execution." Even on a miserly understanding of Congress's incidental authority, Congress may make grants of citizenship "effectual" by providing for the issuance of certificates authenticating them.

One would think that if Congress may grant Zivotofsky a passport and a birth report, it may also require these papers to record his birthplace as "Israel." The birthplace specification promotes the document's citizenship-authenticating function by identifying the bearer, distinguishing people with similar names but different birthplaces from each other, helping authorities uncover identity fraud, and facilitating retrieval of the Government's citizenship records. To be sure, recording Zivotofsky's birthplace as "Jerusalem" rather than "Israel" would fulfill these objectives, but when faced with alternative ways to carry its powers into execution, Congress has the "discretion" to choose the one it deems "most beneficial to the people." It thus has the right to decide that recording birthplaces as "Israel" makes for better foreign policy. Or that regardless of international politics, a passport or birth report should respect its bearer's conscientious belief that Jerusalem belongs to Israel.

The Court frames this case as a debate about recognition. Recognition is a sovereign's official acceptance of a status under international law. A sovereign might recognize a foreign entity as a state, a regime as the other state's government, a place as part of the other state's territory, rebel forces in the other state as a belligerent power, and so on.

The Court holds that the Constitution makes the President alone responsible for recognition and that § 214(d) invades this exclusive power. I agree that the Constitution *empowers* the President to extend recognition on behalf of the United States, but I find it a much harder question whether it makes that power exclusive. The Court tells us that "the weight of historical evidence" supports exclusive executive authority over "the formal determination of recognition." But even with its attention confined to formal recognition, the Court is forced to admit that "history is not all on one side."

To know all this is to realize at once that § 214(d) has nothing to do with recognition. Section 214(d) does not require the Secretary to make a formal declaration about Israel's sovereignty over Jerusalem. And nobody suggests that international custom infers acceptance of sovereignty from the birthplace designation on a passport or birth report, as it does from bilateral treaties or exchanges of ambassadors. Recognition would preclude the United States (as a matter of international law) from later contesting Israeli sovereignty over Jerusalem. But making a notation in a passport or birth report does not encumber the Republic with any international obligations. It leaves the Nation free (so far as international law is concerned) to change its mind in the future. That would be true even if the statute required *all* passports to list "Israel." But in fact it requires only those passports to list "Israel" for which the citizen (or his guardian) *requests* "Israel"; all the rest, under the Secretary's policy, list "Jerusalem." It is utterly impossible for this deference to private requests to constitute an act that unequivocally manifests an intention to grant recognition.

Section 214(d) performs a more prosaic function than extending recognition. Just as foreign countries care about what our Government has to say about their borders, so too American citizens often care about what our Government has to say about their identities. The State Department does not grant or deny recognition in order to accommodate these individuals, but it does make exceptions to its rules about how it records birthplaces.

The Court complains that § 214(d) requires the Secretary of State to issue official documents implying that Jerusalem is a part of Israel; that it appears in a section of the statute bearing the title "United States Policy with Respect to Jerusalem as the Capital of Israel"; and that foreign "observers interpreted [it] as altering United States policy regarding Jerusalem." But these features do not show that § 214(d) recognizes Israel's sovereignty over Jerusalem. They show only that the law displays symbolic support for Israel's territorial claim. That symbolism may have tremendous significance as a matter of international diplomacy, but it makes no difference as a matter of constitutional law.

Even if the Constitution gives the President sole power to extend recognition, it does not give him sole power to make all decisions relating to foreign disputes over sovereignty. The Constitution likewise does not give the President exclusive power to determine which claims to statehood and territory "are legitimate in the eyes of the United States." Congress may express its own views about these matters by declaring war, restricting trade, denying foreign aid, and much else besides.

In the final analysis, the Constitution may well deny Congress power to recognize — the power to make an international commitment accepting a foreign entity as a state, a regime as its government, a place as a part of its territory, and so on. But whatever else § 214(d) may do, it plainly does not make (or require the President to make) a commitment accepting Israel's sovereignty over Jerusalem.

International disputes about statehood and territory are neither rare nor obscure. Leading foreign debates during the 19th century concerned how the United States should respond to revolutions in Latin America, Texas, Mexico, Hawaii, Cuba. During the 20th century, attitudes toward Communist governments in Russia and China became conspicuous subjects of agitation. Disagreements about Taiwan, Kashmir, and Crimea remain prominent today. A President empowered to decide all questions relating to these matters, immune from laws embodying congressional disagreement with his position, would have uncontrolled mastery of a vast share of the Nation's foreign affairs.

That is not the chief magistrate under which the American People agreed to live when they adopted the national charter. They believed that "[t]he accumulation of all powers, legislative, executive, and judiciary, in the same hands, . . . may justly be pronounced the very definition of tyranny." The Federalist No. 47, p. 301 (Madison). For this reason, they did not entrust either the President or Congress with sole power to adopt uncontradictable policies about *any* subject—foreign-sovereignty disputes included. They instead gave each political department its own powers, and with that the freedom to contradict the other's policies. Under the Constitution they approved, Congress may require Zivotofsky's passport and birth report to record his birthplace as Israel, even if that requirement clashes with the President's preference for neutrality about the status of Jerusalem.

Chapter 4

Limits on State Regulatory and Taxing Power

C. The Privileges and Immunities Clause of Article IV, Section 2

2. Analysis Under the Privileges and Immunities Clause (casebook, p. 506)

In *McBurney v. Young,* the Supreme Court rejected a challenge to a Virginia law that limited access to information under Virginia's freedom of information act to requests by Virginia citizens. In doing so, the Court focused on the meaning of the Privileges and Immunities Clause of Article IV, Section 2.

MCBURNEY v. YOUNG

133 S. Ct. 1709 (2013)

Justice ALITO delivered the opinion of the Court.

In this case, we must decide whether the Virginia Freedom of Information Act violates either the Privileges and Immunities Clause of Article IV of the Constitution or the dormant Commerce Clause. The Virginia Freedom of Information Act (FOIA) provides that "all public records shall be open to inspection and copying by any citizens of the Commonwealth," but it grants no such right to non-Virginians.

Petitioners, who are citizens of other States, unsuccessfully sought information under the Act and then brought this constitutional challenge. We hold, however, that petitioners' constitutional rights were not violated. By means other than the state FOIA, Virginia made available to petitioners most of the information that they sought, and the Commonwealth's refusal to furnish the additional information did not abridge any constitutionally protected privilege or immunity. Nor did Virginia violate the dormant Commerce Clause. The state Freedom of Information Act does not regulate commerce in any meaningful sense, but instead provides a service that is related to state citizenship.

I

Petitioners Mark J. McBurney and Roger W. Hurlbert are citizens of Rhode Island and California respectively. McBurney and Hurlbert each requested documents under the Virginia FOIA, but their requests were denied because of their citizenship.

McBurney is a former resident of Virginia whose ex-wife is a Virginia citizen. After his ex-wife defaulted on her child support obligations, McBurney asked the Commonwealth's Division of Child Support Enforcement to file a petition for child support on his behalf. The agency complied, but only after a 9-month delay. McBurney attributes that delay to agency error and says that it cost him nine months of child support. To ascertain the reason for the agency's delay, McBurney filed a Virginia FOIA request seeking "all emails, notes, files, memos, reports, letters, policies, [and] opinions" pertaining to his family, along with all documents "regarding [his] application for child support" and all documents pertaining to the handling of child support claims like his. The agency denied McBurney's request on the ground that he was not a Virginia citizen.

Hurlbert is the sole proprietor of Sage Information Services, a business that requests real estate tax records on clients' behalf from state and local governments across the United States. In 2008, Hurlbert was hired by a land/title company to obtain real estate tax records for properties in Henrico County, Virginia. He filed a Virginia FOIA request for the documents with the Henrico County Real Estate Assessor's Office, but his request was denied because he was not a Virginia citizen.

Like Virginia, several other States have enacted freedom of information laws that are available only to their citizens.

II

Under the Privileges and Immunities Clause, "[t]he Citizens of each State [are] entitled to all Privileges and Immunities of Citizens in the several States." We have said that "[t]he object of the Privileges and Immunities Clause is to 'strongly . . . constitute the citizens of the United States [as] one people,' by 'plac[ing] the citizens of each State upon the same footing with citizens of other States, so far as the advantages resulting from citizenship in those States are concerned.'" This does not mean, we have cautioned, that "state citizenship or residency may never be used by a State to distinguish among persons." "Nor must a State always apply all its laws or all its services equally to anyone, resident or nonresident, who may request it so to do." Rather, we have long held that the Privileges and Immunities Clause protects only those privileges and immunities that are "fundamental."

Petitioners allege that Virginia's citizens-only FOIA provision violates four different "fundamental" privileges or immunities: the opportunity to pursue a common calling, the ability to own and transfer property, access to the Virginia courts, and access to public information. The first three items on that list, however, are not abridged by the Virginia FOIA, and the fourth—framed broadly—is not protected by the Privileges and Immunities Clause.

Hurlbert argues that Virginia's citizens-only FOIA provision abridges his ability to earn a living in his chosen profession, namely, obtaining property records from state and local governments on behalf of clients. He is correct that the Privileges and Immunities Clause protects the right of citizens to "ply their trade, practice their occupation, or pursue a common calling." But the Virginia FOIA does not abridge Hurlbert's ability to engage in a common calling in the sense prohibited by the Privileges and Immunities Clause. Rather, the Court has struck laws down as violating the privilege of pursuing a common calling only when those laws were enacted for the protectionist purpose of burdening out-of-state citizens. In each case, the clear aim of the statute at issue was to advantage in-state workers and commercial interests at the expense of their out-of-state counterparts.

Virginia's FOIA differs sharply from those statutes. By its own terms, Virginia's FOIA was enacted to "ensur[e] the people of the Commonwealth ready access to public records in the custody of a public body or its officers and employees, and free entry to meetings of public bodies wherein the business of the people is being conducted." Rather, it seems clear that the distinction that the statute makes between citizens and noncitizens has a distinctly nonprotectionist aim. The state FOIA essentially represents a mechanism by which those who ultimately hold sovereign power (*i.e.,* the citizens of the Commonwealth) may obtain an accounting from the public officials to whom they delegate the exercise of that power. In addition, the provision limiting the use of the state FOIA to Virginia citizens recognizes that Virginia taxpayers foot the bill for the fixed costs underlying recordkeeping in the Commonwealth. The challenged provision of the state FOIA does not violate the Privileges and Immunities Clause simply because it has the incidental effect of preventing citizens of other States from making a profit by trading on information contained in state records. While the Clause forbids a State from intentionally giving its own citizens a competitive advantage in business or employment, the Clause does not require that a State tailor its every action to avoid any incidental effect on out-of-state tradesmen.

Hurlbert next alleges that the challenged provision of the Virginia FOIA abridges the right to own and transfer property in the Commonwealth. Like the right to pursue a common calling, the right to "take, hold and dispose of property, either real or personal," has long been seen as one of the privileges of citizenship. Virginia, however, does not prevent citizens of other States from obtaining such documents. Under Virginia law, "any records and papers of every circuit court that are maintained by the clerk of the circuit court shall be open to inspection by any person and the clerk shall, when requested, furnish copies thereof."

A similar flaw undermines Hurlbert's claim that Virginia violates the Privileges and Immunities Clause by preventing citizens of other States from accessing real estate tax assessment records. It is true that those records, while available to Virginia citizens under the state FOIA, are not required by statute to be made available to noncitizens. But in fact Virginia and its subdivisions generally make even these less essential records readily available to all. These records are considered nonconfidential under Virginia law and, accordingly, they may be posted online. Henrico County, from which Hurlbert sought real estate tax assessments, follows this practice, as does almost every other county in the Commonwealth. Requiring noncitizens to conduct a few minutes of Internet research in lieu of using a relatively cumbersome state FOIA process cannot be said to impose any significant burden on noncitizens' ability to own or transfer property in Virginia.

McBurney alleges that Virginia's citizens-only FOIA provision impermissibly burdens his "access to public proceedings." McBurney is correct that the Privileges and Immunities Clause "secures citizens of one State the right to resort to the courts of another, equally with the citizens of the latter State." But petitioners do not suggest that the Virginia FOIA slams the courthouse door on noncitizens; rather, the most they claim is that the law creates "[a]n information asymmetry between adversaries based solely on state citizenship."

The challenged provision of the Virginia FOIA clearly does not deprive noncitizens of "reasonable and adequate" access to the Commonwealth's courts. Moreover, Virginia law gives citizens and noncitizens alike access to judicial records.

Finally, we reject petitioners' sweeping claim that the challenged provision of the Virginia FOIA violates the Privileges and Immunities Clause because it denies them the right to access public information on equal terms with citizens of the Commonwealth. We cannot agree that the Privileges and Immunities Clause covers this broad right.

This Court has repeatedly made clear that there is no constitutional right to obtain all the information provided by FOIA laws. It certainly cannot be said that such a broad right has "at all times, been enjoyed by the citizens of the several states which compose this Union, from the time of their becoming free, independent, and sovereign." No such right was recognized at common law. Most founding-era English cases provided that only those persons who had a personal interest in non-judicial records were permitted to access them.

Nineteenth-century American cases, while less uniform, certainly do not support the proposition that a broad-based right to access public information was widely recognized in the early Republic.

Nor is such a sweeping right "basic to the maintenance or well-being of the Union." FOIA laws are of relatively recent vintage. The federal FOIA was enacted in 1966, and Virginia's counterpart was adopted two years later. There is no contention that the Nation's unity foundered in their absence, or that it is suffering now because of the citizens-only FOIA provisions that several States have enacted.

III

In addition to his Privileges and Immunities Clause claim, Hurlbert contends that Virginia's citizens-only FOIA provision violates the dormant Commerce Clause. Our dormant Commerce Clause jurisprudence "significantly limits the ability of States and localities to regulate or otherwise burden the flow of interstate commerce."

Virginia's FOIA law neither "regulates" nor "burdens" interstate commerce; rather, it merely provides a service to local citizens that would not otherwise be available at all. The "common thread" among those cases in which the Court has found a dormant Commerce Clause violation is that "the State interfered with the natural functioning of the interstate market either through prohibition or through burdensome regulation." Here, by contrast, Virginia neither prohibits access to an interstate market nor imposes burdensome regulation on that market. Rather, it merely creates and provides to its own citizens copies — which would not otherwise exist — of state records.

Because Virginia's citizens-only FOIA provision neither abridges any of petitioners' fundamental privileges and immunities nor impermissibly regulates commerce, petitioners' constitutional claims fail.

D.   *The Dormant Commerce Clause* (casebook, p. 445)

3.   The Contemporary Test for the Dormant Commerce Clause (casebook, p. 464)

e.   *State Taxation of Interstate Commerce*

The Court's most recent dormant commerce clause case considered it in the context of state taxation of interstate commerce. It also was the occasion for renewed disagreement among the justices as to whether there should be a dormant commerce clause.

COMPTROLLER OF THE TREASURY OF
MARYLAND v. WYNNE
135 S. Ct. 1787 (2015)

Justice ALITO delivered the opinion of the Court.

This case involves the constitutionality of an unusual feature of Maryland's personal income tax scheme. Like many other States, Maryland taxes the income its residents earn both within and outside the State, as well as the income that nonresidents earn from sources within Maryland. But unlike most other States, Maryland does not offer its residents a full credit against the income taxes that they pay to other States. The effect of this scheme is that some of the income earned by Maryland residents outside the State is taxed twice. Maryland's scheme creates an incentive for taxpayers to opt for intrastate rather than interstate economic activity.

We have long held that States cannot subject corporate income to tax schemes similar to Maryland's, and we see no reason why income earned by individuals should be treated less favorably. Maryland admits that its law has the same economic effect as a state tariff, the quintessential evil targeted by the dormant Commerce Clause. We therefore affirm the decision of Maryland's highest court and hold that this feature of the State's tax scheme violates the Federal Constitution.

I

Maryland, like most States, raises revenue in part by levying a personal income tax. The income tax that Maryland imposes upon its own residents has two parts: a "state" income tax, which is set at a graduated rate, and a so-called "county" income tax, which is set at a rate that varies by county but is capped at 3.2%. Despite the names that Maryland has assigned to these taxes, both are State taxes, and both are collected by the State's Comptroller of the Treasury. Of course, some Maryland residents earn income in other States, and some of those States also tax this income. If Maryland residents pay income tax to another jurisdiction for income earned there, Maryland allows them a credit against the "state" tax but not the "county" tax. As a result, part of the income that a Maryland resident earns outside the State may be taxed twice.

Maryland also taxes the income of nonresidents. This tax has two parts. First, nonresidents must pay the "state" income tax on all the income that they earn from sources within Maryland. Second, nonresidents not subject to the county tax must pay a "special nonresident tax" in lieu of the "county" tax. The "special nonresident tax" is levied on income earned from sources within Maryland, and its rate is "equal to the lowest county income tax rate set by any Maryland county." Maryland does not tax the income that nonresidents earn from sources outside Maryland.

The Court of Appeals of Maryland [held the double taxing of income unconstitutional under the four-part test of *Complete Auto Transit, Inc. v. Brady* (1977), which asks whether a "tax is applied to an activity with a substantial nexus with the taxing State, is fairly apportioned, does not discriminate against interstate commerce, and is fairly related to the services provided by the State." The Court of Appeals held that the tax failed both the fair apportionment and nondiscrimination parts of the *Complete Auto* test. With respect to fair apportionment, the court first held that the tax failed the "internal consistency" test because if every State adopted Maryland's tax scheme, interstate commerce would be taxed at a higher rate than intrastate commerce. It then held that the tax failed the "external consistency" test because it created a risk of multiple taxation. With respect to nondiscrimination, the court held that the tax discriminated against interstate commerce because it denied residents a credit on income taxes paid to other States and so taxed income earned interstate at a rate higher than income earned intrastate. The court thus concluded that Maryland's tax scheme was unconstitutional insofar as it denied the Wynnes a credit against the "county" tax for income taxes they paid to other States.

II

The Commerce Clause grants Congress power to "regulate Commerce
. . . among the several States." These "few simple words . . . reflected a
central concern of the Framers that was an immediate reason for calling the Constitutional Convention: the conviction that in order to succeed, the new Union would have to avoid the tendencies toward economic
Balkanization that had plagued relations among the Colonies and later
among the States under the Articles of Confederation." Although the
Clause is framed as a positive grant of power to Congress, "we have
consistently held this language to contain a further, negative command,
known as the dormant Commerce Clause, prohibiting certain state taxation even when Congress has failed to legislate on the subject."

Under our precedents, the dormant Commerce Clause precludes States
from "discriminat[ing] between transactions on the basis of some interstate element." This means, among other things, that a State "may not
tax a transaction or incident more heavily when it crosses state lines than
when it occurs entirely within the State." "Nor may a State impose a tax
which discriminates against interstate commerce either by providing a
direct commercial advantage to local business, or by subjecting interstate
commerce to the burden of 'multiple taxation.' "

Our existing dormant Commerce Clause cases all but dictate the result
reached in this case by Maryland's highest court. In addition, the notion
that the victims of such discrimination have a complete remedy at the
polls is fanciful. It is likely that only a distinct minority of a State's residents earns income out of State. Schemes that discriminate against income
earned in other States may be attractive to legislators and a majority of
their constituents for precisely this reason. It is even more farfetched to
suggest that natural persons with out-of-state income are better able to
influence state lawmakers than large corporations headquartered in the
State. In short, petitioner's argument would leave no security where the
majority of voters prefer protectionism at the expense of the few who
earn income interstate.

In attempting to justify Maryland's unusual tax scheme, the principal
dissent argues that the Commerce Clause imposes no limit on Maryland's
ability to tax the income of its residents, no matter where that income is
earned. It argues that Maryland has the sovereign power to tax all of the
income of its residents, wherever earned, and it therefore reasons that
the dormant Commerce Clause cannot constrain Maryland's ability to
expose its residents (and nonresidents) to the threat of double taxation.

This argument confuses what a State may do without violating the Due Process Clause of the Fourteenth Amendment with what it may do without violating the Commerce Clause. The Due Process Clause allows a State to tax "*all* the income of its residents, even income earned outside the taxing jurisdiction." But "while a State may, consistent with the Due Process Clause, have the authority to tax a particular taxpayer, imposition of the tax may nonetheless violate the Commerce Clause."

One good reason why we have never accepted the principal dissent's logic is that it would lead to plainly untenable results. Imagine that Maryland taxed the income that its residents earned in other States but exempted income earned out of State from any business that primarily served Maryland residents. Such a tax would violate the dormant Commerce Clause, and it cannot be saved by the principal dissent's admonition that Maryland has the power to tax all the income of its residents. There is no principled difference between that hypothetical Commerce Clause challenge and this one.

The principal dissent, if accepted, would work a sea change in our Commerce Clause jurisprudence. Legion are the cases in which we have considered and even upheld dormant Commerce Clause challenges brought by residents to taxes that the State had the jurisdictional power to impose.

Critically — and this dispels a central argument made by petitioner and the principal dissent — the Maryland scheme's discriminatory treatment of interstate commerce is not simply the result of its interaction with the taxing schemes of other States. Instead, the internal consistency test reveals what the undisputed economic analysis shows: Maryland's tax scheme is inherently discriminatory and operates as a tariff. This identity between Maryland's tax and a tariff is fatal because tariffs are "[t]he paradigmatic example of a law discriminating against interstate commerce." But Maryland has offered no reason why our analysis should change because we deal with an income tax rather than a formal tariff, and we see none. After all, "tariffs against the products of other States are so patently unconstitutional that our cases reveal not a single attempt by any State to enact one. Instead, the cases are filled with state laws that aspire to reap some of the benefits of tariffs by other means."

Justice SCALIA, with whom Justice THOMAS joins as to Parts I and II, dissenting.

The Court holds unconstitutional Maryland's refusal to give its residents full credits against income taxes paid to other States. It does this by invoking the negative Commerce Clause, a judge-invented rule under which judges may set aside state laws that they think impose too much of a burden upon interstate commerce. I join the principal dissent, which demonstrates the incompatibility of this decision with our prior negative Commerce Clause cases. The principal purpose of my writing separately is to point out how wrong our negative Commerce Clause jurisprudence is in the first place, and how well today's decision illustrates its error.

The fundamental problem with our negative Commerce Clause cases is that the Constitution does not contain a negative Commerce Clause. It contains only a Commerce Clause. Unlike the negative Commerce Clause adopted by the judges, the real Commerce Clause adopted by the People merely empowers Congress to "regulate Commerce with foreign Nations, and among the several States, and with the Indian Tribes." The Clause says nothing about prohibiting state laws that burden commerce. Much less does it say anything about authorizing judges to set aside state laws *they believe* burden commerce. The clearest sign that the negative Commerce Clause is a judicial fraud is the utterly illogical holding that congressional consent enables States to enact laws that would otherwise constitute impermissible burdens upon interstate commerce. How could congressional consent lift a constitutional prohibition?

The Court's efforts to justify this judicial economic veto come to naught. The Court claims that the doctrine "has deep roots." So it does, like many weeds. But age alone does not make up for brazen invention. And the doctrine in any event is not quite as old as the Court makes it seem. The idea that the Commerce Clause of its own force limits state power "finds no expression" in discussions surrounding the Constitution's ratification. For years after the adoption of the Constitution, States continually made regulations that burdened interstate commerce (like pilotage laws and quarantine laws) without provoking any doubts about their constitutionality. This Court's earliest allusions to a negative Commerce Clause came only in dicta — ambiguous dicta, at that — and were vigorously contested at the time. Our first clear *holding* setting aside a state law under the negative Commerce Clause came after the Civil War, more than 80 years after the Constitution's adoption. Since then, we have tended to revamp the doctrine every couple of decades upon finding existing decisions unworkable or unsatisfactory. The negative Commerce Clause applied today has little in common with the negative Commerce Clause of the 19th century, except perhaps for incoherence.

The Court adds that "tariffs and other laws that burdened interstate commerce" were among "the chief evils that led to the adoption of the Constitution." This line of reasoning forgets that interpretation requires heeding more than the Constitution's purposes; it requires heeding the means the Constitution uses to achieve those purposes. The Constitution addresses the evils of local impediments to commerce by prohibiting States from imposing certain especially burdensome taxes — "Imposts or Duties on Imports or Exports" and "Dut[ies] of Tonnage" — without congressional consent. Art. I, § 10, cls. 2–3. It also addresses these evils by giving Congress a commerce power under which *it* may prohibit other burdensome taxes and laws. As the Constitution's text shows, however, it does not address these evils by empowering the *judiciary* to set aside state taxes and laws that *it* deems too burdensome. By arrogating this power anyway, our negative Commerce Clause cases have disrupted the balance the Constitution strikes between the goal of protecting commerce and competing goals like preserving local autonomy and promoting democratic responsibility.

The failings of negative Commerce Clause doctrine go beyond its lack of a constitutional foundation, as today's decision well illustrates.

1. One glaring defect of the negative Commerce Clause is its lack of governing principle. Neither the Constitution nor our legal traditions offer guidance about how to separate improper state interference with commerce from permissible state taxation or regulation of commerce. So we must make the rules up as we go along. That is how we ended up with the bestiary of ad hoc tests and ad hoc exceptions that we apply nowadays.

For reasons of *stare decisis,* I will vote to set aside a tax under the negative Commerce Clause if (but only if) it discriminates on its face against interstate commerce or cannot be distinguished from a tax this Court has already held unconstitutional. The income tax before us does not discriminate on its face against interstate commerce; a resident pays no less to Maryland when he works in Maryland than when he works elsewhere. Neither is the tax before us indistinguishable from one that we have previously held unconstitutional. To the contrary, as the principal dissent establishes, our prior cases validate this tax.

Maryland's refusal to give residents full tax credits against income taxes paid to other States has its disadvantages. It threatens double taxation and encourages residents to work in Maryland. But Maryland's law also has its advantages. It allows the State to collect equal revenue from taxpayers with equal incomes, avoids the administrative burdens of verifying tax payments to other States, and ensures that every resident pays the State at least some income tax. Nothing in the Constitution precludes Maryland from deciding that the benefits of its tax scheme are worth the costs.

Justice THOMAS, with whom Justice SCALIA joins except as to the first paragraph, dissenting.

"I continue to adhere to my view that the negative Commerce Clause has no basis in the text of the Constitution, makes little sense, and has proved virtually unworkable in application, and, consequently, cannot serve as a basis for striking down a state statute." For that reason, I would uphold Maryland's tax scheme.

In reaching the contrary conclusion, the Court proves just how far our negative Commerce Clause jurisprudence has departed from the actual Commerce Clause. According to the majority, a state income tax that fails to provide residents with "a full credit against the income taxes that they pay to other States" violates the Commerce Clause. That news would have come as a surprise to those who penned and ratified the Constitution. As this Court observed some time ago, "Income taxes . . . were imposed by several of the States at or shortly after the adoption of the Federal Constitution." There is no indication that those early state income tax schemes provided credits for income taxes paid elsewhere. Thus, under the majority's reasoning, all of those state laws would have contravened the newly ratified Commerce Clause.

It seems highly implausible that those who ratified the Commerce Clause understood it to conflict with the income tax laws of their States and nonetheless adopted it without a word of concern. That silence is particularly deafening given the importance of such taxes for raising revenues at the time.

Justice GINSBURG, with whom Justice SCALIA and Justice KAGAN join, dissenting.

Today's decision veers from a principle of interstate and international taxation repeatedly acknowledged by this Court: A nation or State "may tax *all* the income of its residents, even income earned outside the taxing jurisdiction." In accord with this principle, the Court has regularly rejected claims that taxes on a resident's out-of-state income violate the Due Process Clause for lack of a sufficient "connection" to the taxing State. But under dormant Commerce Clause jurisprudence, the Court decides, a State is not really empowered to tax a resident's income from whatever source derived. In taxing personal income, the Court holds, source-based authority, *i.e.,* authority to tax commerce conducted within a State's territory, boxes in the taxing authority of a taxpayer's domicile.

As I see it, nothing in the Constitution or in prior decisions of this Court dictates that one of two States, the domiciliary State or the source State, must recede simply because both have lawful tax regimes reaching the same income. True, Maryland elected to deny a credit for income taxes paid to other States in computing a resident's county tax liability. It is equally true, however, that the other States that taxed the Wynnes' income elected not to offer them a credit for their Maryland county income taxes. In this situation, the Constitution does not prefer one lawful basis for state taxation of a person's income over the other. Nor does it require one State, in this case Maryland, to limit its residence-based taxation, should the State also choose to exercise, to the full extent, its source-based authority. States often offer their residents credits for income taxes paid to other States, as Maryland does for state income tax purposes. States do so, however, as a matter of tax "policy," not because the Constitution compels that course.

This case is, at bottom, about policy choices: Should States prioritize ensuring that all who live or work within the State shoulder their fair share of the costs of government? Or must States prioritize avoidance of double taxation? As I have demonstrated, achieving even the latter goal is beyond this Court's competence. Resolving the competing tax policy considerations this case implicates is something the Court is even less well equipped to do. For a century, we have recognized that state legislatures and the Congress are constitutionally assigned and institutionally better equipped to balance such issues. I would reverse, so that we may leave that task where it belongs.

Chapter 6

Economic Liberties

D. The Takings Clause

2. Is There a "Taking"? (casebook, p. 658)

In *Nollan v. California Coastal Commission* (casebook, p. 676) and *Dolan v. City of Tigard* (casebook, p. 677), the Court held that conditions on the development of property must be justified by a benefit roughly proportionate to the burden imposed. Otherwise, it is a taking. In Koontz v. St. Johns River Water Management District, the Court applied this rule to a situation in which the government denies a permit (as opposed to granting it) with conditions that are challenged as a taking.

KOONTZ v. ST. JOHNS RIVER WATER
MANAGEMENT DISTRICT
133 S. Ct. 2586 (2013)

Justice ALITO delivered the opinion of the Court.

Our decisions in *Nollan v. California Coastal Comm'n* (1987), and *Dolan v. City of Tigard* (1994), provide important protection against the misuse of the power of land-use regulation. In those cases, we held that a unit of government may not condition the approval of a land-use permit on the owner's relinquishment of a portion of his property unless there is a "nexus" and "rough proportionality" between the government's demand and the effects of the proposed land use. In this case, the St. Johns River Water Management District (District) believes that it circumvented Nollan and Dolan because of the way in which it structured its handling of a permit application submitted by Coy Koontz, Sr., whose estate is represented in this Court by Coy Koontz, Jr. The District did not approve his application on the condition that he surrender an interest in his land. Instead, the District, after suggesting that he could obtain approval by signing over such an interest, denied his application because he refused to yield. The Florida Supreme Court blessed this maneuver and thus effectively interred those important decisions. Because we conclude that Nollan and Dolan cannot be evaded in this way, the Florida Supreme Court's decision must be reversed.

I

In 1972, petitioner purchased an undeveloped 14.9-acre tract of land on the south side of Florida State Road 50, a divided four-lane highway east of Orlando. The property is located less than 1,000 feet from that road's intersection with Florida State Road 408, a tolled expressway that is one of Orlando's major thoroughfares.

Petitioner decided to develop the 3.7-acre northern section of his property, and in 1994 he applied to the District for MSSW and WRM permits. To mitigate the environmental effects of his proposal, petitioner offered to foreclose any possible future development of the approximately 11-acre southern section of his land by deeding to the District a conservation easement on that portion of his property.

The District considered the 11-acre conservation easement to be inadequate, and it informed petitioner that it would approve construction only if he agreed to one of two concessions. First, the District proposed that petitioner reduce the size of his development to 1 acre and deed to the District a conservation easement on the remaining 13.9 acres. To reduce the development area, the District suggested that petitioner could eliminate the dry-bed pond from his proposal and instead install a more costly subsurface stormwater management system beneath the building site. The District also suggested that petitioner install retaining walls rather than gradually sloping the land from the building site down to the elevation of the rest of his property to the south.

In the alternative, the District told petitioner that he could proceed with the development as proposed, building on 3.7 acres and deeding a conservation easement to the government on the remainder of the property, if he also agreed to hire contractors to make improvements to District-owned land several miles away. Specifically, petitioner could pay to replace culverts on one parcel or fill in ditches on another. Either of those projects would have enhanced approximately 50 acres of District-owned wetlands.

Believing the District's demands for mitigation to be excessive in light of the environmental effects that his building proposal would have caused, petitioner filed suit in state court. Among other claims, he argued that he was entitled to relief under Fla. Stat. § 373.617(2), which allows owners to recover "monetary damages" if a state agency's action is "an unreasonable exercise of the state's police power constituting a taking without just compensation."

II

We have said in a variety of contexts that "the government may not deny a benefit to a person because he exercises a constitutional right." Nollan and Dolan "involve a special application" of this doctrine that protects the Fifth Amendment right to just compensation for property the government takes when owners apply for land-use permits.

Our decisions in those cases reflect two realities of the permitting process. The first is that land-use permit applicants are especially vulnerable to the type of coercion that the unconstitutional conditions doctrine prohibits because the government often has broad discretion to deny a permit that is worth far more than property it would like to take. By conditioning a building permit on the owner's deeding over a public right-of-way, for example, the government can pressure an owner into voluntarily giving up property for which the Fifth Amendment would otherwise require just compensation.

A second reality of the permitting process is that many proposed land uses threaten to impose costs on the public that dedications of property can offset. Where a building proposal would substantially increase traffic congestion, for example, officials might condition permit approval on the owner's agreement to deed over the land needed to widen a public road.

Nollan and Dolan accommodate both realities by allowing the government to condition approval of a permit on the dedication of property to the public so long as there is a "nexus" and "rough proportionality" between the property that the government demands and the social costs of the applicant's proposal. Under Nollan and Dolan the government may choose whether and how a permit applicant is required to mitigate the impacts of a proposed development, but it may not leverage its legitimate interest in mitigation to pursue governmental ends that lack an essential nexus and rough proportionality to those impacts.

The principles that undergird our decisions in Nollan and Dolan do not change depending on whether the government approves a permit on the condition that the applicant turn over property or denies a permit because the applicant refuses to do so. We have often concluded that denials of governmental benefits were impermissible under the unconstitutional conditions doctrine. In so holding, we have recognized that regardless of whether the government ultimately succeeds in pressuring someone into forfeiting a constitutional right, the unconstitutional conditions doctrine forbids burdening the Constitution's enumerated rights by coercively withholding benefits from those who exercise them.

A contrary rule would be especially untenable in this case because it would enable the government to evade the limitations of Nollan and Dolan simply by phrasing its demands for property as conditions precedent to permit approval. Under the Florida Supreme Court's approach, a government order stating that a permit is "approved if" the owner turns over property would be subject to Nollan and Dolan, but an identical order that uses the words "denied until" would not. Our unconstitutional conditions cases have long refused to attach significance to the distinction between conditions precedent and conditions subsequent.

That is not to say, however, that there is no relevant difference between a consummated taking and the denial of a permit based on an unconstitutionally extortionate demand. Where the permit is denied and the condition is never imposed, nothing has been taken. While the unconstitutional conditions doctrine recognizes that this burdens a constitutional right, the Fifth Amendment mandates a particular remedy — just compensation — only for takings. In cases where there is an excessive demand but no taking, whether money damages are available is not a question of federal constitutional law but of the cause of action — whether state or federal — on which the landowner relies. Because petitioner brought his claim pursuant to a state law cause of action, the Court has no occasion to discuss what remedies might be available for a Nollan/Dolan unconstitutional conditions violation either here or in other cases.

We hold that the government's demand for property from a land-use permit applicant must satisfy the requirements of Nollan and Dolan even when the government denies the permit and even when its demand is for money. The Court expresses no view on the merits of petitioner's claim that respondent's actions here failed to comply with the principles set forth in this opinion and those two cases. The Florida Supreme Court's judgment is reversed, and this case is remanded for further proceedings not inconsistent with this opinion.

Justice KAGAN, with whom Justice GINSBURG, Justice BREYER, and Justice SOTOMAYOR join, dissenting.

In the paradigmatic case triggering review under *Nollan v. California Coastal Comm'n* (1987), and *Dolan v. City of Tigard* (1994), the government approves a building permit on the condition that the land-owner relinquish an interest in real property, like an easement. The significant legal questions that the Court resolves today are whether Nollan and Dolan also apply when that case is varied in two ways. First, what if the government does not approve the permit, but instead demands that the condition be fulfilled before it will do so? Second, what if the condition entails not transferring real property, but simply paying money?

I think the Court gets the first question it addresses right. The Nollan-Dolan standard applies not only when the government approves a development permit conditioned on the owner's conveyance of a property interest (i.e., imposes a condition subsequent), but also when the government denies a permit until the owner meets the condition (i.e., imposes a condition precedent). That means an owner may challenge the denial of a permit on the ground that the government's condition lacks the "nexus" and "rough proportionality" to the development's social costs that Nollan and Dolan require. Still, the condition-subsequent and condition-precedent situations differ in an important way. When the government grants a permit subject to the relinquishment of real property, and that condition does not satisfy Nollan and Dolan, then the government has taken the property and must pay just compensation under the Fifth Amendment. But when the government denies a permit because an owner has refused to accede to that same demand, nothing has actually been taken. The owner is entitled to have the improper condition removed; and he may be entitled to a monetary remedy created by state law for imposing such a condition; but he cannot be entitled to constitutional compensation for a taking of property. So far, we all agree.

Our core disagreement concerns the second question the Court addresses. The majority extends Nollan and Dolan to cases in which the government conditions a permit not on the transfer of real property, but instead on the payment or expenditure of money. The boundaries of the majority's new rule are uncertain. But it threatens to subject a vast array of land-use regulations, applied daily in States and localities throughout the country, to heightened constitutional scrutiny. I would not embark on so unwise an adventure.

I also would affirm for two independent reasons establishing that Koontz cannot get the money damages he seeks. First, respondent St. Johns River Water Management District (District) never demanded anything (including money) in exchange for a permit; the Nollan-Dolan standard therefore does not come into play (even assuming that test applies to demands for money). Second, no taking occurred in this case because

Koontz never acceded to a demand (even had there been one), and so no property changed hands; as just noted, Koontz therefore cannot claim just compensation under the Fifth Amendment. The majority does not take issue with my first conclusion, and affirmatively agrees with my second. But the majority thinks Koontz might still be entitled to money damages, and remands to the Florida Supreme Court on that question. I do not see how, and expect that court will so rule.

Nollan and Dolan are important decisions, designed to curb governments from using their power over land-use permitting to extract for free what the Takings Clause would otherwise require them to pay for. But for no fewer than three independent reasons, this case does not present that problem. First and foremost, the government commits a taking only when it appropriates a specific property interest, not when it requires a person to pay or spend money. Here, the District never took or threatened such an interest; it tried to extract from Koontz solely a commitment to spend money to repair public wetlands. Second, Nollan and Dolan can operate only when the government makes a demand of the permit applicant; the decisions' prerequisite, in other words, is a condition. Here, the District never made such a demand: It informed Koontz that his applications did not meet legal requirements; it offered suggestions for bringing those applications into compliance; and it solicited further proposals from Koontz to achieve the same end. That is not the stuff of which an unconstitutional condition is made. And third, the Florida statute at issue here does not, in any event, offer a damages remedy for imposing such a condition. It provides relief only for a consummated taking, which did not occur here.

The majority's errors here are consequential. The majority turns a broad array of local land-use regulations into federal constitutional questions. It deprives state and local governments of the flexibility they need to enhance their communities — to ensure environmentally sound and economically productive development. It places courts smack in the middle of the most everyday local government activity. As those consequences play out across the country, I believe the Court will rue today's decision. I respectfully dissent.

The Court also considered the definition of a "taking" in a very different context: that is, whether a federal program requiring that raisin producers set aside part of their crops for use by the federal government is a taking. In considering this, the Court also addressed what "just compensation" requires.

HORNE v. DEPARTMENT OF AGRICULTURE
135 S. Ct. ___ (2015)

Chief Justice ROBERTS delivered the opinion of the Court.

Under the United States Department of Agriculture's California Raisin Marketing Order, a percentage of a grower's crop must be physically set aside in certain years for the account of the Government, free of charge. The Government then sells, allocates, or otherwise disposes of the raisins in ways it determines are best suited to maintaining an orderly market. The question is whether the Takings Clause of the Fifth Amendment bars the Government from imposing such a demand on the growers without just compensation.

I

The Agricultural Marketing Agreement Act of 1937 authorizes the Secretary of Agriculture to promulgate "marketing orders" to help maintain stable markets for particular agricultural products. The marketing order for raisins requires growers in certain years to give a percentage of their crop to the Government, free of charge. The required allocation is determined by the Raisin Administrative Committee, a Government entity composed largely of growers and others in the raisin business appointed by the Secretary of Agriculture. In 2002–2003, this Committee ordered raisin growers to turn over 47 percent of their crop. In 2003–2004, 30 percent.

Growers generally ship their raisins to a raisin "handler," who physically separates the raisins due the Government (called "reserve raisins"), pays the growers only for the remainder ("free-tonnage raisins"), and packs and sells the free-tonnage raisins. The Raisin Committee acquires title to the reserve raisins that have been set aside, and decides how to dispose of them in its discretion. It sells them in noncompetitive markets, for example to exporters, federal agencies, or foreign governments; donates them to charitable causes; releases them to growers who agree to reduce their raisin production; or disposes of them by "any other means" consistent with the purposes of the raisin program. Proceeds from Committee sales are principally used to subsidize handlers who sell raisins for export (not including the Hornes, who are not raisin exporters). Raisin growers retain an interest in any net proceeds from sales the Raisin Committee makes, after deductions for the export subsidies and the Committee's administrative expenses. In the years at issue in this case, those proceeds were less than the cost of producing the crop one year, and nothing at all the next.

The Hornes — Marvin Horne, Laura Horne, and their family — are both raisin growers and handlers. They "handled" not only their own raisins but also those produced by other growers, paying those growers in full for all of their raisins, not just the free-tonnage portion. In 2002, the Hornes refused to set aside any raisins for the Government, believing they were not legally bound to do so. The Government sent trucks to the Hornes' facility at eight o'clock one morning to pick up the raisins, but the Hornes refused entry. The Government then assessed against the Hornes a fine equal to the market value of the missing raisins — some $480,000 — as well as an additional civil penalty of just over $200,000 for disobeying the order to turn them over.

When the Government sought to collect the fine, the Hornes turned to the courts, arguing that the reserve requirement was an unconstitutional taking of their property under the Fifth Amendment.

II

The petition for certiorari poses three questions, which we answer in turn.

A

The first question presented asks "Whether the government's 'categorical duty' under the Fifth Amendment to pay just compensation when it 'physically takes possession of an interest in property,' applies only to real property and not to personal property." The answer is no.

There is no dispute that the "classic taking [is one] in which the government directly appropriates private property for its own use." Nor is there any dispute that, in the case of real property, such an appropriation is a *per se* taking that requires just compensation.

Nothing in the text or history of the Takings Clause, or our precedents, suggests that the rule is any different when it comes to appropriation of personal property. The Government has a categorical duty to pay just compensation when it takes your car, just as when it takes your home.

The reserve requirement imposed by the Raisin Committee is a clear physical taking. Actual raisins are transferred from the growers to the Government. Title to the raisins passes to the Raisin Committee. The Committee's raisins must be physically segregated from free-tonnage raisins. Reserve raisins are sometimes left on the premises of handlers, but they are held "for the account" of the Government. The Committee disposes of what become its raisins as it wishes, to promote the purposes of the raisin marketing order.

Raisin growers subject to the reserve requirement thus lose the entire "bundle" of property rights in the appropriated raisins — "the rights to possess, use and dispose of" them, — with the exception of the speculative hope that some residual proceeds may be left when the Government is done with the raisins and has deducted the expenses of implementing all aspects of the marketing order. The Government's "actual taking of possession and control" of the reserve raisins gives rise to a taking as clearly "as if the Government held full title and ownership," as it essentially does. The Government's formal demand that the Hornes turn over a percentage of their raisin crop without charge, for the Government's control and use, is "of such a unique character that it is a taking without regard to other factors that a court might ordinarily examine."

B

The second question presented asks "Whether the government may avoid the categorical duty to pay just compensation for a physical taking of property by reserving to the property owner a contingent interest in a portion of the value of the property, set at the government's discretion." The answer is no.

The Government and dissent argue that raisins are fungible goods whose only value is in the revenue from their sale. According to the Government, the raisin marketing order leaves that interest with the raisin growers: After selling reserve raisins and deducting expenses and subsidies for exporters, the Raisin Committee returns any net proceeds to the growers. The Government contends that because growers are entitled to these net proceeds, they retain the most important property interest in the reserve raisins, so there is no taking in the first place.

But when there has been a physical appropriation, "we do not ask . . . whether it deprives the owner of all economically valuable use" of the item taken. The Government and dissent again confuse our inquiry concerning *per se* takings with our analysis for regulatory takings. A regulatory restriction on use that does not entirely deprive an owner of property rights may not be a taking under *Penn Central*. But once there is a taking, as in the case of a physical appropriation, any payment from the Government in connection with that action goes, at most, to the question of just compensation.

C

The third question presented asks "Whether a governmental mandate to relinquish specific, identifiable property as a 'condition' on permission to engage in commerce effects a per se taking." The answer, at least in this case, is yes.

The Government contends that the reserve requirement is not a taking because raisin growers voluntarily choose to participate in the raisin market. According to the Government, if raisin growers don't like it, they can "plant different crops," or "sell their raisin-variety grapes as table grapes or for use in juice or wine."

"Let them sell wine" is probably not much more comforting to the raisin growers than similar retorts have been to others throughout history. In any event, the Government is wrong as a matter of law. In *Loretto* [*v. Teleprompter*], we rejected the argument that the New York law was not a taking because a landlord could avoid the requirement by ceasing to be a landlord. We held instead that "a landlord's ability to rent his property may not be conditioned on his forfeiting the right to compensation for a physical occupation."

The taking here cannot reasonably be characterized as part of a similar voluntary exchange. In one of the years at issue here, the Government insisted that the Hornes turn over 47 percent of their raisin crop, in exchange for the "benefit" of being allowed to sell the remaining 53 percent. The next year, the toll was 30 percent. Selling produce in interstate commerce, although certainly subject to reasonable government regulation, is similarly not a special governmental benefit that the Government may hold hostage, to be ransomed by the waiver of constitutional protection.

III

The Government correctly points out that a taking does not violate the Fifth Amendment unless there is no just compensation Finally, the Government briefly argues that if we conclude that the reserve requirement effects a taking, we should remand for the Court of Appeals to calculate "what compensation would have been due if petitioners had complied with the reserve requirement." The Government contends that the calculation must consider what the value of the reserve raisins would have been without the price support program, as well as "other benefits . . . from the regulatory program, such as higher consumer demand for raisins spurred by enforcement of quality standards and promotional activities." Indeed, according to the Government, the Hornes would "likely" have a net gain under this theory.

The best defense may be a good offense, but the Government cites no support for its hypothetical-based approach, or its notion that general regulatory activity such as enforcement of quality standards can constitute just compensation for a specific physical taking. Instead, our cases have set forth a clear and administrable rule for just compensation: "The Court has repeatedly held that just compensation normally is to be measured by 'the market value of the property at the time of the taking.'"

The Government has already calculated the amount of just compensation in this case, when it fined the Hornes the fair market value of the raisins: $483,843.53. The Government cannot now disavow that valuation, and does not suggest that the marketing order affords the Hornes compensation in that amount. There is accordingly no need for a remand; the Hornes should simply be relieved of the obligation to pay the fine and associated civil penalty they were assessed when they resisted the Government's effort to take their raisins. This case, in litigation for more than a decade, has gone on long enough.

Justice BREYER, with whom Justice GINSBURG and Justice KAGAN join, concurring in part and dissenting in part.

I agree with Parts I and II of the Court's opinion. However, I cannot agree with the Court's rejection, in Part III, of the Government's final argument. The Government contends that we should remand the case for a determination of whether any compensation would have been due if the Hornes had complied with the California Raisin Marketing Order's reserve requirement. In my view, a remand for such a determination is necessary.

The question of just compensation was not presented in the Hornes' petition for certiorari. It was barely touched on in the briefs. And the courts below did not decide it. At the same time, the case law that I have found indicates that the Government may well be right: The marketing order may afford just compensation for the takings of raisins that it imposes. If that is correct, then the reserve requirement does not violate the Takings Clause.

On the record before us, the Hornes have not established that the Government, through the raisin reserve program, takes raisins *without just compensation*. When the Government takes as reserve raisins a percentage of the annual crop, the raisin owners retain the remaining, free-tonnage, raisins. The reserve requirement is intended, at least in part, to enhance the price that free-tonnage raisins will fetch on the open market.

And any such enhancement matters. This Court's precedents indicate that, when calculating the just compensation that the Fifth Amendment requires, a court should deduct from the value of the taken (reserve) raisins any enhancement caused by the taking to the value of the remaining (free-tonnage) raisins.

Ultimately, the majority rejects the Government's request for a remand because it believes that the Government "does not suggest that the marketing order affords the Hornes compensation" in the amount of the fine that the Government assessed. In my view, however, the relevant precedent indicates that the Takings Clause requires compensation in an amount equal to the value of the reserve raisins adjusted to account for the benefits received. And the Government does, indeed, suggest that the marketing order affords just compensation. Further, the Hornes have not demonstrated the contrary. Before granting judgment in favor of the Hornes, a court should address the issue in light of all of the relevant facts and law.

Justice SOTOMAYOR, dissenting.

The Hornes claim, and the Court agrees, that the Raisin Marketing Order, effects a *per se* taking under our decision in *Loretto v. Teleprompter Manhattan CATV Corp.* (1982). But *Loretto* sets a high bar for such claims: It requires that each and every property right be destroyed by governmental action before that action can be said to have effected a *per se* taking. Because the Order does not deprive the Hornes of all of their property rights, it does not effect a *per se* taking. I respectfully dissent from the Court's contrary holding.

I

What our jurisprudence thus makes plain is that a claim of a *Loretto* taking is a bold accusation that carries with it a heavy burden. To qualify as a *per se* taking under *Loretto,* the governmental action must be so completely destructive to the property owner's rights — all of them — as to render the ordinary, generally applicable protections of the *Penn Central* framework either a foregone conclusion or unequal to the task. Simply put, the retention of even one property right that is not destroyed is sufficient to defeat a claim of a *per se* taking under *Loretto.*

II

When evaluating the Order under this rubric, it is important to bear two things in mind. The first is that *Loretto* is not concerned with whether the

Order is a good idea now, whether it was ever a good idea, or whether it intrudes upon some property rights. The Order may well be an outdated, and by some lights downright silly, regulation. It is also no doubt intrusive. But whatever else one can say about the Order, it is not a *per se* taking if it does not result in the destruction of every property right.

The second thing to keep in mind is the need for precision about whose property rights are at issue and about what property is at issue. Here, what is at issue are the Hornes' property rights in the raisins they own and that are subject to the reserve requirement. The Order therefore effects a *per se* taking under *Loretto* if and only if each of the Hornes' property rights in the portion of raisins that the Order designated as reserve has been destroyed. If not, then whatever fate the Order may reach under some other takings test, it is not a *per se* taking.

The Hornes, however, retain at least one meaningful property interest in the reserve raisins: the right to receive some money for their disposition. The Order explicitly provides that raisin producers retain the right to "[t]he net proceeds from the disposition of reserve tonnage raisins," and ensures that reserve raisins will be sold "at prices and in a manner intended to maxim[ize] producer returns." Granted, this equitable distribution may represent less income than what some or all of the reserve raisins could fetch if sold in an unregulated market. In some years, it may even turn out (and has turned out) to represent no net income. But whether and when that occurs turns on market forces for which the Government cannot be blamed and to which all commodities — indeed, all property — are subject. In any event, we have emphasized that "a reduction in the value of property is not necessarily equated with a taking." Moreover, when, as here, the property at issue is a fungible commodity for sale, the income that the property may yield is the property owner's most central interest.

III

The Court's contrary conclusion rests upon two fundamental errors. The first is the Court's breezy assertion that a *per se* taking has occurred because the Hornes "lose the entire 'bundle' of property rights in the appropriated raisins . . . with the exception of" the retained interest in the equitable distribution of the proceeds from the disposition of the reserve raisins. But if there is a property right that has not been lost, as the Court concedes there is, then the Order has *not* destroyed each of the Hornes' rights in the reserve raisins and does *not* effect a *per se* taking. The Court protests that the retained interest is not substantial or certain enough. But while I see more value in that interest than the Court does, the bottom line is that *Loretto* does not distinguish among retained property interests that are substantial or certain enough to count and others that are not. Nor is it at all clear how the Court's approach will be administrable. How, after all, are courts, governments, or individuals supposed to know how much a property owner must be left with before this Court will bless the retained interest as sufficiently meaningful and certain?

One virtue of the *Loretto* test was, at least until today, its clarity. Under *Loretto,* a total destruction of all property rights constitutes a *per se* taking; anything less does not. Among the most significant doctrinal damage that the Court causes is the blurring of this otherwise bright line and the expansion of this otherwise narrow category. By the Court's lights, perhaps a 95 percent destruction of property rights can be a *per se* taking. Perhaps 90? Perhaps 60, so long as the remaining 40 is viewed by a reviewing court as less than meaningful? And what makes a retained right meaningful enough? One wonders. Indeed, it is not at all clear what test the Court has actually applied. Such confusion would be bad enough in any context, but it is especially pernicious in the area of property rights. Property owners should be assured of where they stand, and the government needs to know how far it can permissibly go without tripping over a categorical rule.

The second overarching error in the Court's opinion arises from its reliance on what it views as the uniquely physical nature of the taking effected by the Order. This, it says, is why many of the cases having to do with so-called regulatory takings are inapposite. It is not the case, however, that Government agents acting pursuant to the Order are storming raisin farms in the dark of night to load raisins onto trucks. The Order simply requires the Hornes to set aside a portion of their raisins — a requirement with which the Hornes refused to comply. And it does so to facilitate two classic regulatory goals. One is the regulatory purpose of limiting the quantity of raisins that can be sold on the market. The other is the regulatory purpose of arranging the orderly disposition of those raisins whose sale would otherwise exceed the cap.

Because a straightforward application of our precedents reveals that the Hornes have not suffered a *per se* taking, I would affirm the judgment of the Ninth Circuit. The Court reaches a contrary conclusion only by expanding our *per se* takings doctrine in a manner that is as unwarranted as it is vague. I respectfully dissent.

Chapter 7

Equal Protection

C. Classifications Based on Race and National Origin

5. Racial Classifications Benefiting Minorities

In *Grutter v. Bollinger* (2003) (casebook, p. 838), the Court held that colleges and universities have a compelling interest in having a diverse student body and may use race as a factor in admissions decisions to benefit minorities and enhance diversity. In *Fisher v. University of Texas at Austin*, the Court did not reconsider Grutter, but clarified the burden on colleges and universities to justify such programs.

FISHER v. UNIVERSITY OF TEXAS AT AUSTIN
133 S. Ct. 2411 (2013)

Justice KENNEDY delivered the opinion of the Court.

The University of Texas at Austin considers race as one of various factors in its undergraduate admissions process. Race is not itself assigned a numerical value for each applicant, but the University has committed itself to increasing racial minority enrollment on campus. It refers to this goal as a "critical mass." Petitioner, who is Caucasian, sued the University after her application was rejected. She contends that the University's use of race in the admissions process violated the Equal Protection Clause of the Fourteenth Amendment.

The parties asked the Court to review whether the judgment below was consistent with "this Court's decisions interpreting the Equal Protection Clause of the Fourteenth Amendment, including *Grutter v. Bollinger* (2003)." The Court concludes that the Court of Appeals did not hold the University to the demanding burden of strict scrutiny articulated in *Grutter* and *Regents of Univ. of Cal. v. Bakke* (1978) (opinion of Powell, J.). Because the Court of Appeals did not apply the correct standard of strict scrutiny, its decision affirming the District Court's grant of summary judgment to the University was incorrect. That decision is vacated, and the case is remanded for further proceedings.

I

Located in Austin, Texas, on the most renowned campus of the Texas state university system, the University is one of the leading institutions of higher education in the Nation. Admission is prized and competitive. In 2008, when petitioner sought admission to the University's entering class, she was 1 of 29,501 applicants. From this group 12,843 were admitted, and 6,715 accepted and enrolled. Petitioner was denied admission.

Following this Court's decisions in *Grutter v. Bollinger*, supra, and *Gratz v. Bollinger* (2003), the University adopted an admissions program, the 2004 program in which the University reverted to explicit consideration of race. This is the program here at issue.

The University's plan to resume race-conscious admissions was given formal expression in June 2004 in an internal document entitled Proposal to Consider Race and Ethnicity in Admissions (Proposal). The Proposal relied in substantial part on a study of a subset of undergraduate classes containing between 5 and 24 students. It showed that few of these classes had significant enrollment by members of racial minorities.

To implement the Proposal the University included a student's race as a component of the [Personal Achievement Index] score, beginning with applicants in the fall of 2004. The University asks students to classify themselves from among five predefined racial categories on the application. Race is not assigned an explicit numerical value, but it is undisputed that race is a meaningful factor.

Once applications have been scored, they are plotted on a grid with the Academic Index on the x-axis and the Personal Achievement Index on the y-axis. On that grid students are assigned to so-called cells based on their individual scores. All students in the cells falling above a certain line are admitted. All students below the line are not. Each college — such as Liberal Arts or Engineering — admits students separately. So a student is considered initially for her first-choice college, then for her second choice, and finally for general admission as an undeclared major.

Petitioner applied for admission to the University's 2008 entering class and was rejected. She sued the University and various University officials in the United States District Court for the Western District of Texas. She alleged that the University's consideration of race in admissions violated the Equal Protection Clause. The parties cross-moved for summary judgment. The District Court granted summary judgment to the University. The United States Court of Appeals for the Fifth Circuit affirmed.

B

Among the Court's cases involving racial classifications in education, there are three decisions that directly address the question of considering racial minority status as a positive or favorable factor in a university's admissions process, with the goal of achieving the educational benefits of a more diverse student body: Bakke, Gratz, and Grutter. We take those cases as given for purposes of deciding this case.

While these are the cases that most specifically address the central issue in this case, additional guidance may be found in the Court's broader equal protection jurisprudence which applies in this context. "Distinctions between citizens solely because of their ancestry are by their very nature odious to a free people," and therefore "are contrary to our traditions and hence constitutionally suspect." " '[B]ecause racial characteristics so seldom provide a relevant basis for disparate treatment,' " "the Equal Protection Clause demands that racial classifications . . . be subjected to the 'most rigid scrutiny.' "

To implement these canons, judicial review must begin from the position that "any official action that treats a person differently on account of his race or ethnic origin is inherently suspect." Strict scrutiny is a searching examination, and it is the government that bears the burden to prove " 'that the reasons for any [racial] classification [are] clearly identified and unquestionably legitimate.' "

II

Grutter made clear that racial "classifications are constitutional only if they are narrowly tailored to further compelling governmental interests." And Grutter endorsed Justice Powell's conclusion in Bakke that "the attainment of a diverse student body . . . is a constitutionally permissible goal for an institution of higher education." Thus, under Grutter, strict scrutiny must be applied to any admissions program using racial categories or classifications.

According to Grutter, a university's "educational judgment that such diversity is essential to its educational mission is one to which we defer." Grutter concluded that the decision to pursue "the educational benefits that flow from student body diversity," that the University deems integral to its mission is, in substantial measure, an academic judgment to which some, but not complete, judicial deference is proper under Grutter. A court, of course, should ensure that there is a reasoned, principled explanation for the academic decision. On this point, the District Court and Court of Appeals were correct in finding that Grutter calls for deference to the University's conclusion, " 'based on its experience and expertise,' " that a diverse student body would serve its educational goals. There is disagreement about whether Grutter was consistent with the principles of equal protection in approving this compelling interest in diversity. But the parties here do not ask the Court to revisit that aspect of *Grutter*'s holding.

A university is not permitted to define diversity as "some specified percentage of a particular group merely because of its race or ethnic origin." "That would amount to outright racial balancing, which is patently unconstitutional." "Racial balancing is not transformed from 'patently unconstitutional' to a compelling state interest simply by relabeling it 'racial diversity.' "

Once the University has established that its goal of diversity is consistent with strict scrutiny, however, there must still be a further judicial determination that the admissions process meets strict scrutiny in its implementation. The University must prove that the means chosen by the University to attain diversity are narrowly tailored to that goal. On this point, the University receives no deference. Grutter made clear that it is for the courts, not for university administrators, to ensure that "[t]he means chosen to accomplish the [government's] asserted purpose must be specifically and narrowly framed to accomplish that purpose." True, a court can take account of a university's experience and expertise in adopting or rejecting certain admissions processes. But, as the Court said in Grutter, it remains at all times the University's obligation to demonstrate, and the Judiciary's obligation to determine, that admissions processes "ensure that each applicant is evaluated as an individual and not in a way that makes an applicant's race or ethnicity the defining feature of his or her application."

Narrow tailoring also requires that the reviewing court verify that it is "necessary" for a university to use race to achieve the educational benefits of diversity. This involves a careful judicial inquiry into whether a university could achieve sufficient diversity without using racial classifications. Although "[n]arrow tailoring does not require exhaustion of every conceivable race-neutral alternative," strict scrutiny does require a court to examine with care, and not defer to, a university's "serious, good faith consideration of workable race-neutral alternatives." Consideration by the university is of course necessary, but it is not sufficient to satisfy strict scrutiny: The reviewing court must ultimately be satisfied that no workable race-neutral alternatives would produce the educational benefits of diversity. If "'a nonracial approach . . . could promote the substantial interest about as well and at tolerable administrative expense,'" then the university may not consider race. A plaintiff, of course, bears the burden of placing the validity of a university's adoption of an affirmative action plan in issue. But strict scrutiny imposes on the university the ultimate burden of demonstrating, before turning to racial classifications, that available, workable race-neutral alternatives do not suffice.

Rather than perform this searching examination, however, the Court of Appeals held petitioner could challenge only "whether [the University's] decision to reintroduce race as a factor in admissions was made in good faith." And in considering such a challenge, the court would "presume the University acted in good faith" and place on petitioner the burden of rebutting that presumption. The Court of Appeals held that to "second-guess the merits" of this aspect of the University's decision was a task it was "ill-equipped to perform" and that it would attempt only to "ensure that [the University's] decision to adopt a race-conscious admissions policy followed from [a process of] good faith consideration." The Court of Appeals thus concluded that "the narrow-tailoring inquiry — like the compelling-interest inquiry — is undertaken with a degree of deference to the Universit[y]."

These expressions of the controlling standard are at odds with *Grutter*'s command that "all racial classifications imposed by government 'must be analyzed by a reviewing court under strict scrutiny.'" Grutter did not hold that good faith would forgive an impermissible consideration of race. It must be remembered that "the mere recitation of a 'benign' or legitimate purpose for a racial classification is entitled to little or no weight." Strict scrutiny does not permit a court to accept a school's assertion that its admissions process uses race in a permissible way without a court giving close analysis to the evidence of how the process works in practice.

The higher education dynamic does not change the narrow tailoring analysis of strict scrutiny applicable in other contexts. "[T]he analysis and level of scrutiny applied to determine the validity of [a racial] classification do not vary simply because the objective appears acceptable. . . . While the validity and importance of the objective may affect the outcome of the analysis, the analysis itself does not change."

The District Court and Court of Appeals confined the strict scrutiny inquiry in too narrow a way by deferring to the University's good faith in its use of racial classifications and affirming the grant of summary judgment on that basis. The Court vacates that judgment, but fairness to the litigants and the courts that heard the case requires that it be remanded so that the admissions process can be considered and judged under a correct analysis.

Strict scrutiny must not be 'strict in theory, but fatal in fact.'" But the opposite is also true. Strict scrutiny must not be strict in theory but feeble in fact. In order for judicial review to be meaningful, a university must make a showing that its plan is narrowly tailored to achieve the only interest that this Court has approved in this context: the benefits of a student body diversity that "encompasses a . . . broa[d] array of qualifications and characteristics of which racial or ethnic origin is but a single though important element." The judgment of the Court of Appeals is vacated, and the case is remanded for further proceedings consistent with this opinion.

Justice SCALIA, concurring.

I adhere to the view I expressed in *Grutter v. Bollinger*: "The Constitution proscribes government discrimination on the basis of race, and state-provided education is no exception." The petitioner in this case did not ask us to overrule *Grutter*'s holding that a "compelling interest" in the educational benefits of diversity can justify racial preferences in university admissions. I therefore join the Court's opinion in full.

Justice THOMAS, concurring.

I join the Court's opinion because I agree that the Court of Appeals did not apply strict scrutiny to the University of Texas at Austin's (University) use of racial discrimination in admissions decisions. I write separately to explain that I would overrule *Grutter v. Bollinger* (2003), and hold that a State's use of race in higher education admissions decisions is categorically prohibited by the Equal Protection Clause.

Justice GINSBURG, dissenting.

The University of Texas at Austin (University) is candid about what it is endeavoring to do: It seeks to achieve student-body diversity through an admissions policy patterned after the Harvard plan referenced as exemplary in Justice Powell's opinion in *Regents of Univ. of Cal. v. Bakke* (1978). The University has steered clear of a quota system like the one struck down in *Bakke*, which excluded all nonminority candidates from competition for a fixed number of seats. And, like so many educational institutions across the Nation, the University has taken care to follow the model approved by the Court in *Grutter v. Bollinger* (2003).

Petitioner urges that Texas' Top Ten Percent Law and race-blind holistic review of each application achieve significant diversity, so the University must be content with those alternatives. I have said before and reiterate here that only an ostrich could regard the supposedly neutral alternatives as race unconscious.

Texas' percentage plan was adopted with racially segregated neighborhoods and schools front and center stage. It is race consciousness, not blindness to race, that drives such plans. As for holistic review, if universities cannot explicitly include race as a factor, many may "resort to camouflage" to "maintain their minority enrollment."

I have several times explained why government actors, including state universities, need not be blind to the lingering effects of "an overtly discriminatory past," the legacy of "centuries of law-sanctioned inequality." Among constitutionally permissible options, I remain convinced, "those that candidly disclose their consideration of race [are] preferable to those that conceal it."

Accordingly, I would not return this case for a second look. As the thorough opinions below show, the University's admissions policy flexibly considers race only as a "factor of a factor of a factor of a factor" in the calculus; followed a yearlong review through which the University reached the reasonable, good-faith judgment that supposedly race-neutral initiatives were insufficient to achieve, in appropriate measure, the educational benefits of student-body diversity; and is subject to periodic review to ensure that the consideration of race remains necessary and proper to achieve the University's educational objectives. Justice Powell's opinion in Bakke and the Court's decision in Grutter require no further determinations.

The Court rightly declines to cast off the equal protection framework settled in Grutter. Yet it stops short of reaching the conclusion that framework warrants. Instead, the Court vacates the Court of Appeals' judgment and remands for the Court of Appeals to "assess whether the University has offered sufficient evidence [to] prove that its admissions program is narrowly tailored to obtain the educational benefits of diversity." As I see it, the Court of Appeals has already completed that inquiry, and its judgment, trained on this Court's Bakke and Grutter pathmarkers, merits our approbation.

On remand, the United States Court of Appeals for the Fifth Circuit ruled in favor of the University of Texas, concluding that it had sufficiently demonstrated that no race neutral alternative could yield diversity. The Supreme Court has again granted review of the case, to be heard in the October 2015 Term.

In Schuette v. Coalition to Defend Affirmative Action, 134 S. Ct. 1623 (2014), the Court considered the constitutionality of a voter-passed initiative that prohibits affirmative action. In 2006, Michigan voters passed an initiative, Proposal 2, which amended the state constitution to prohibit the state or its political subdivisions from discriminating or giving preference based on race or gender in education, contracting, or employment.

Two lawsuits were brought challenging this in the area of education. The district court upheld Proposal 2, but the Sixth Circuit declared it unconstitutional in a panel decision and then in an 8-7 *en banc* ruling.

The Sixth Circuit, relying on earlier Supreme Court decisions in *Hunter v. Erickson* and *Washington v. Seattle Schools* concluded that the initiative impermissibly restructured the political process along racial lines. Under Proposal 2, groups other than racial minorities can continue to go to the Michigan Board of Regents or the Michigan state legislature to obtain preferences in admissions. These bodies could award, preferences to those who come from Michigan, or from a particular part of the state, or those whose parents attended the university, or those with particular interests.

However, if racial minorities want a preference in admission, they need to go through the arduous process of amending the state constitution. In other words, the initiative singles out race and says that it is to be treated differently from all other types of preferences. In practical reality, this means that racial minorities face a significant barrier to using the political process that is not imposed on other groups.

The Supreme Court, in a 6-2 decision, without a majority opinion reversed the Sixth Circuit and upheld the Michigan initiative. Justice Kennedy wrote a plurality opinion joined by Chief Justice Roberts and Justice Alito. Justice Kennedy said that no state is required to have affirmative action and it may eliminate it, including by an initiative. Justice Kennedy distinguished *Hunter v. Erickson* and *Washington v. Seattle Schools* saying that they had the serious risk, if not purpose, of causing specific injuries on account of race. Justice Scalia concurred in the judgment, joined by Justice Thomas and said that *Hunter* and *Washington* are not distinguishable and should be overruled. Justice Breyer concurred in the judgment and stressed the importance of deference to the political process and the initiative process.

Justice Sotomayor wrote a lengthy, vehement dissent, joined by Justice Ginsburg. Justice Sotomayor argued that affirmative action is essential to remedy the history of discrimination and contended that Michigan's Proposal 2 impermissibly restructured the political process to the detriment of racial minorities.

G. Other Types of Discrimination

4. Discrimination Based on Sexual Orientation (casebook, p. 930)

In *United States v. Windsor* (2013), the Court declared unconstitutional Section 3 of the Defense of Marriage Act, which provided that for federal law marriage must be between a man and a woman. The portion of the majority opinion and the dissents concerning the jurisdictional issues, including standing, are presented in Chapter 1. In *Obergefell v. Hodges* (2015), the Court declared unconstitutional state laws prohibiting same-sex marriage and focused primarily on the right to marry. Because both cases involve marriage equality for gays and lesbians, both are presented here.

UNITED STATES v. WINDSOR
133 S. Ct. 2675 (2013)

Justice KENNEDY delivered the opinion of the Court.

Two women then resident in New York were married in a lawful ceremony in Ontario, Canada, in 2007. Edith Windsor and Thea Spyer returned to their home in New York City. When Spyer died in 2009, she left her entire estate to Windsor. Windsor sought to claim the estate tax exemption for surviving spouses. She was barred from doing so, however, by a federal law, the Defense of Marriage Act, which excludes a same-sex partner from the definition of "spouse" as that term is used in federal statutes. Windsor paid the taxes but filed suit to challenge the constitutionality of this provision. The United States District Court and the Court of Appeals ruled that this portion of the statute is unconstitutional and ordered the United States to pay Windsor a refund. This Court granted certiorari and now affirms the judgment in Windsor's favor.

I

In 1996, as some States were beginning to consider the concept of same-sex marriage, and before any State had acted to permit it, Congress enacted the Defense of Marriage Act (DOMA). DOMA contains two operative sections: Section 2, which has not been challenged here, allows States to refuse to recognize same-sex marriages performed under the laws of other States.

Section 3 is at issue here. It amends the Dictionary Act in Title 1, § 7, of the United States Code to provide a federal definition of "marriage" and "spouse." Section 3 of DOMA provides as follows:

In determining the meaning of any Act of Congress, or of any ruling, regulation, or interpretation of the various administrative bureaus and agencies of the United States, the word "marriage" means only a legal union between one man and one woman as husband and wife, and the word "spouse" refers only to a person of the opposite sex who is a husband or a wife.

The definitional provision does not by its terms forbid States from enacting laws permitting same-sex marriages or civil unions or providing state benefits to residents in that status. The enactment's comprehensive definition of marriage for purposes of all federal statutes and other regulations or directives covered by its terms, however, does control over 1,000 federal laws in which marital or spousal status is addressed as a matter of federal law.

Edith Windsor and Thea Spyer met in New York City in 1963 and began a long-term relationship. Windsor and Spyer registered as domestic partners when New York City gave that right to same-sex couples in 1993. Concerned about Spyer's health, the couple made the 2007 trip to Canada for their marriage, but they continued to reside in New York City. The State of New York deems their Ontario marriage to be a valid one.

Spyer died in February 2009, and left her entire estate to Windsor. Because DOMA denies federal recognition to same-sex spouses, Windsor did not qualify for the marital exemption from the federal estate tax, which excludes from taxation "any interest in property which passes or has passed from the decedent to his surviving spouse." Windsor paid $363,053 in estate taxes and sought a refund. The Internal Revenue Service denied the refund, concluding that, under DOMA, Windsor was not a "surviving spouse." Windsor commenced this refund suit in the United States District Court for the Southern District of New York. She contended that DOMA violates the guarantee of equal protection, as applied to the Federal Government through the Fifth Amendment.

[II]

Slowly at first and then in rapid course, the laws of New York came to acknowledge the urgency of this issue for same-sex couples who wanted to affirm their commitment to one another before their children, their family, their friends, and their community. And so New York recognized same-sex marriages performed elsewhere; and then it later amended its own marriage laws to permit same-sex marriage. New York, in common with, as of this writing, 11 other States and the District of Columbia, decided that same-sex couples should have the right to marry and so live with pride in themselves and their union and in a status of equality with all other married persons. After a statewide deliberative process that enabled its citizens to discuss and weigh arguments for and against same-sex marriage, New York acted to enlarge the definition of marriage to correct what its citizens and elected representatives perceived to be an injustice that they had not earlier known or understood.

Against this background of lawful same-sex marriage in some States, the design, purpose, and effect of DOMA should be considered as the beginning point in deciding whether it is valid under the Constitution. By history and tradition the definition and regulation of marriage, as will be discussed in more detail, has been treated as being within the authority and realm of the separate States. Yet it is further established that Congress, in enacting discrete statutes, can make determinations that bear on marital rights and privileges.

Other precedents involving congressional statutes which affect marriages and family status further illustrate this point. In addressing the interaction of state domestic relations and federal immigration law Congress determined that marriages "entered into for the purpose of procuring an alien's admission [to the United States] as an immigrant" will not qualify the noncitizen for that status, even if the noncitizen's marriage is valid and proper for state-law purposes. And in establishing income-based criteria for Social Security benefits, Congress decided that although state law would determine in general who qualifies as an applicant's spouse, common-law marriages also should be recognized, regardless of any particular State's view on these relationships.

Though these discrete examples establish the constitutionality of limited federal laws that regulate the meaning of marriage in order to further federal policy, DOMA has a far greater reach; for it enacts a directive applicable to over 1,000 federal statutes and the whole realm of federal regulations. And its operation is directed to a class of persons that the laws of New York, and of 11 other States, have sought to protect.

In order to assess the validity of that intervention it is necessary to discuss the extent of the state power and authority over marriage as a matter of history and tradition. State laws defining and regulating marriage, of course, must respect the constitutional rights of persons, but, subject to those guarantees, "regulation of domestic relations" is "an area that has long been regarded as a virtually exclusive province of the States."

The recognition of civil marriages is central to state domestic relations law applicable to its residents and citizens. The definition of marriage is the foundation of the State's broader authority to regulate the subject of domestic relations with respect to the "[p]rotection of offspring, property interests, and the enforcement of marital responsibilities."

Consistent with this allocation of authority, the Federal Government, through our history, has deferred to state-law policy decisions with respect to domestic relations.

The significance of state responsibilities for the definition and regulation of marriage dates to the Nation's beginning; for "when the Constitution was adopted the common understanding was that the domestic relations of husband and wife and parent and child were matters reserved to the States." *Ohio ex rel. Popovici v. Agler* (1930). Marriage laws vary in some respects from State to State. For example, the required minimum age is 16 in Vermont, but only 13 in New Hampshire. Likewise the permissible degree of consanguinity can vary (most States permit first cousins to marry, but a handful — such as Iowa and Washington — prohibit the practice).

Despite these considerations, it is unnecessary to decide whether this federal intrusion on state power is a violation of the Constitution because it disrupts the federal balance. The State's power in defining the marital relation is of central relevance in this case quite apart from principles of federalism. Here the State's decision to give this class of persons the right to marry conferred upon them a dignity and status of immense import. When the State used its historic and essential authority to define the marital relation in this way, its role and its power in making the decision enhanced the recognition, dignity, and protection of the class in their own community. DOMA, because of its reach and extent, departs from this history and tradition of reliance on state law to define marriage. "'[D]iscriminations of an unusual character especially suggest careful consideration to determine whether they are obnoxious to the constitutional provision.'"

The Federal Government uses this state-defined class for the opposite purpose — to impose restrictions and disabilities. That result requires this Court now to address whether the resulting injury and indignity is a deprivation of an essential part of the liberty protected by the Fifth Amendment. What the State of New York treats as alike the federal law deems unlike by a law designed to injure the same class the State seeks to protect.

The States' interest in defining and regulating the marital relation, subject to constitutional guarantees, stems from the understanding that marriage is more than a routine classification for purposes of certain statutory benefits. Private, consensual sexual intimacy between two adult persons of the same sex may not be punished by the State, and it can form "but one element in a personal bond that is more enduring." *Lawrence v. Texas* (2003). By its recognition of the validity of same-sex marriages performed in other jurisdictions and then by authorizing same-sex unions and same-sex marriages, New York sought to give further protection and dignity to that bond. For same-sex couples who wished to be married, the State acted to give their lawful conduct a lawful status. This status is a far-reaching legal acknowledgment of the intimate relationship between two people, a relationship deemed by the State worthy of dignity in the community equal with all other marriages. It reflects both the community's considered perspective on the historical roots of the institution of marriage and its evolving understanding of the meaning of equality.

IV

DOMA seeks to injure the very class New York seeks to protect. By doing so it violates basic due process and equal protection principles applicable to the Federal Government. The Constitution's guarantee of equality "must at the very least mean that a bare congressional desire to harm a politically unpopular group cannot" justify disparate treatment of that group. In determining whether a law is motived by an improper animus or purpose, " [d]iscriminations of an unusual character' " especially require careful consideration. DOMA cannot survive under these principles. The avowed purpose and practical effect of the law here in question are to impose a disadvantage, a separate status, and so a stigma upon all who enter into same-sex marriages made lawful by the unquestioned authority of the States.

The history of DOMA's enactment and its own text demonstrate that interference with the equal dignity of same-sex marriages, a dignity conferred by the States in the exercise of their sovereign power, was more than an incidental effect of the federal statute. It was its essence. The House Report announced its conclusion that "it is both appropriate and necessary for Congress to do what it can to defend the institution of traditional heterosexual marriage. . . . H.R. 3396 is appropriately entitled the 'Defense of Marriage Act.' The effort to redefine 'marriage' to extend to homosexual couples is a truly radical proposal that would fundamentally alter the institution of marriage." The House concluded that DOMA expresses "both moral disapproval of homosexuality, and a moral conviction that heterosexuality better comports with traditional (especially

Judeo-Christian) morality." The stated purpose of the law was to promote an "interest in protecting the traditional moral teachings reflected in heterosexual-only marriage laws." Were there any doubt of this far-reaching purpose, the title of the Act confirms it: The Defense of Marriage.

The Act's demonstrated purpose is to ensure that if any State decides to recognize same-sex marriages, those unions will be treated as second-class marriages for purposes of federal law. This raises a most serious question under the Constitution's Fifth Amendment.

DOMA's operation in practice confirms this purpose. When New York adopted a law to permit same-sex marriage, it sought to eliminate inequality; but DOMA frustrates that objective through a system-wide enactment with no identified connection to any particular area of federal law. DOMA writes inequality into the entire United States Code. The particular case at hand concerns the estate tax, but DOMA is more than a simple determination of what should or should not be allowed as an estate tax refund. Among the over 1,000 statutes and numerous federal regulations that DOMA controls are laws pertaining to Social Security, housing, taxes, criminal sanctions, copyright, and veterans' benefits.

DOMA's principal effect is to identify a subset of state-sanctioned marriages and make them unequal. The principal purpose is to impose inequality, not for other reasons like governmental efficiency. Responsibilities, as well as rights, enhance the dignity and integrity of the person. And DOMA contrives to deprive some couples married under the laws of their State, but not other couples, of both rights and responsibilities. By creating two contradictory marriage regimes within the same State, DOMA forces same-sex couples to live as married for the purpose of state law but unmarried for the purpose of federal law, thus diminishing the stability and predictability of basic personal relations the State has found it proper to acknowledge and protect. By this dynamic DOMA undermines both the public and private significance of state-sanctioned same-sex marriages; for it tells those couples, and all the world, that their otherwise valid marriages are unworthy of federal recognition. This places same-sex couples in an unstable position of being in a second-tier marriage. The differentiation demeans the couple, whose moral and sexual choices the Constitution protects, and whose relationship the State has sought to dignify. And it humiliates tens of thousands of children now being raised by same-sex couples. The law in question makes it even more difficult for the children to understand the integrity and closeness of their own family and its concord with other families in their community and in their daily lives.

Under DOMA, same-sex married couples have their lives burdened, by reason of government decree, in visible and public ways. By its great reach, DOMA touches many aspects of married and family life, from the mundane to the profound.

The power the Constitution grants it also restrains. And though Congress has great authority to design laws to fit its own conception of sound national policy, it cannot deny the liberty protected by the Due Process Clause of the Fifth Amendment.

What has been explained to this point should more than suffice to establish that the principal purpose and the necessary effect of this law are to demean those persons who are in a lawful same-sex marriage. This requires the Court to hold, as it now does, that DOMA is unconstitutional as a deprivation of the liberty of the person protected by the Fifth Amendment of the Constitution.

The liberty protected by the Fifth Amendment's Due Process Clause contains within it the prohibition against denying to any person the equal protection of the laws. While the Fifth Amendment itself withdraws from Government the power to degrade or demean in the way this law does, the equal protection guarantee of the Fourteenth Amendment makes that Fifth Amendment right all the more specific and all the better understood and preserved.

The class to which DOMA directs its restrictions and restraints are those persons who are joined in same-sex marriages made lawful by the State. DOMA singles out a class of persons deemed by a State entitled to recognition and protection to enhance their own liberty. It imposes a disability on the class by refusing to acknowledge a status the State finds to be dignified and proper. DOMA instructs all federal officials, and indeed all persons with whom same-sex couples interact, including their own children, that their marriage is less worthy than the marriages of others. The federal statute is invalid, for no legitimate purpose overcomes the purpose and effect to disparage and to injure those whom the State, by its marriage laws, sought to protect in personhood and dignity. By seeking to displace this protection and treating those persons as living in marriages less respected than others, the federal statute is in violation of the Fifth Amendment. This opinion and its holding are confined to those lawful marriages.

Chief Justice ROBERTS, dissenting.

On the merits of the constitutional dispute the Court decides to decide, I also agree with Justice Scalia that Congress acted constitutionally in passing the Defense of Marriage Act (DOMA). Interests in uniformity and stability amply justified Congress's decision to retain the definition of marriage that, at that point, had been adopted by every State in our Nation, and every nation in the world.

The majority sees a more sinister motive, pointing out that the Federal Government has generally (though not uniformly) deferred to state definitions of marriage in the past. That is true, of course, but none of those prior state-by-state variations had involved differences over something — as the majority puts it — "thought of by most people as essential to the very definition of [marriage] and to its role and function throughout the history of civilization." That the Federal Government treated this fundamental question differently than it treated variations over consanguinity or minimum age is hardly surprising — and hardly enough to support a conclusion that the "principal purpose," of the 342 Representatives and 85 Senators who voted for it, and the President who signed it, was a bare desire to harm. Nor do the snippets of legislative history and the banal title of the Act to which the majority points suffice to make such a showing. At least without some more convincing evidence that the Act's principal purpose was to codify malice, and that it furthered no legitimate government interests, I would not tar the political branches with the brush of bigotry.

But while I disagree with the result to which the majority's analysis leads it in this case, I think it more important to point out that its analysis leads no further. The Court does not have before it, and the logic of its opinion does not decide, the distinct question whether the States, in the exercise of their "historic and essential authority to define the marital relation," may continue to utilize the traditional definition of marriage.

We may in the future have to resolve challenges to state marriage definitions affecting same-sex couples. That issue, however, is not before us in this case.

Justice SCALIA, with whom Justice THOMAS joins, and with whom THE CHIEF JUSTICE joins as to Part I [concerning jurisdiction], dissenting.

This case is about power in several respects. It is about the power of our people to govern themselves, and the power of this Court to pronounce the law. Today's opinion aggrandizes the latter, with the predictable consequence of diminishing the former. We have no power to decide this case. And even if we did, we have no power under the Constitution to invalidate this democratically adopted legislation. The Court's errors on both points spring forth from the same diseased root: an exalted conception of the role of this institution in America.

[I]f this is meant to be an equal-protection opinion, it is a confusing one. The opinion does not resolve and indeed does not even mention what had been the central question in this litigation: whether, under the Equal Protection Clause, laws restricting marriage to a man and a woman are reviewed for more than mere rationality. That is the issue that divided the parties and the court below. In accord with my previously expressed skepticism about the Court's "tiers of scrutiny" approach, I would review this classification only for its rationality. As nearly as I can tell, the Court agrees with that; its opinion does not apply strict scrutiny, and its central propositions are taken from rational-basis cases like Moreno. But the Court certainly does not apply anything that resembles that deferential framework.

Some might conclude that this loaf could have used a while longer in the oven. But that would be wrong; it is already overcooked. The most expert care in preparation cannot redeem a bad recipe. The sum of all the Court's nonspecific hand-waving is that this law is invalid (maybe on equal-protection grounds, maybe on substantive-due-process grounds, and perhaps with some amorphous federalism component playing a role) because it is motivated by a " 'bare . . . desire to harm' " couples in same-sex marriages. It is this proposition with which I will therefore engage.

As I have observed before, the Constitution does not forbid the government to enforce traditional moral and sexual norms. I will not swell the U.S. Reports with restatements of that point. It is enough to say that the Constitution neither requires nor forbids our society to approve of same-sex marriage, much as it neither requires nor forbids us to approve of no-fault divorce, polygamy, or the consumption of alcohol.

However, even setting aside traditional moral disapproval of same-sex marriage (or indeed same-sex sex), there are many perfectly valid — indeed, downright boring — justifying rationales for this legislation. Their existence ought to be the end of this case. For they give the lie to the Court's conclusion that only those with hateful hearts could have voted "aye" on this Act. And more importantly, they serve to make the contents of the legislators' hearts quite irrelevant: "It is a familiar principle of constitutional law that this Court will not strike down an otherwise constitutional statute on the basis of an alleged illicit legislative motive." Or at least it was a familiar principle. By holding to the contrary, the majority has declared open season on any law that (in the opinion of the law's opponents and any panel of like-minded federal judges) can be characterized as mean-spirited.

The majority concludes that the only motive for this Act was the "bare . . . desire to harm a politically unpopular group." Bear in mind that the object of this condemnation is not the legislature of some once-Confederate Southern state (familiar objects of the Court's scorn), but our respected coordinate branches, the Congress and Presidency of the United States. Laying such a charge against them should require the most extraordinary evidence, and I would have thought that every attempt would be made to indulge a more anodyne explanation for the statute. The majority does the opposite — affirmatively concealing from the reader the arguments that exist in justification. It makes only a passing mention of the "arguments put forward" by the Act's defenders, and does not even trouble to paraphrase or describe them. I imagine that this is because it is harder to maintain the illusion of the Act's supporters as unhinged members of a wild-eyed lynch mob when one first describes their views as they see them.

To choose just one of these defenders' arguments, DOMA avoids difficult choice-of-law issues that will now arise absent a uniform federal definition of marriage. Imagine a pair of women who marry in Albany and then move to Alabama, which does not "recognize as valid any marriage of parties of the same sex." When the couple files their next federal tax return, may it be a joint one? Which State's law controls, for federal-law purposes: their State of celebration (which recognizes the marriage) or their State of domicile (which does not)? (Does the answer depend on whether they were just visiting in Albany?) Are these questions to be answered as a matter of federal common law, or perhaps by borrowing a State's choice-of-law rules? If so, which State's? And what about States where the status of an out-of-state same-sex marriage is an unsettled question under local law? DOMA avoided all of this uncertainty by specifying which marriages would be recognized for federal purposes. That is a classic purpose for a definitional provision.

The Court mentions none of this. Instead, it accuses the Congress that enacted this law and the President who signed it of something much worse than, for example, having acted in excess of enumerated federal powers — or even having drawn distinctions that prove to be irrational. Those legal errors may be made in good faith, errors though they are. But the majority says that the supporters of this Act acted with malice — with the "purpose" "to disparage and to injure" same-sex couples.

I am sure these accusations are quite untrue. To be sure (as the majority points out), the legislation is called the Defense of Marriage Act. But to defend traditional marriage is not to condemn, demean, or humiliate those who would prefer other arrangements, any more than to defend the Constitution of the United States is to condemn, demean, or humiliate other constitutions. To hurl such accusations so casually demeans this institution. In the majority's judgment, any resistance to its holding is beyond the pale of reasoned disagreement. To question its high-handed invalidation of a presumptively valid statute is to act (the majority is sure) with *the purpose* to "disparage," "injure," "degrade," "demean," and "humiliate" our fellow human beings, our fellow citizens, who are homosexual. All that, simply for supporting an Act that did no more than codify an aspect of marriage that had been unquestioned in our society for most of its existence—indeed, had been unquestioned in virtually all societies for virtually all of human history. It is one thing for a society to elect change; it is another for a court of law to impose change by adjudging those who oppose it *hostes humani generis,* enemies of the human race.

The penultimate sentence of the majority's opinion is a naked declaration that "[t]his opinion and its holding are confined" to those couples "joined in same-sex marriages made lawful by the State." I have heard such "bald, unreasoned disclaimer[s]" before. When the Court declared a constitutional right to homosexual sodomy, we were assured that the case had nothing, nothing at all to do with "whether the government must give formal recognition to any relationship that homosexual persons seek to enter." It takes real cheek for today's majority to assure us, as it is going out the door, that a constitutional requirement to give formal recognition to same-sex marriage is not at issue here—when what has preceded that assurance is a lecture on how superior the majority's moral judgment in favor of same-sex marriage is to the Congress's hateful moral judgment against it. I promise you this: The only thing that will "confine" the Court's holding is its sense of what it can get away with.

In my opinion, however, the view that *this* Court will take of state prohibition of same-sex marriage is indicated beyond mistaking by today's opinion. As I have said, the real rationale of today's opinion, whatever disappearing trail of its legalistic argle-bargle one chooses to follow, is that DOMA is motivated by " 'bare . . . desire to harm' " couples in same-sex marriages. How easy it is, indeed how inevitable, to reach the same conclusion with regard to state laws denying same-sex couples marital status.

By formally declaring anyone opposed to same-sex marriage an enemy of human decency, the majority arms well every challenger to a state law restricting marriage to its traditional definition. Henceforth those challengers will lead with this Court's declaration that there is "no legitimate purpose" served by such a law, and will claim that the traditional definition has "the purpose and effect to disparage and to injure" the "personhood and dignity" of same-sex couples. The majority's limiting assurance will be meaningless in the face of language like that, as the majority well knows. That is why the language is there. The result will be a judicial distortion of our society's debate over marriage—a debate that can seem in need of our clumsy "help" only to a member of this institution.

In the majority's telling, this story is black-and-white: Hate your neighbor or come along with us. The truth is more complicated. It is hard to admit that one's political opponents are not monsters, especially in a struggle like this one, and the challenge in the end proves more than today's Court can handle. Too bad. A reminder that disagreement over something so fundamental as marriage can still be politically legitimate would have been a fit task for what in earlier times was called the judicial temperament. We might have covered ourselves with honor today, by promising all sides of this debate that it was theirs to settle and that we would respect their resolution. We might have let the People decide.

But that the majority will not do. Some will rejoice in today's decision, and some will despair at it; that is the nature of a controversy that matters so much to so many. But the Court has cheated both sides, robbing the winners of an honest victory, and the losers of the peace that comes from a fair defeat. We owed both of them better. I dissent.

Justice ALITO, with whom Justice THOMAS joins as to Parts II and III, dissenting.

Our Nation is engaged in a heated debate about same-sex marriage. That debate is, at bottom, about the nature of the institution of marriage. Respondent Edith Windsor, supported by the United States, asks this Court to intervene in that debate, and although she couches her argument in different terms, what she seeks is a holding that enshrines in the Constitution a particular understanding of marriage under which the sex of the partners makes no difference. The Constitution, however, does not dictate that choice. It leaves the choice to the people, acting through their elected representatives at both the federal and state levels. I would therefore hold that Congress did not violate Windsor's constitutional rights by enacting § 3 of the Defense of Marriage Act (DOMA), which defines the meaning of marriage under federal statutes that either confer upon married persons certain federal benefits or impose upon them certain federal obligations.

Same-sex marriage presents a highly emotional and important question of public policy—but not a difficult question of constitutional law. The Constitution does not guarantee the right to enter into a same-sex marriage. Indeed, no provision of the Constitution speaks to the issue.

The Court has sometimes found the Due Process Clauses to have a substantive component that guarantees liberties beyond the absence of physical restraint. And the Court's holding that "DOMA is unconstitutional as a deprivation of the liberty of the person protected by the Fifth Amendment of the Constitution" suggests that substantive due process may partially underlie the Court's decision today. But it is well established that any "substantive" component to the Due Process Clause protects only "those fundamental rights and liberties which are, objectively, 'deeply rooted in this Nation's history and tradition.'"

It is beyond dispute that the right to same-sex marriage is not deeply rooted in this Nation's history and tradition. In this country, no State permitted same-sex marriage until the Massachusetts Supreme Judicial Court held in 2003 that limiting marriage to opposite-sex couples violated the State Constitution. Nor is the right to same-sex marriage deeply rooted in the traditions of other nations. No country allowed same-sex couples to marry until the Netherlands did so in 2000.

What Windsor and the United States seek, therefore, is not the protection of a deeply rooted right but the recognition of a very new right, and they seek this innovation not from a legislative body elected by the people, but from unelected judges. Faced with such a request, judges have cause for both caution and humility.

At present, no one—including social scientists, philosophers, and historians—can predict with any certainty what the long-term ramifications of widespread acceptance of same-sex marriage will be. And judges are certainly not equipped to make such an assessment. The Members of this Court have the authority and the responsibility to interpret and apply the Constitution. Thus, if the Constitution contained a provision guaranteeing the right to marry a person of the same sex, it would be our duty to enforce that right. But the Constitution simply does not speak to the issue of same-sex marriage. In our system of government, ultimate sovereignty rests with the people, and the people have the right to control their own destiny. Any change on a question so fundamental should be made by the people through their elected officials.

Perhaps because they cannot show that same-sex marriage is a fundamental right under our Constitution, Windsor and the United States couch their arguments in equal protection terms. They argue that § 3 of DOMA discriminates on the basis of sexual orientation, that classifications based on sexual orientation should trigger a form of "heightened" scrutiny, and that § 3 cannot survive such scrutiny.

In my view, the approach that Windsor and the United States advocate is misguided. Our equal protection framework, upon which Windsor and the United States rely, is a judicial construct that provides a useful mechanism for analyzing a certain universe of equal protection cases. But that framework is ill suited for use in evaluating the constitutionality of laws based on the traditional understanding of marriage, which fundamentally turn on what marriage is.

Underlying our equal protection jurisprudence is the central notion that "[a] classification 'must be reasonable, not arbitrary, and must rest upon some ground of difference having a fair and substantial relation to the object of the legislation, so that all persons similarly circumstanced shall be treated alike.' "

In asking the Court to determine that § 3 of DOMA is subject to and violates heightened scrutiny, Windsor and the United States thus ask us to rule that the presence of two members of the opposite sex is as rationally related to marriage as white skin is to voting or a Y-chromosome is to the ability to administer an estate. That is a striking request and one that unelected judges should pause before granting. Acceptance of the argument would cast all those who cling to traditional beliefs about the nature of marriage in the role of bigots or superstitious fools.

To the extent that the Court takes the position that the question of same-sex marriage should be resolved primarily at the state level, I wholeheartedly agree. I hope that the Court will ultimately permit the people of each State to decide this question for themselves. Unless the Court is willing to allow this to occur, the whiffs of federalism in the today's opinion of the Court will soon be scattered to the wind.

In any event, § 3 of DOMA, in my view, does not encroach on the prerogatives of the States, assuming of course that the many federal statutes affected by DOMA have not already done so. Section 3 does not prevent any State from recognizing same-sex marriage or from extending to same-sex couples any right, privilege, benefit, or obligation stemming from state law. All that § 3 does is to define a class of persons to whom federal law extends certain special benefits and upon whom federal law imposes certain special burdens. In these provisions, Congress used marital status as a way of defining this class—in part, I assume, because it viewed marriage as a valuable institution to be fostered and in part because it viewed married couples as comprising a unique type of economic unit that merits special regulatory treatment. Assuming that Congress has the power under the Constitution to enact the laws affected by § 3, Congress has the power to define the category of persons to whom those laws apply.

For these reasons, I would hold that § 3 of DOMA does not violate the Fifth Amendment. I respectfully dissent.

OBERGEFELL v. HODGES
135 S. Ct. ___ (2015)

Justice KENNEDY delivered the opinion of the Court.

The Constitution promises liberty to all within its reach, a liberty that includes certain specific rights that allow persons, within a lawful realm, to define and express their identity. The petitioners in these cases seek to find that liberty by marrying someone of the same sex and having their marriages deemed lawful on the same terms and conditions as marriages between persons of the opposite sex.

I

These cases come from Michigan, Kentucky, Ohio, and Tennessee, States that define marriage as a union between one man and one woman. The petitioners are 14 same-sex couples and two men whose same-sex partners are deceased. The respondents are state officials responsible for enforcing the laws in question. The petitioners claim the respondents violate the Fourteenth Amendment by denying them the right to marry or to have their marriages, lawfully performed in another State, given full recognition.

II

Before addressing the principles and precedents that govern these cases, it is appropriate to note the history of the subject now before the Court.

From their beginning to their most recent page, the annals of human history reveal the transcendent importance of marriage. The lifelong union of a man and a woman always has promised nobility and dignity to all persons, without regard to their station in life. Marriage is sacred to those who live by their religions and offers unique fulfillment to those who find meaning in the secular realm. Its dynamic allows two people to find a life that could not be found alone, for a marriage becomes greater than just the two persons. Rising from the most basic human needs, marriage is essential to our most profound hopes and aspirations.

The centrality of marriage to the human condition makes it unsurprising that the institution has existed for millennia and across civilizations. Since the dawn of history, marriage has transformed strangers into relatives, binding families and societies together. It is fair and necessary to say these references were based on the understanding that marriage is a union between two persons of the opposite sex.

That history is the beginning of these cases. The respondents say it should be the end as well. To them, it would demean a timeless institution if the concept and lawful status of marriage were extended to two persons of the same sex. Marriage, in their view, is by its nature a gender-differentiated union of man and woman. This view long has been held—and continues to be held—in good faith by reasonable and sincere people here and throughout the world.

The petitioners acknowledge this history but contend that these cases cannot end there. Were their intent to demean the revered idea and reality of marriage, the petitioners' claims would be of a different order. But that is neither their purpose nor their submission. To the contrary, it is the enduring importance of marriage that underlies the petitioners' contentions. This, they say, is their whole point. Far from seeking to devalue marriage, the petitioners seek it for themselves because of their respect—and need—for its privileges and responsibilities. And their immutable nature dictates that same-sex marriage is their only real path to this profound commitment.

Recounting the circumstances of three of these cases illustrates the urgency of the petitioners' cause from their perspective.

Petitioner James Obergefell, a plaintiff in the Ohio case, met John Arthur over two decades ago. They fell in love and started a life together, establishing a lasting, committed relation. In 2011, however, Arthur was diagnosed with amyotrophic lateral sclerosis, or ALS. This debilitating disease is progressive, with no known cure. Two years ago, Obergefell and Arthur decided to commit to one another, resolving to marry before Arthur died. To fulfill their mutual promise, they traveled from Ohio to Maryland, where same-sex marriage was legal. It was difficult for Arthur to move, and so the couple were wed inside a medical transport plane as it remained on the tarmac in Baltimore. Three months later, Arthur died. Ohio law does not permit Obergefell to be listed as the surviving spouse on Arthur's death certificate. By statute, they must remain strangers even in death, a state-imposed separation Obergefell deems "hurtful for the rest of time." He brought suit to be shown as the surviving spouse on Arthur's death certificate.

The ancient origins of marriage confirm its centrality, but it has not stood in isolation from developments in law and society. The history of marriage is one of both continuity and change. That institution—even as confined to opposite-sex relations—has evolved over time.

These new insights have strengthened, not weakened, the institution of marriage. Indeed, changed understandings of marriage are characteristic of a Nation where new dimensions of freedom become apparent to new generations, often through perspectives that begin in pleas or protests and then are considered in the political sphere and the judicial process.

This dynamic can be seen in the Nation's experiences with the rights of gays and lesbians. Until the mid–20th century, same-sex intimacy long had been condemned as immoral by the state itself in most Western nations, a belief often embodied in the criminal law. For this reason, among others, many persons did not deem homosexuals to have dignity in their own distinct identity. A truthful declaration by same-sex couples of what was in their hearts had to remain unspoken. Even when a greater awareness of the humanity and integrity of homosexual persons came in the period after World War II, the argument that gays and lesbians had a just claim to dignity was in conflict with both law and widespread social conventions. Same-sex intimacy remained a crime in many States. Gays and lesbians were prohibited from most government employment, barred from military service, excluded under immigration laws, targeted by police, and burdened in their rights to associate.

For much of the 20th century, moreover, homosexuality was treated as an illness. When the American Psychiatric Association published the first Diagnostic and Statistical Manual of Mental Disorders in 1952, homosexuality was classified as a mental disorder, a position adhered to until 1973. Only in more recent years have psychiatrists and others recognized that sexual orientation is both a normal expression of human sexuality and immutable.

III

Under the Due Process Clause of the Fourteenth Amendment, no State shall "deprive any person of life, liberty, or property, without due process of law." The fundamental liberties protected by this Clause include most of the rights enumerated in the Bill of Rights. In addition these liberties extend to certain personal choices central to individual dignity and autonomy, including intimate choices that define personal identity and beliefs.

The identification and protection of fundamental rights is an enduring part of the judicial duty to interpret the Constitution. That responsibility, however, "has not been reduced to any formula." *Poe v. Ullman* (1961) (Harlan, J., dissenting). Rather, it requires courts to exercise reasoned judgment in identifying interests of the person so fundamental that the State must accord them its respect. That process is guided by many of the same considerations relevant to analysis of other constitutional provisions that set forth broad principles rather than specific requirements. History and tradition guide and discipline this inquiry but do not set its outer boundaries. That method respects our history and learns from it without allowing the past alone to rule the present.

The nature of injustice is that we may not always see it in our own times. The generations that wrote and ratified the Bill of Rights and the Fourteenth Amendment did not presume to know the extent of freedom in all of its dimensions, and so they entrusted to future generations a charter protecting the right of all persons to enjoy liberty as we learn its meaning. When new insight reveals discord between the Constitution's central protections and a received legal stricture, a claim to liberty must be addressed.

Applying these established tenets, the Court has long held the right to marry is protected by the Constitution. In *Loving v. Virginia* (1967), which invalidated bans on interracial unions, a unanimous Court held marriage is "one of the vital personal rights essential to the orderly pursuit of happiness by free men." The Court reaffirmed that holding in *Zablocki v. Redhail* (1978), which held the right to marry was burdened by a law prohibiting fathers who were behind on child support from marrying. The Court again applied this principle in *Turner v. Safley* (1987), which held the right to marry was abridged by regulations limiting the privilege of prison inmates to marry. Over time and in other contexts, the Court has reiterated that the right to marry is fundamental under the Due Process Clause.

It cannot be denied that this Court's cases describing the right to marry presumed a relationship involving opposite-sex partners. The Court, like many institutions, has made assumptions defined by the world and time of which it is a part.

Still, there are other, more instructive precedents. This Court's cases have expressed constitutional principles of broader reach. In defining the right to marry these cases have identified essential attributes of that right based in history, tradition, and other constitutional liberties inherent in this intimate bond. And in assessing whether the force and rationale of its cases apply to same-sex couples, the Court must respect the basic reasons why the right to marry has been long protected.

This analysis compels the conclusion that same-sex couples may exercise the right to marry. The four principles and traditions to be discussed demonstrate that the reasons marriage is fundamental under the Constitution apply with equal force to same-sex couples.

A first premise of the Court's relevant precedents is that the right to personal choice regarding marriage is inherent in the concept of individual autonomy. This abiding connection between marriage and liberty is why Like choices concerning contraception, family relationships, procreation, and childrearing, all of which are protected by the Constitution, decisions concerning marriage are among the most intimate that an individual can make. Indeed, the Court has noted it would be contradictory "to recognize a right of privacy with respect to other matters of family life and not with respect to the decision to enter the relationship that is the foundation of the family in our society."

Choices about marriage shape an individual's destiny. The nature of marriage is that, through its enduring bond, two persons together can find other freedoms, such as expression, intimacy, and spirituality. This is true for all persons, whatever their sexual orientation. There is dignity in the bond between two men or two women who seek to marry and in their autonomy to make such profound choices.

A second principle in this Court's jurisprudence is that the right to marry is fundamental because it supports a two-person union unlike any other in its importance to the committed individuals. This point was central to *Griswold v. Connecticut* [1965], which held the Constitution protects the right of married couples to use contraception.

Marriage responds to the universal fear that a lonely person might call out only to find no one there. It offers the hope of companionship and understanding and assurance that while both still live there will be someone to care for the other.

As this Court held in *Lawrence,* same-sex couples have the same right as opposite-sex couples to enjoy intimate association. *Lawrence* invalidated laws that made same-sex intimacy a criminal act. But while *Lawrence* confirmed a dimension of freedom that allows individuals to engage in intimate association without criminal liability, it does not follow that freedom stops there. Outlaw to outcast may be a step forward, but it does not achieve the full promise of liberty.

A third basis for protecting the right to marry is that it safeguards children and families and thus draws meaning from related rights of childrearing, procreation, and education. By giving recognition and legal structure to their parents' relationship, marriage allows children "to understand the integrity and closeness of their own family and its concord with other families in their community and in their daily lives." Marriage also affords the permanency and stability important to children's best interests.

As all parties agree, many same-sex couples provide loving and nurturing homes to their children, whether biological or adopted. And hundreds of thousands of children are presently being raised by such couples. Most States have allowed gays and lesbians to adopt, either as individuals or as couples, and many adopted and foster children have same-sex parents. This provides powerful confirmation from the law itself that gays and lesbians can create loving, supportive families.

Excluding same-sex couples from marriage thus conflicts with a central premise of the right to marry. Without the recognition, stability, and predictability marriage offers, their children suffer the stigma of knowing their families are somehow lesser. They also suffer the significant material costs of being raised by unmarried parents, relegated through no fault of their own to a more difficult and uncertain family life. The marriage laws at issue here thus harm and humiliate the children of same-sex couples.

That is not to say the right to marry is less meaningful for those who do not or cannot have children. An ability, desire, or promise to procreate is not and has not been a prerequisite for a valid marriage in any State. In light of precedent protecting the right of a married couple not to procreate, it cannot be said the Court or the States have conditioned the right to marry on the capacity or commitment to procreate. The constitutional marriage right has many aspects, of which childbearing is only one.

Fourth and finally, this Court's cases and the Nation's traditions make clear that marriage is a keystone of our social order. For that reason, just as a couple vows to support each other, so does society pledge to support the couple, offering symbolic recognition and material benefits to protect and nourish the union. Indeed, while the States are in general free to vary the benefits they confer on all married couples, they have throughout our history made marriage the basis for an expanding list of governmental rights, benefits, and responsibilities. These aspects of marital status include: taxation; inheritance and property rights; rules of intestate succession; spousal privilege in the law of evidence; hospital access; medical decisionmaking authority; adoption rights; the rights and benefits of survivors; birth and death certificates; professional ethics rules; campaign finance restrictions; workers' compensation benefits; health insurance; and child custody, support, and visitation rules.

There is no difference between same- and opposite-sex couples with respect to this principle. Yet by virtue of their exclusion from that institution, same-sex couples are denied the constellation of benefits that the States have linked to marriage. This harm results in more than just material burdens. Same-sex couples are consigned to an instability many opposite-sex couples would deem intolerable in their own lives. As the State itself makes marriage all the more precious by the significance it attaches to it, exclusion from that status has the effect of teaching that gays and lesbians are unequal in important respects. It demeans gays and lesbians for the State to lock them out of a central institution of the Nation's society. Same-sex couples, too, may aspire to the transcendent purposes of marriage and seek fulfillment in its highest meaning.

The limitation of marriage to opposite-sex couples may long have seemed natural and just, but its inconsistency with the central meaning of the fundamental right to marry is now manifest. With that knowledge must come the recognition that laws excluding same-sex couples from the marriage right impose stigma and injury of the kind prohibited by our basic charter.

If rights were defined by who exercised them in the past, then received practices could serve as their own continued justification and new groups could not invoke rights once denied. This Court has rejected that approach, both with respect to the right to marry and the rights of gays and lesbians.

The right of same-sex couples to marry that is part of the liberty promised by the Fourteenth Amendment is derived, too, from that Amendment's guarantee of the equal protection of the laws. It is now clear that the challenged laws burden the liberty of same-sex couples, and it must be further acknowledged that they abridge central precepts of equality. Here the marriage laws enforced by the respondents are in essence unequal: same-sex couples are denied all the benefits afforded to opposite-sex couples and are barred from exercising a fundamental right. Especially against a long history of disapproval of their relationships, this denial to same-sex couples of the right to marry works a grave and continuing harm. The imposition of this disability on gays and lesbians serves to disrespect and subordinate them. And the Equal Protection Clause, like the Due Process Clause, prohibits this unjustified infringement of the fundamental right to marry.

These considerations lead to the conclusion that the right to marry is a fundamental right inherent in the liberty of the person, and under the Due Process and Equal Protection Clauses of the Fourteenth Amendment couples of the same-sex may not be deprived of that right and that liberty. The Court now holds that same-sex couples may exercise the fundamental right to marry. No longer may this liberty be denied to them.

IV

There may be an initial inclination in these cases to proceed with caution — to await further legislation, litigation, and debate. Yet there has been far more deliberation than this argument acknowledges. There have been referenda, legislative debates, and grassroots campaigns, as well as countless studies, papers, books, and other popular and scholarly writings. There has been extensive litigation in state and federal courts.

Of course, the Constitution contemplates that democracy is the appropriate process for change, so long as that process does not abridge fundamental rights.

The dynamic of our constitutional system is that individuals need not await legislative action before asserting a fundamental right. The Nation's courts are open to injured individuals who come to them to vindicate their own direct, personal stake in our basic charter. An individual can invoke a right to constitutional protection when he or she is harmed, even if the broader public disagrees and even if the legislature refuses to act.

Finally, it must be emphasized that religions, and those who adhere to religious doctrines, may continue to advocate with utmost, sincere conviction that, by divine precepts, same-sex marriage should not be condoned. The First Amendment ensures that religious organizations and persons are given proper protection as they seek to teach the principles that are so fulfilling and so central to their lives and faiths, and to their own deep aspirations to continue the family structure they have long revered. The same is true of those who oppose same-sex marriage for other reasons. In turn, those who believe allowing same-sex marriage is proper or indeed essential, whether as a matter of religious conviction or secular belief, may engage those who disagree with their view in an open and searching debate. The Constitution, however, does not permit the State to bar same-sex couples from marriage on the same terms as accorded to couples of the opposite sex.

No union is more profound than marriage, for it embodies the highest ideals of love, fidelity, devotion, sacrifice, and family. In forming a marital union, two people become something greater than once they were. As some of the petitioners in these cases demonstrate, marriage embodies a love that may endure even past death. It would misunderstand these men and women to say they disrespect the idea of marriage. Their plea is that they do respect it, respect it so deeply that they seek to find its fulfillment for themselves. Their hope is not to be condemned to live in loneliness, excluded from one of civilization's oldest institutions. They ask for equal dignity in the eyes of the law. The Constitution grants them that right.

Chief Justice ROBERTS, with whom Justice SCALIA and Justice THOMAS join, dissenting.

Petitioners make strong arguments rooted in social policy and considerations of fairness. They contend that same-sex couples should be allowed to affirm their love and commitment through marriage, just like opposite-sex couples. That position has undeniable appeal; over the past six years, voters and legislators in eleven States and the District of Columbia have revised their laws to allow marriage between two people of the same sex.

But this Court is not a legislature. Whether same-sex marriage is a good idea should be of no concern to us. Under the Constitution, judges have power to say what the law is, not what it should be.

Although the policy arguments for extending marriage to same-sex couples may be compelling, the legal arguments for requiring such an extension are not. The fundamental right to marry does not include a right to make a State change its definition of marriage. And a State's decision to maintain the meaning of marriage that has persisted in every culture throughout human history can hardly be called irrational. In short, our Constitution does not enact any one theory of marriage. The people of a State are free to expand marriage to include same-sex couples, or to retain the historic definition.

Today, however, the Court takes the extraordinary step of ordering every State to license and recognize same-sex marriage. Many people will rejoice at this decision, and I begrudge none their celebration. But for those who believe in a government of laws, not of men, the majority's approach is deeply disheartening. Supporters of same-sex marriage have achieved considerable success persuading their fellow citizens—through the democratic process—to adopt their view. That ends today. Five lawyers have closed the debate and enacted their own vision of marriage as a matter of constitutional law. Stealing this issue from the people will for many cast a cloud over same-sex marriage, making a dramatic social change that much more difficult to accept.

The majority's decision is an act of will, not legal judgment. The right it announces has no basis in the Constitution or this Court's precedent. The majority expressly disclaims judicial "caution" and omits even a pretense of humility, openly relying on its desire to remake society according to its own "new insight" into the "nature of injustice." As a result, the Court invalidates the marriage laws of more than half the States and orders the transformation of a social institution that has formed the basis of human society for millennia, for the Kalahari Bushmen and the Han Chinese, the Carthaginians and the Aztecs. Just who do we think we are?

It can be tempting for judges to confuse our own preferences with the requirements of the law. But as this Court has been reminded throughout our history, the Constitution "is made for people of fundamentally differing views." *Lochner v. New York* (1905) (Holmes, J., dissenting). Accordingly, "courts are not concerned with the wisdom or policy of legislation." *Id.* The majority today neglects that restrained conception of the judicial role. It seizes for itself a question the Constitution leaves to the people, at a time when the people are engaged in a vibrant debate on that question. And it answers that question based not on neutral principles of constitutional law, but on its own "understanding of what freedom is and must become." I have no choice but to dissent.

Understand well what this dissent is about: It is not about whether, in my judgment, the institution of marriage should be changed to include same-sex couples. It is instead about whether, in our democratic republic, that decision should rest with the people acting through their elected representatives, or with five lawyers who happen to hold commissions authorizing them to resolve legal disputes according to law. The Constitution leaves no doubt about the answer.

It is striking how much of the majority's reasoning would apply with equal force to the claim of a fundamental right to plural marriage. If "[t]here is dignity in the bond between two men or two women who seek to marry and in their autonomy to make such profound choices," why would there be any less dignity in the bond between three people who, in exercising their autonomy, seek to make the profound choice to marry? If a same-sex couple has the constitutional right to marry because their children would otherwise "suffer the stigma of knowing their families are somehow lesser," why wouldn't the same reasoning apply to a family of three or more persons raising children? If not having the opportunity to marry "serves to disrespect and subordinate" gay and lesbian couples, why wouldn't the same "imposition of this disability," serve to disrespect and subordinate people who find fulfillment in polyamorous relationships?

I do not mean to equate marriage between same-sex couples with plural marriages in all respects. There may well be relevant differences that compel different legal analysis. But if there are, petitioners have not pointed to any. When asked about a plural marital union at oral argument, petitioners asserted that a State "doesn't have such an institution." But that is exactly the point: the States at issue here do not have an institution of same-sex marriage, either.

The majority's understanding of due process lays out a tantalizing vision of the future for Members of this Court: If an unvarying social institution enduring over all of recorded history cannot inhibit judicial policymaking, what can? But this approach is dangerous for the rule of law. The purpose of insisting that implied fundamental rights have roots in the history and tradition of our people is to ensure that when unelected judges strike down democratically enacted laws, they do so based on something more than their own beliefs. The Court today not only overlooks our country's entire history and tradition but actively repudiates it, preferring to live only in the heady days of the here and now. I agree with the majority that the "nature of injustice is that we may not always see it in our own times." As petitioners put it, "times can blind." But to blind yourself to history is both prideful and unwise. "The past is never dead. It's not even past." W. Faulkner, Requiem for a Nun 92 (1951).

III

In addition to their due process argument, petitioners contend that the Equal Protection Clause requires their States to license and recognize same-sex marriages. The majority does not seriously engage with this claim. Its discussion is, quite frankly, difficult to follow.

The majority goes on to assert in conclusory fashion that the Equal Protection Clause provides an alternative basis for its holding. Yet the majority fails to provide even a single sentence explaining how the Equal Protection Clause supplies independent weight for its position, nor does it attempt to justify its gratuitous violation of the canon against unnecessarily resolving constitutional questions.

IV

Those who founded our country would not recognize the majority's conception of the judicial role. They after all risked their lives and fortunes for the precious right to govern themselves. They would never have imagined yielding that right on a question of social policy to unaccountable and unelected judges. And they certainly would not have been satisfied by a system empowering judges to override policy judgments so long as they do so after "a quite extensive discussion." In our democracy, debate about the content of the law is not an exhaustion requirement to be checked off before courts can impose their will.

The Court's accumulation of power does not occur in a vacuum. It comes at the expense of the people. And they know it. Here and abroad, people are in the midst of a serious and thoughtful public debate on the issue of same-sex marriage. They see voters carefully considering same-sex marriage, casting ballots in favor or opposed, and sometimes changing their minds. They see political leaders similarly reexamining their positions, and either reversing course or explaining adherence to old convictions confirmed anew. They see governments and businesses modifying policies and practices with respect to same-sex couples, and participating actively in the civic discourse. They see countries overseas democratically accepting profound social change, or declining to do so. This deliberative process is making people take seriously questions that they may not have even regarded as questions before.

When decisions are reached through democratic means, some people will inevitably be disappointed with the results. But those whose views do not prevail at least know that they have had their say, and accordingly are—in the tradition of our political culture—reconciled to the result of a fair and honest debate. In addition, they can gear up to raise the issue later, hoping to persuade enough on the winning side to think again. "That is exactly how our system of government is supposed to work."

But today the Court puts a stop to all that. By deciding this question under the Constitution, the Court removes it from the realm of democratic decision. There will be consequences to shutting down the political process on an issue of such profound public significance. Closing debate tends to close minds. People denied a voice are less likely to accept the ruling of a court on an issue that does not seem to be the sort of thing courts usually decide. As a thoughtful commentator observed about another issue, "The political process was moving . . . , not swiftly enough for advocates of quick, complete change, but majoritarian institutions were listening and acting. Heavy-handed judicial intervention was difficult to justify and appears to have provoked, not resolved, conflict." Ginsburg, Some Thoughts on Autonomy and Equality in Relation to Roe v. Wade, 63 N.C. L. Rev. 375, 385–386 (1985). Indeed, however heartened the proponents of same-sex marriage might be on this day, it is worth acknowledging what they have lost, and lost forever: the opportunity to win the true acceptance that comes from persuading their fellow citizens of the justice of their cause. And they lose this just when the winds of change were freshening at their backs.

Federal courts are blunt instruments when it comes to creating rights. They have constitutional power only to resolve concrete cases or controversies; they do not have the flexibility of legislatures to address concerns of parties not before the court or to anticipate problems that may arise from the exercise of a new right. Today's decision, for example, creates serious questions about religious liberty. Many good and decent people oppose same-sex marriage as a tenet of faith, and their freedom to exercise religion is—unlike the right imagined by the majority—actually spelled out in the Constitution. Amdt. 1.

Respect for sincere religious conviction has led voters and legislators in every State that has adopted same-sex marriage democratically to include accommodations for religious practice. The majority's decision imposing same-sex marriage cannot, of course, create any such accommodations. The majority graciously suggests that religious believers may continue to "advocate" and "teach" their views of marriage. The First Amendment guarantees, however, the freedom to "*exercise* " religion. Ominously, that is not a word the majority uses.

If you are among the many Americans—of whatever sexual orientation— who favor expanding same-sex marriage, by all means celebrate today's decision. Celebrate the achievement of a desired goal. Celebrate the opportunity for a new expression of commitment to a partner. Celebrate the availability of new benefits. But do not celebrate the Constitution. It had nothing to do with it.

Justice SCALIA, with whom Justice THOMAS joins, dissenting.

I join The Chief Justice's opinion in full. I write separately to call attention to this Court's threat to American democracy.

The substance of today's decree is not of immense personal importance to me. The law can recognize as marriage whatever sexual attachments and living arrangements it wishes, and can accord them favorable civil consequences, from tax treatment to rights of inheritance. Those civil consequences — and the public approval that conferring the name of marriage evidences — can perhaps have adverse social effects, but no more adverse than the effects of many other controversial laws. So it is not of special importance to me what the law says about marriage. It is of overwhelming importance, however, who it is that rules me. Today's decree says that my Ruler, and the Ruler of 320 million Americans coast-to-coast, is a majority of the nine lawyers on the Supreme Court. The opinion in these cases is the furthest extension in fact — and the furthest extension one can even imagine — of the Court's claimed power to create "liberties" that the Constitution and its Amendments neglect to mention. This practice of constitutional revision by an unelected committee of nine, always accompanied (as it is today) by extravagant praise of liberty, robs the People of the most important liberty they asserted in the Declaration of Independence and won in the Revolution of 1776: the freedom to govern themselves.

I

Until the courts put a stop to it, public debate over same-sex marriage displayed American democracy at its best. Individuals on both sides of the issue passionately, but respectfully, attempted to persuade their fellow citizens to accept their views. Americans considered the arguments and put the question to a vote. The electorates of 11 States, either directly or through their representatives, chose to expand the traditional definition of marriage. Many more decided not to. Win or lose, advocates for both sides continued pressing their cases, secure in the knowledge that an electoral loss can be negated by a later electoral win. That is exactly how our system of government is supposed to work.

The Constitution places some constraints on self-rule — constraints adopted *by the People themselves* when they ratified the Constitution and its Amendments. These cases ask us to decide whether the Fourteenth Amendment contains a limitation that requires the States to license and recognize marriages between two people of the same sex. Does it remove *that* issue from the political process?

Of course not. It would be surprising to find a prescription regarding marriage in the Federal Constitution since, as the author of today's opinion reminded us only two years ago (in an opinion joined by the same Justices who join him today): "[R]egulation of domestic relations is an area that has long been regarded as a virtually exclusive province of the States." "[T]he Federal Government, through our history, has deferred to state-law policy decisions with respect to domestic relations."[11]

But we need not speculate. When the Fourteenth Amendment was ratified in 1868, every State limited marriage to one man and one woman, and no one doubted the constitutionality of doing so. That resolves these cases. We have no basis for striking down a practice that is not expressly prohibited by the Fourteenth Amendment's text, and that bears the endorsement of a long tradition of open, widespread, and unchallenged use dating back to the Amendment's ratification. Since there is no doubt whatever that the People never decided to prohibit the limitation of marriage to opposite-sex couples, the public debate over same-sex marriage must be allowed to continue.

But the Court ends this debate, in an opinion lacking even a thin veneer of law. Buried beneath the mummeries and straining-to-be-memorable passages of the opinion is a candid and startling assertion: No matter *what* it was the People ratified, the Fourteenth Amendment protects those rights that the Judiciary, in its "reasoned judgment," thinks the Fourteenth Amendment ought to protect.

This is a naked judicial claim to legislative—indeed, *super*-legislative—power; a claim fundamentally at odds with our system of government. Except as limited by a constitutional prohibition agreed to by the People, the States are free to adopt whatever laws they like, even those that offend the esteemed Justices' "reasoned judgment." A system of government that makes the People subordinate to a committee of nine unelected lawyers does not deserve to be called a democracy.

II

But what really astounds is the hubris reflected in today's judicial Putsch. The five Justices who compose today's majority are entirely comfortable concluding that every State violated the Constitution for all of the 135 years between the Fourteenth Amendment's ratification and Massachusetts' permitting of same-sex marriages in 2003. They have discovered in the Fourteenth Amendment a "fundamental right" overlooked by every person alive at the time of ratification, and almost everyone else in the time since. They see what lesser legal minds — minds like Thomas Cooley, John Marshall Harlan, Oliver Wendell Holmes, Jr., Learned Hand, Louis Brandeis, William Howard Taft, Benjamin Cardozo, Hugo Black, Felix Frankfurter, Robert Jackson, and Henry Friendly — could not.

Hubris is sometimes defined as o'erweening pride; and pride, we know, goeth before a fall. The Judiciary is the "least dangerous" of the federal branches because it has "neither Force nor Will, but merely judgment; and must ultimately depend upon the aid of the executive arm" and the States, "even for the efficacy of its judgments." With each decision of ours that takes from the People a question properly left to them — with each decision that is unabashedly based not on law, but on the "reasoned judgment" of a bare majority of this Court — we move one step closer to being reminded of our impotence.

Justice THOMAS, with whom Justice SCALIA joins, dissenting.

The Court's decision today is at odds not only with the Constitution, but with the principles upon which our Nation was built. Since well before 1787, liberty has been understood as freedom from government action, not entitlement to government benefits. The Framers created our Constitution to preserve that understanding of liberty. Yet the majority invokes our Constitution in the name of a "liberty" that the Framers would not have recognized, to the detriment of the liberty they sought to protect. Along the way, it rejects the idea — captured in our Declaration of Independence — that human dignity is innate and suggests instead that it comes from the Government. This distortion of our Constitution not only ignores the text, it inverts the relationship between the individual and the state in our Republic. I cannot agree with it.

The majority's decision today will require States to issue marriage licenses to same-sex couples and to recognize same-sex marriages entered in other States largely based on a constitutional provision guaranteeing "due process" before a person is deprived of his "life, liberty, or property." I have elsewhere explained the dangerous fiction of treating the Due Process Clause as a font of substantive rights. It distorts the constitutional text, which guarantees only whatever "process" is "due" before a person is deprived of life, liberty, and property. Worse, it invites judges to do exactly what the majority has done here — " 'roa[m] at large in the constitutional field' guided only by their personal views" as to the " 'fundamental rights' " protected by that document.

By straying from the text of the Constitution, substantive due process exalts judges at the expense of the People from whom they derive their authority. Petitioners argue that by enshrining the traditional definition of marriage in their State Constitutions through voter-approved amendments, the States have put the issue "beyond the reach of the normal democratic process." But the result petitioners seek is far less democratic. They ask nine judges on this Court to enshrine their definition of marriage in the Federal Constitution and thus put it beyond the reach of the normal democratic process for the entire Nation. That a "bare majority" of this Court, is able to grant this wish, wiping out with a stroke of the keyboard the results of the political process in over 30 States, based on a provision that guarantees only "due process" is but further evidence of the danger of substantive due process.

Even if the doctrine of substantive due process were somehow defensible — it is not — petitioners still would not have a claim. To invoke the protection of the Due Process Clause at all — whether under a theory of "substantive" or "procedural" due process — a party must first identify a deprivation of "life, liberty, or property." The majority claims these state laws deprive petitioners of "liberty," but the concept of "liberty" it conjures up bears no resemblance to any plausible meaning of that word as it is used in the Due Process Clauses.

Even assuming that the "liberty" in those Clauses encompasses something more than freedom from physical restraint, it would not include the types of rights claimed by the majority. In the American legal tradition, liberty has long been understood as individual freedom *from* governmental action, not as a right *to* a particular governmental entitlement.

Whether we define "liberty" as locomotion or freedom from governmental action more broadly, petitioners have in no way been deprived of it. Petitioners cannot claim, under the most plausible definition of "liberty," that they have been imprisoned or physically restrained by the States for participating in same-sex relationships. To the contrary, they have been able to cohabitate and raise their children in peace. They have been able to hold civil marriage ceremonies in States that recognize same-sex marriages and private religious ceremonies in all States. They have been able to travel freely around the country, making their homes where they please. Far from being incarcerated or physically restrained, petitioners have been left alone to order their lives as they see fit.

Nor, under the broader definition, can they claim that the States have restricted their ability to go about their daily lives as they would be able to absent governmental restrictions. Petitioners do not ask this Court to order the States to stop restricting their ability to enter same-sex relationships, to engage in intimate behavior, to make vows to their partners in public ceremonies, to engage in religious wedding ceremonies, to hold themselves out as married, or to raise children. The States have imposed no such restrictions. Nor have the States prevented petitioners from approximating a number of incidents of marriage through private legal means, such as wills, trusts, and powers of attorney.

Instead, the States have refused to grant them governmental entitlements. Petitioners claim that as a matter of "liberty," they are entitled to access privileges and benefits that exist solely *because of* the government. They want, for example, to receive the State's *imprimatur* on their marriages—on state issued marriage licenses, death certificates, or other official forms. And they want to receive various monetary benefits, including reduced inheritance taxes upon the death of a spouse, compensation if a spouse dies as a result of a work-related injury, or loss of consortium damages in tort suits. But receiving governmental recognition and benefits has nothing to do with any understanding of "liberty" that the Framers would have recognized.

Our Constitution—like the Declaration of Independence before it—was predicated on a simple truth: One's liberty, not to mention one's dignity, was something to be shielded from—not provided by—the State. Today's decision casts that truth aside. In its haste to reach a desired result, the majority misapplies a clause focused on "due process" to afford substantive rights, disregards the most plausible understanding of the "liberty" protected by that clause, and distorts the principles on which this Nation was founded. Its decision will have inestimable consequences for our Constitution and our society. I respectfully dissent.

Justice ALITO, with whom Justice SCALIA and Justice THOMAS join, dissenting.

Until the federal courts intervened, the American people were engaged in a debate about whether their States should recognize same-sex marriage. The question in these cases, however, is not what States *should* do about same-sex marriage but whether the Constitution answers that question for them. It does not. The Constitution leaves that question to be decided by the people of each State.

The Constitution says nothing about a right to same-sex marriage, but the Court holds that the term "liberty" in the Due Process Clause of the Fourteenth Amendment encompasses this right. To prevent five unelected Justices from imposing their personal vision of liberty upon the American people, the Court has held that "liberty" under the Due Process Clause should be understood to protect only those rights that are " 'deeply rooted in this Nation's history and tradition.' " *Washington* v. *Glucksberg* (1997).

And it is beyond dispute that the right to same-sex marriage is not among those rights. See *United States v. Windsor* (2013) (Alito, J., dissenting).

For today's majority, it does not matter that the right to same-sex marriage lacks deep roots or even that it is contrary to long-established tradition. The Justices in the majority claim the authority to confer constitutional protection upon that right simply because they believe that it is fundamental.

Attempting to circumvent the problem presented by the newness of the right found in these cases, the majority claims that the issue is the right to equal treatment. Noting that marriage is a fundamental right, the majority argues that a State has no valid reason for denying that right to same-sex couples. This reasoning is dependent upon a particular understanding of the purpose of civil marriage. This understanding of marriage, which focuses almost entirely on the happiness of persons who choose to marry, is shared by many people today, but it is not the traditional one. For millennia, marriage was inextricably linked to the one thing that only an opposite-sex couple can do: procreate.

Today's decision usurps the constitutional right of the people to decide whether to keep or alter the traditional understanding of marriage. The decision will also have other important consequences.

It will be used to vilify Americans who are unwilling to assent to the new orthodoxy. In the course of its opinion, the majority compares traditional marriage laws to laws that denied equal treatment for African-Americans and women. The implications of this analogy will be exploited by those who are determined to stamp out every vestige of dissent.

Perhaps recognizing how its reasoning may be used, the majority attempts, toward the end of its opinion, to reassure those who oppose same-sex marriage that their rights of conscience will be protected. We will soon see whether this proves to be true. I assume that those who cling to old beliefs will be able to whisper their thoughts in the recesses of their homes, but if they repeat those views in public, they will risk being labeled as bigots and treated as such by governments, employers, and schools.

The system of federalism established by our Constitution provides a way for people with different beliefs to live together in a single nation. If the issue of same-sex marriage had been left to the people of the States, it is likely that some States would recognize same-sex marriage and others would not. It is also possible that some States would tie recognition to protection for conscience rights. The majority today makes that impossible. By imposing its own views on the entire country, the majority facilitates the marginalization of the many Americans who have traditional ideas. Recalling the harsh treatment of gays and lesbians in the past, some may think that turnabout is fair play. But if that sentiment prevails, the Nation will experience bitter and lasting wounds.

Today's decision will also have a fundamental effect on this Court and its ability to uphold the rule of law. If a bare majority of Justices can invent a new right and impose that right on the rest of the country, the only real limit on what future majorities will be able to do is their own sense of what those with political power and cultural influence are willing to tolerate. Even enthusiastic supporters of same-sex marriage should worry about the scope of the power that today's majority claims.

Today's decision shows that decades of attempts to restrain this Court's abuse of its authority have failed. A lesson that some will take from today's decision is that preaching about the proper method of interpreting the Constitution or the virtues of judicial self-restraint and humility cannot compete with the temptation to achieve what is viewed as a noble end by any practicable means. I do not doubt that my colleagues in the majority sincerely see in the Constitution a vision of liberty that happens to coincide with their own. But this sincerity is cause for concern, not comfort. What it evidences is the deep and perhaps irremediable corruption of our legal culture's conception of constitutional interpretation.

Most Americans—understandably—will cheer or lament today's decision because of their views on the issue of same-sex marriage. But all Americans, whatever their thinking on that issue, should worry about what the majority's claim of power portends.

Chapter 8

Fundamental Rights Under Due Process and Equal Protection

C. The Constitutional Protection for Family Autonomy

1. The Right to Marry (casebook, p. 939)

In *Obergefell v. Hodges* (2015), the Court ruled that state laws prohibiting same sex marriage infringe the right to marry and deny equal protection. This decision is presented in the prior chapter.

I. The Right to Vote (casebook, p. 1069)

5. Independent Districting Commissions (new)

Partisan gerrymandering occurs when the political party that controls a legislative body draws election districts to maximize safe seats for that party. Is it constitutional for the voters of a state to assign this task to an independent commission?

ARIZONA STATE LEGISLATURE v. ARIZONA INDEPENDENT REDISTRICTING COMMISSION
135 S. Ct. ___ (2015)

Justice GINSBURG delivered the opinion of the Court.

This case concerns an endeavor by Arizona voters to address the problem of partisan gerrymandering—the drawing of legislative district lines to subordinate adherents of one political party and entrench a rival party in power. "[P]artisan gerrymanders," this Court has recognized, "[are incompatible] with democratic principles." *Vieth v. Jubelirer* (2004)

In 2000, Arizona voters adopted an initiative, Proposition 106, aimed at "ending the practice of gerrymandering and improving voter and candidate participation in elections." Proposition 106 amended Arizona's Constitution to remove redistricting authority from the Arizona Legislature and vest that authority in an independent commission, the Arizona Independent Redistricting Commission (AIRC or Commission). After the 2010 census, as after the 2000 census, the AIRC adopted redistricting maps for congressional as well as state legislative districts.

The Arizona Legislature challenged the map the Commission adopted in January 2012 for congressional districts. Recognizing that the voters could control redistricting for state legislators, the Arizona Legislature sued the AIRC in federal court seeking a declaration that the Commission and its map for congressional districts violated the "Elections Clause" of the U.S. Constitution. That Clause, critical to the resolution of this case, provides: "The Times, Places and Manner of holding Elections for Senators and Representatives, shall be prescribed in each State by the Legislature thereof; but the Congress may at any time by Law make or alter such Regulations. . . ." Art. I, § 4, cl. 1.

The Arizona Legislature's complaint alleged that "[t]he word 'Legislature' in the Elections Clause means [specifically and only] the representative body which makes the laws of the people"; so read, the Legislature urges, the Clause precludes resort to an independent commission, created by initiative, to accomplish redistricting. The AIRC responded that, for Elections Clause purposes, "the Legislature" is not confined to the elected representatives; rather, the term encompasses all legislative authority conferred by the State Constitution, including initiatives adopted by the people themselves.

We hold, first, that the Arizona Legislature, having lost authority to draw congressional districts, has standing to contest the constitutionality of Proposition 106. Next, we hold that lawmaking power in Arizona includes the initiative process, and that both § 2a(c) and the Elections Clause permit use of the AIRC in congressional districting in the same way the Commission is used in districting for Arizona's own Legislature.

I

Proposition 106, vesting redistricting authority in the AIRC, was adopted by citizen initiative in 2000 against a "background of recurring redistricting turmoil" in Arizona. Redistricting plans adopted by the Arizona Legislature sparked controversy in every redistricting cycle since the 1970's, and several of those plans were rejected by a federal court or refused preclearance by the Department of Justice under the Voting Rights Act of 1965.

Aimed at "ending the practice of gerrymandering and improving voter and candidate participation in elections," Proposition 106 amended the Arizona Constitution to remove congressional redistricting authority from the state legislature, lodging that authority, instead, in a new entity, the AIRC. The AIRC convenes after each census, establishes final district boundaries, and certifies the new districts to the Arizona Secretary of State. The legislature may submit nonbinding recommendations to the AIRC, and is required to make necessary appropriations for its operation.

Several other States, as a means to curtail partisan gerrymandering, have also provided for the participation of commissions in redistricting. Some States, in common with Arizona, have given nonpartisan or bipartisan commissions binding authority over redistricting. Still other States have given commissions an auxiliary role, advising the legislatures on redistricting, or serving as a "backup" in the event the State's representative body fails to complete redistricting. Studies report that nonpartisan and bipartisan commissions generally draw their maps in a timely fashion and create districts both more competitive and more likely to survive legal challenge.

II

We turn first to the threshold question: Does the Arizona Legislature have standing to bring this suit? Trained on "whether the plaintiff is [a] proper party to bring [a particular lawsuit,]" standing is "[o]ne element" of the Constitution's case-or-controversy limitation on federal judicial authority, expressed in Article III of the Constitution. "To qualify as a party with standing to litigate," the Arizona Legislature "must show, first and foremost," injury in the form of " 'invasion of a legally protected interest' that is 'concrete and particularized' and 'actual or imminent.' " The Legislature's injury also must be "fairly traceable to the challenged action" and "redressable by a favorable ruling."

The Arizona Legislature maintains that the Elections Clause vests in it "primary responsibility" for redistricting. To exercise that responsibility, the Legislature urges, it must have at least the opportunity to engage (or decline to engage) in redistricting before the State may involve other actors in the redistricting process. Although we conclude that the Arizona Legislature does not have the exclusive, constitutionally guarded role it asserts, one must not "confus[e] weakness on the merits with absence of Article III standing."

Closer to the mark is this Court's decision in *Coleman v. Miller* (1939). There, plaintiffs were 20 (of 40) Kansas State Senators, whose votes "would have been sufficient to defeat [a] resolution ratifying [a] proposed [federal] constitutional amendment." We held they had standing to challenge, as impermissible under Article V of the Federal Constitution, the State Lieutenant Governor's tie-breaking vote for the amendment. *Coleman,* as we later explained in *Raines,* stood "for the proposition that legislators whose votes would have been sufficient to defeat (or enact) a specific legislative Act have standing to sue if that legislative action goes into effect (or does not go into effect), on the ground that their votes have been completely nullified." Our conclusion that the Arizona Legislature has standing fits that bill. Proposition 106, together with the Arizona Constitution's ban on efforts to undermine the purposes of an initiative, would "completely nullif[y]" any vote by the Legislature, now or "in the future," purporting to adopt a redistricting plan. This dispute, in short, "will be resolved . . . in a concrete factual context conducive to a realistic appreciation of the consequences of judicial action."

III

On the merits, we instructed the parties to address this question: Do the Elections Clause of the United States Constitution and 2 U.S.C. § 2a(c) permit Arizona's use of a commission to adopt congressional districts? The Elections Clause is set out at the start of this opinion. Section 2a(c) provides: "Until a State is redistricted in the manner provided by the law thereof after any apportionment, the Representatives to which such State is entitled under such apportionment shall be elected in the following manner: [setting out five federally prescribed redistricting procedures]."

Constantly resisted by The Chief Justice but well understood in opinions that speak for the Court: "[T]he meaning of the word 'legislature,' used several times in the Federal Constitution, differs according to the connection in which it is employed, depend[ent] upon the character of the function which that body in each instance is called upon to exercise." Thus "the Legislature" comprises the referendum and the Governor's veto in the context of regulating congressional elections. In the context of ratifying constitutional amendments, in contrast, "the Legislature" has a different identity, one that excludes the referendum and the Governor's veto.

In sum, our precedent teaches that redistricting is a legislative function, to be performed in accordance with the State's prescriptions for lawmaking, which may include the referendum and the Governor's veto.

The exercise of the initiative, we acknowledge, was not at issue in our prior decisions. But as developed below, we see no constitutional barrier to a State's empowerment of its people by embracing that form of lawmaking.

In accord with the District Court, see *supra,* at ——, we hold that the Elections Clause permits the people of Arizona to provide for redistricting by independent commission. To restate the key question in this case, the issue centrally debated by the parties: Absent congressional authorization, does the Elections Clause preclude the people of Arizona from creating a commission operating independently of the state legislature to establish congressional districts? The history and purpose of the Clause weigh heavily against such preclusion, as does the animating principle of our Constitution that the people themselves are the originating source of all the powers of government.

We note, preliminarily, that dictionaries, even those in circulation during the founding era, capaciously define the word "legislature." Samuel Johnson defined "legislature" simply as "[t]he power that makes laws." 2 A Dictionary of the English Language (1st ed. 1755). Thomas Sheridan's dictionary defined "legislature" exactly as Dr. Johnson did: "The power that makes laws." 2 A Complete Dictionary of the English Language (4th ed. 1797). Noah Webster defined the term precisely that way as well. Compendious Dictionary of the English Language 174 (1806). And Nathan Bailey similarly defined "legislature" as "the Authority of making Laws, or Power which makes them." An Universal Etymological English Dictionary (20th ed. 1763).

As to the "power that makes laws" in Arizona, initiatives adopted by the voters legislate for the State just as measures passed by the representative body do. As well in Arizona, the people may delegate their legislative authority over redistricting to an independent commission just as the representative body may choose to do.

The dominant purpose of the Elections Clause, the historical record bears out, was to empower Congress to override state election rules, not to restrict the way States enact legislation. The Clause was also intended to act as a safeguard against manipulation of electoral rules by politicians and factions in the States to entrench themselves or place their interests over those of the electorate.

The Arizona Legislature maintains that, by specifying "the Legislature thereof," the Elections Clause renders the State's representative body the sole "component of state government authorized to prescribe . . . regulations . . . for congressional redistricting." But it is characteristic of our federal system that States retain autonomy to establish their own governmental processes. Arizona engaged in definition of that kind when its people placed both the initiative power and the AIRC's redistricting authority in the portion of the Arizona Constitution delineating the State's legislative authority.

This Court has "long recognized the role of the States as laboratories for devising solutions to difficult legal problems." We resist reading the Elections Clause to single out federal elections as the one area in which States may not use citizen initiatives as an alternative legislative process.

Banning lawmaking by initiative to direct a State's method of apportioning congressional districts would do more than stymie attempts to curb partisan gerrymandering, by which the majority in the legislature draws district lines to their party's advantage. It would also cast doubt on numerous other election laws adopted by the initiative method of legislating.

Invoking the Elections Clause, the Arizona Legislature instituted this lawsuit to disempower the State's voters from serving as the legislative power for redistricting purposes. But the Clause surely was not adopted to diminish a State's authority to determine its own lawmaking processes. Article I, § 4, stems from a different view. Both parts of the Elections Clause are in line with the fundamental premise that all political power flows from the people. *McCulloch v. Maryland* (1819). So comprehended, the Clause doubly empowers the people. They may control the State's lawmaking processes in the first instance, as Arizona voters have done, and they may seek Congress' correction of regulations prescribed by state legislatures.

The people of Arizona turned to the initiative to curb the practice of gerrymandering and, thereby, to ensure that Members of Congress would have "an habitual recollection of their dependence on the people." The Federalist No. 57, at 350 (J. Madison). In so acting, Arizona voters sought to restore "the core principle of republican government," namely, "that the voters should choose their representatives, not the other way around." The Elections Clause does not hinder that endeavor.

Chief Justice ROBERTS, with whom Justice SCALIA, Justice THOMAS, and Justice ALITO join, dissenting.

Just over a century ago, Arizona became the second State in the Union to ratify the Seventeenth Amendment. That Amendment transferred power to choose United States Senators from "the Legislature" of each State, Art. I, § 3, to "the people thereof." The Amendment resulted from an arduous, decades-long campaign in which reformers across the country worked hard to garner approval from Congress and three-quarters of the States.

What chumps! Didn't they realize that all they had to do was interpret the constitutional term "the Legislature" to mean "the people"? The Court today performs just such a magic trick with the Elections Clause. Art. I, § 4. That Clause vests congressional redistricting authority in "the Legislature" of each State. An Arizona ballot initiative transferred that authority from "the Legislature" to an "Independent Redistricting Commission." The majority approves this deliberate constitutional evasion by doing what the proponents of the Seventeenth Amendment dared not: revising "the Legislature" to mean "the people."

The Court's position has no basis in the text, structure, or history of the Constitution, and it contradicts precedents from both Congress and this Court. The Constitution contains seventeen provisions referring to the "Legislature" of a State, many of which cannot possibly be read to mean "the people." Indeed, several provisions expressly distinguish "the Legislature" from "the People." See Art. I, § 2; Amdt. 17. This Court has accordingly defined "the Legislature" in the Elections Clause as *"the representative body* which ma[kes] the laws of the people."

The majority largely ignores this evidence, relying instead on disconnected observations about direct democracy, a contorted interpretation of an irrelevant statute, and naked appeals to public policy. Nowhere does the majority explain how a constitutional provision that vests redistricting authority in "the Legislature" permits a State to wholly exclude "the Legislature" from redistricting. Arizona's Commission might be a noble endeavor—although it does not seem so "independent" in practice—but the "fact that a given law or procedure is efficient, convenient, and useful . . . will not save it if it is contrary to the Constitution." No matter how concerned we may be about partisanship in redistricting, this Court has no power to gerrymander the Constitution. I respectfully dissent.

I

The majority begins by discussing policy. I begin with the Constitution. The Elections Clause provides:

> The Times, Places and Manner of holding Elections for Senators and Representatives, shall be prescribed in each State by the Legislature thereof; but the Congress may at any time by Law make or alter such Regulations, except as to the Places of chusing Senators. Art. I, § 4, cl. 1.

The Elections Clause both imposes a duty on States and assigns that duty to a particular state actor: In the absence of a valid congressional directive to the contrary, States must draw district lines for their federal representatives. And that duty "shall" be carried out "in each State by the Legislature thereof."

In Arizona, however, redistricting is not carried out by the legislature. Instead, as the result of a ballot initiative, an unelected body called the Independent Redistricting Commission draws the lines. See *ante,* at ——— – ———. The key question in the case is whether the Commission can conduct congressional districting consistent with the directive that such authority be exercised "by the Legislature."

The majority concedes that the unelected Commission is not "the Legislature" of Arizona. The Court contends instead that the people of Arizona as a whole constitute "the Legislature" for purposes of the Elections Clause, and that they may delegate the congressional districting authority conferred by that Clause to the Commission. *Ante,* at ———. The majority provides no support for the delegation part of its theory, and I am not sure whether the majority's analysis is correct on that issue. But even giving the Court the benefit of the doubt in that regard, the Commission is still unconstitutional. Both the Constitution and our cases make clear that "the Legislature" in the Elections Clause is the representative body which makes the laws of the people.

A

The majority devotes much of its analysis to establishing that the people of Arizona may exercise lawmaking power under their State Constitution. See *ante,* at ——— – ———, ———, ——— – ———. Nobody doubts that. This case is governed, however, by the Federal Constitution. The States do not, in the majority's words, "retain autonomy to establish their own governmental processes," *ante,* at ———, if those "processes" violate the United States Constitution. In a conflict between the Arizona Constitution and the Elections Clause, the State Constitution must give way. Art. VI, cl. 2; Cook v. Gralike, 531 U.S. 510, 523, 121 S. Ct. 1029, 149 L. Ed.2d 44 (2001). The majority opinion therefore largely misses the point.

The relevant question in this case is how to define "the Legislature" under the Elections Clause. Any ambiguity about the meaning of "the Legislature" is removed by other founding era sources. "[E]very state constitution from the Founding Era that used the term *legislature* defined it as a distinct multimember entity comprised of representatives." The Federalist Papers are replete with references to "legislatures" that can only be understood as referring to representative institutions.

I could go on, but the Court has said this before. As we put it nearly a century ago, "Legislature" was "not a term of uncertain meaning when incorporated into the Constitution." "What it meant when adopted it still means for the purpose of interpretation." "A Legislature" is "the representative body which ma[kes] the laws of the people."

The unambiguous meaning of "the Legislature" in the Elections Clause as a representative body is confirmed by other provisions of the Constitution that use the same term in the same way. When seeking to discern the meaning of a word in the Constitution, there is no better dictionary than the rest of the Constitution itself. Our precedents new and old have employed this structural method of interpretation to read the Constitution in the manner it was drafted and ratified—as a unified, coherent whole.

The Constitution includes seventeen provisions referring to a State's "Legislature." Every one of those references is consistent with the understanding of a legislature as a representative body. More importantly, many of them are only consistent with an institutional legislature — and flatly incompatible with the majority's reading of "the Legislature" to refer to the people as a whole.

The history of the Elections Clause further supports the conclusion that "the Legislature" is a representative body. The first known draft of the Clause to appear at the Constitutional Convention provided that "Each state shall prescribe the time and manner of holding elections." 1 Debates on the Federal Constitution 146 (J. Elliot ed. 1836). After revision by the Committee of Detail, the Clause included the important limitation at issue here: "The times and places, and the manner, of holding the elections of the members of each house, shall be prescribed *by the legislature of each state*; but their provisions concerning them may, at any time, be altered *by the legislature of the United States*." *Id.,* at 225 (emphasis added). The insertion of "the legislature" indicates that the Framers thought carefully about which entity within the State was to perform congressional districting. And the parallel between "the legislature of each state" and "the legislature of the United States" further suggests that they meant "the legislature" as a representative body.

As the majority explains, the debate over the ratification of the Elections Clause centered on its second part, which empowers Congress to "make or alter" regulations prescribed by "the Legislature" of a State. Importantly for our purposes, however, both sides in this debate "recognized the distinction between the state legislature and the people themselves."

The constitutional text, structure, history, and precedent establish a straightforward rule: Under the Elections Clause, "the Legislature" is a representative body that, when it prescribes election regulations, may be required to do so within the ordinary lawmaking process, but may not be cut out of that process. Put simply, the state legislature need not be exclusive in congressional districting, but neither may it be excluded.

The majority's contrary understanding requires it to accept a definition of "the Legislature" that contradicts the term's plain meaning, creates discord with the Seventeenth Amendment and the Constitution's many other uses of the term, makes nonsense of the drafting and ratification of the Elections Clause, and breaks with the relevant precedents. In short, the effect of the majority's decision is to erase the words "by the Legislature thereof" from the Elections Clause. That is a judicial error of the most basic order. "It cannot be presumed that any clause in the constitution is intended to be without effect; and therefore such a construction is inadmissible." *Marbury v. Madison* (1803).

For the reasons I have explained, there is no real doubt about what "the Legislature" means. The Framers of the Constitution were "practical men, dealing with the facts of political life as they understood them, putting into form the government they were creating, and prescribing in language clear and intelligible the powers that government was to take." We ought to give effect to the words they used.

Justice SCALIA, with whom Justice THOMAS joins, dissenting.

I do not believe that the question the Court answers is properly before us. Disputes between governmental branches or departments regarding the allocation of political power do not in my view constitute "cases" or "controversies" committed to our resolution by Art. III, § 2, of the Constitution.

What those who framed and ratified the Constitution had in mind when they entrusted the "judicial Power" to a separate and coequal branch of the Federal Government was the judicial power they were familiar with—that traditionally exercised by English and American courts. The "cases" and "controversies" that those courts entertained did not include suits between units of government regarding their legitimate powers. The job of the courts was, in Chief Justice Marshall's words, "solely, to decide on the rights of individuals," *Marbury v. Madison* (1803).

What history and judicial tradition show is that courts do not resolve direct disputes between two political branches of the same government regarding their respective powers. Nearly every separation-of-powers case presents questions like the ones in this case. But we have *never* passed on a separation-of-powers question raised directly by a governmental subunit's complaint. We have *always* resolved those questions in the context of a private lawsuit in which the claim or defense depends on the constitutional validity of action by one of the governmental subunits that has caused a private party concrete harm.

Normally, having arrived at that conclusion, I would express no opinion on the merits unless my vote was necessary to enable the Court to produce a judgment. In the present case, however, the majority's resolution of the merits question ("legislature" means "the people") is so outrageously wrong, so utterly devoid of textual or historic support, so flatly in contradiction of prior Supreme Court cases, so obviously the willful product of hostility to districting by state legislatures, that I cannot avoid adding my vote to the devastating dissent of the Chief Justice.

Chapter 9

First Amendment: Freedom of Expression

B. Free Speech Methodology

1. The Distinction Between Content-Based and Content-Neutral Laws

a. The importance of the Distinction (casebook, p. 1206)

The Court's decision in *Reed v. Town of Gilbert* illustrates the importance of this distinction and also how different justices want to treat it.

REED v. TOWN OF GILBERT
135 S. Ct. 2218 (2015)

Justice THOMAS delivered the opinion of the Court.

The town of Gilbert, Arizona (or Town), has adopted a comprehensive code governing the manner in which people may display outdoor signs. The Sign Code identifies various categories of signs based on the type of information they convey, then subjects each category to different restrictions. One of the categories is "Temporary Directional Signs Relating to a Qualifying Event," loosely defined as signs directing the public to a meeting of a nonprofit group. The Code imposes more stringent restrictions on these signs than it does on signs conveying other messages. We hold that these provisions are content-based regulations of speech that cannot survive strict scrutiny.

I

The Sign Code prohibits the display of outdoor signs anywhere within the Town without a permit, but it then exempts 23 categories of signs from that requirement. These exemptions include everything from bazaar signs to flying banners. Three categories of exempt signs are particularly relevant here.

The first is "Ideological Sign[s]." This category includes any "sign communicating a message or ideas for noncommercial purposes that is not a Construction Sign, Directional Sign, Temporary Directional Sign Relating to a Qualifying Event, Political Sign, Garage Sale Sign, or a sign owned or required by a governmental agency." Of the three categories discussed here, the Code treats ideological signs most favorably, allowing them to be up to 20 square feet in area and to be placed in all "zoning districts" without time limits.

The second category is "Political Sign[s]." This includes any "temporary sign designed to influence the outcome of an election called by a public body." The Code treats these signs less favorably than ideological signs. The Code allows the placement of political signs up to 16 square feet on residential property and up to 32 square feet on nonresidential property, undeveloped municipal property, and "rights-of-way." These signs may be displayed up to 60 days before a primary election and up to 15 days following a general election.

The third category is "Temporary Directional Signs Relating to a Qualifying Event." This includes any "Temporary Sign intended to direct pedestrians, motorists, and other passersby to a 'qualifying event.'" A "qualifying event" is defined as any "assembly, gathering, activity, or meeting sponsored, arranged, or promoted by a religious, charitable, community service, educational, or other similar non-profit organization." The Code treats temporary directional signs even less favorably than political signs. Temporary directional signs may be no larger than six square feet. They may be placed on private property or on a public right-of-way, but no more than four signs may be placed on a single property at any time. And, they may be displayed no more than 12 hours before the "qualifying event" and no more than 1 hour afterward.

Petitioners Good News Community Church (Church) and its pastor, Clyde Reed, wish to advertise the time and location of their Sunday church services. The Church is a small, cash-strapped entity that owns no building, so it holds its services at elementary schools or other locations in or near the Town. In order to inform the public about its services, which are held in a variety of different locations, the Church began placing 15 to 20 temporary signs around the Town, frequently in the public right-of-way abutting the street. The signs typically displayed the Church's name, along with the time and location of the upcoming service. Church members would post the signs early in the day on Saturday and then remove them around midday on Sunday. The display of these signs requires little money and manpower, and thus has proved to be an economical and effective way for the Church to let the community know where its services are being held each week.

This practice caught the attention of the Town's Sign Code compliance manager, who twice cited the Church for violating the Code. The first citation noted that the Church exceeded the time limits for displaying its temporary directional signs. The second citation referred to the same problem, along with the Church's failure to include the date of the event on the signs. Town officials even confiscated one of the Church's signs, which Reed had to retrieve from the municipal offices.

Reed contacted the Sign Code Compliance Department in an attempt to reach an accommodation. His efforts proved unsuccessful. The Town's Code compliance manager informed the Church that there would be "no leniency under the Code" and promised to punish any future violations. Shortly thereafter, petitioners filed a complaint in the United States District Court for the District of Arizona, arguing that the Sign Code abridged their freedom of speech in violation of the First and Fourteenth Amendments.

II

The First Amendment, applicable to the States through the Fourteenth Amendment, prohibits the enactment of laws "abridging the freedom of speech." Under that Clause, a government, including a municipal government vested with state authority, "has no power to restrict expression because of its message, its ideas, its subject matter, or its content." Content-based laws—those that target speech based on its communicative content—are presumptively unconstitutional and may be justified only if the government proves that they are narrowly tailored to serve compelling state interests.

Government regulation of speech is content based if a law applies to particular speech because of the topic discussed or the idea or message expressed. This commonsense meaning of the phrase "content based" requires a court to consider whether a regulation of speech "on its face" draws distinctions based on the message a speaker conveys. Some facial distinctions based on a message are obvious, defining regulated speech by particular subject matter, and others are more subtle, defining regulated speech by its function or purpose. Both are distinctions drawn based on the message a speaker conveys, and, therefore, are subject to strict scrutiny.

Our precedents have also recognized a separate and additional category of laws that, though facially content neutral, will be considered content-based regulations of speech: laws that cannot be " 'justified without reference to the content of the regulated speech,' " or that were adopted by the government "because of disagreement with the message [the speech] conveys." Those laws, like those that are content based on their face, must also satisfy strict scrutiny.

The Town's Sign Code is content based on its face. It defines "Temporary Directional Signs" on the basis of whether a sign conveys the message of directing the public to church or some other "qualifying event." It defines "Political Signs" on the basis of whether a sign's message is "designed to influence the outcome of an election." And it defines "Ideological Signs" on the basis of whether a sign "communicat[es] a message or ideas" that do not fit within the Code's other categories. It then subjects each of these categories to different restrictions.

The restrictions in the Sign Code that apply to any given sign thus depend entirely on the communicative content of the sign. If a sign informs its reader of the time and place a book club will discuss John Locke's Two Treatises of Government, that sign will be treated differently from a sign expressing the view that one should vote for one of Locke's followers in an upcoming election, and both signs will be treated differently from a sign expressing an ideological view rooted in Locke's theory of government. More to the point, the Church's signs inviting people to attend its worship services are treated differently from signs conveying other types of ideas. On its face, the Sign Code is a content-based regulation of speech. We thus have no need to consider the government's justifications or purposes for enacting the Code to determine whether it is subject to strict scrutiny.

The Court of Appeals first determined that the Sign Code was content neutral because the Town "did not adopt its regulation of speech [based on] disagree[ment] with the message conveyed," and its justifications for regulating temporary directional signs were "unrelated to the content of the sign."

But this analysis skips the crucial first step in the content-neutrality analysis: determining whether the law is content neutral on its face. A law that is content based on its face is subject to strict scrutiny regardless of the government's benign motive, content-neutral justification, or lack of "animus toward the ideas contained" in the regulated speech.

The First Amendment requires no less. Innocent motives do not eliminate the danger of censorship presented by a facially content-based statute, as future government officials may one day wield such statutes to suppress disfavored speech. That is why the First Amendment expressly targets the operation of the laws—*i.e.,* the "abridg[ment] of speech"—rather than merely the motives of those who enacted them. "'The vice of content-based legislation . . . is not that it is always used for invidious, thought-control purposes, but that it lends itself to use for those purposes.'"

III

Because the Town's Sign Code imposes content-based restrictions on speech, those provisions can stand only if they survive strict scrutiny, "'which requires the Government to prove that the restriction furthers a compelling interest and is narrowly tailored to achieve that interest.'" Thus, it is the Town's burden to demonstrate that the Code's differentiation between temporary directional signs and other types of signs, such as political signs and ideological signs, furthers a compelling governmental interest and is narrowly tailored to that end.

The Town cannot do so. It has offered only two governmental interests in support of the distinctions the Sign Code draws: preserving the Town's aesthetic appeal and traffic safety. Assuming for the sake of argument that those are compelling governmental interests, the Code's distinctions fail as hopelessly underinclusive.

Starting with the preservation of aesthetics, temporary directional signs are "no greater an eyesore," than ideological or political ones. Yet the Code allows unlimited proliferation of larger ideological signs while strictly limiting the number, size, and duration of smaller directional ones. The Town cannot claim that placing strict limits on temporary directional signs is necessary to beautify the Town while at the same time allowing unlimited numbers of other types of signs that create the same problem.

The Town similarly has not shown that limiting temporary directional signs is necessary to eliminate threats to traffic safety, but that limiting other types of signs is not. The Town has offered no reason to believe that directional signs pose a greater threat to safety than do ideological or political signs. If anything, a sharply worded ideological sign seems more likely to distract a driver than a sign directing the public to a nearby church meeting.

In light of this underinclusiveness, the Town has not met its burden to prove that its Sign Code is narrowly tailored to further a compelling government interest. Because a "'law cannot be regarded as protecting an interest of the highest order, and thus as justifying a restriction on truthful speech, when it leaves appreciable damage to that supposedly vital interest unprohibited,'" the Sign Code fails strict scrutiny.

IV

Our decision today will not prevent governments from enacting effective sign laws. The Town asserts that an " 'absolutist' " content-neutrality rule would render "virtually all distinctions in sign laws . . . subject to strict scrutiny," but that is not the case. Not "all distinctions" are subject to strict scrutiny, only *content-based* ones are. Laws that are *content neutral* are instead subject to lesser scrutiny.

The Town has ample content-neutral options available to resolve problems with safety and aesthetics. For example, its current Code regulates many aspects of signs that have nothing to do with a sign's message: size, building materials, lighting, moving parts, and portability. And on public property, the Town may go a long way toward entirely forbidding the posting of signs, so long as it does so in an evenhanded, content-neutral manner.

At the same time, the presence of certain signs may be essential, both for vehicles and pedestrians, to guide traffic or to identify hazards and ensure safety. A sign ordinance narrowly tailored to the challenges of protecting the safety of pedestrians, drivers, and passengers — such as warning signs marking hazards on private property, signs directing traffic, or street numbers associated with private houses — well might survive strict scrutiny. The signs at issue in this case, including political and ideological signs and signs for events, are far removed from those purposes. As discussed above, they are facially content based and are neither justified by traditional safety concerns nor narrowly tailored.

Justice ALITO, with whom Justice KENNEDY and Justice SOTOMAYOR join, concurring.

I join the opinion of the Court but add a few words of further explanation.

As the Court holds, what we have termed "content-based" laws must satisfy strict scrutiny. Content-based laws merit this protection because they present, albeit sometimes in a subtler form, the same dangers as laws that regulate speech based on viewpoint. Limiting speech based on its "topic" or "subject" favors those who do not want to disturb the status quo. Such regulations may interfere with democratic self-government and the search for truth.

As the Court shows, the regulations at issue in this case are replete with content-based distinctions, and as a result they must satisfy strict scrutiny. This does not mean, however, that municipalities are powerless to enact and enforce reasonable sign regulations. I will not attempt to provide anything like a comprehensive list, but here are some rules that would not be content based:

> Rules regulating the size of signs. These rules may distinguish among signs based on any content-neutral criteria, including any relevant criteria listed below.
>
> Rules regulating the locations in which signs may be placed. These rules may distinguish between free-standing signs and those attached to buildings.
>
> Rules distinguishing between lighted and unlighted signs.
>
> Rules distinguishing between signs with fixed messages and electronic signs with messages that change.
>
> Rules that distinguish between the placement of signs on private and public property.
>
> Rules distinguishing between the placement of signs on commercial and residential property.
>
> Rules distinguishing between on-premises and off-premises signs.
>
> Rules restricting the total number of signs allowed per mile of roadway.
>
> Rules imposing time restrictions on signs advertising a one-time event. Rules of this nature do not discriminate based on topic or subject and are akin to rules restricting the times within which oral speech or music is allowed.*

In addition to regulating signs put up by private actors, government entities may also erect their own signs consistent with the principles that allow governmental speech. They may put up all manner of signs to promote safety, as well as directional signs and signs pointing out historic sites and scenic spots.

Properly understood, today's decision will not prevent cities from regulating signs in a way that fully protects public safety and serves legitimate esthetic objectives.

Justice KAGAN, with whom Justice GINSBURG and Justice BREYER join, concurring in the judgment.

Countless cities and towns across America have adopted ordinances regulating the posting of signs, while exempting certain categories of signs based on their subject matter. For example, some municipalities generally prohibit illuminated signs in residential neighborhoods, but lift that ban for signs that identify the address of a home or the name of its owner or occupant. In other municipalities, safety signs such as "Blind Pedestrian Crossing" and "Hidden Driveway" can be posted without a permit, even as other permanent signs require one. Elsewhere, historic site markers—for example, "George Washington Slept Here"—are also exempt from general regulations. And similarly, the federal Highway Beautification Act limits signs along interstate highways unless, for instance, they direct travelers to "scenic and historical attractions" or advertise free coffee.

Given the Court's analysis, many sign ordinances of that kind are now in jeopardy. And although the majority holds out hope that some sign laws with subject-matter exemptions "might survive" that stringent review, the likelihood is that most will be struck down. After all, it is the "rare case[ ] in which a speech restriction withstands strict scrutiny." To clear that high bar, the government must show that a content-based distinction "is necessary to serve a compelling state interest and is narrowly drawn to achieve that end." So on the majority's view, courts would have to determine that a town has a compelling interest in informing passersby where George Washington slept. And likewise, courts would have to find that a town has no other way to prevent hidden-driveway mishaps than by specially treating hidden-driveway signs. (Well-placed speed bumps? Lower speed limits? Or how about just a ban on hidden driveways?) The consequence — unless courts water down strict scrutiny to something unrecognizable — is that our communities will find themselves in an unenviable bind: They will have to either repeal the exemptions that allow for helpful signs on streets and sidewalks, or else lift their sign restrictions altogether and resign themselves to the resulting clutter.*

Although the majority insists that applying strict scrutiny to all such ordinances is "essential" to protecting First Amendment freedoms, I find it challenging to understand why that is so. This Court's decisions articulate two important and related reasons for subjecting content-based speech regulations to the most exacting standard of review. The first is "to preserve an uninhibited marketplace of ideas in which truth will ultimately prevail." The second is to ensure that the government has not regulated speech "based on hostility — or favoritism — towards the underlying message expressed." Yet the subject-matter exemptions included in many sign ordinances do not implicate those concerns. Allowing residents, say, to install a light bulb over "name and address" signs but no others does not distort the marketplace of ideas. Nor does that different treatment give rise to an inference of impermissible government motive.

We apply strict scrutiny to facially content-based regulations of speech, in keeping with the rationales just described, when there is any "realistic possibility that official suppression of ideas is afoot." That is always the case when the regulation facially differentiates on the basis of viewpoint. It is also the case (except in non-public or limited public forums) when a law restricts "discussion of an entire topic" in public debate.)

But when that is not realistically possible, we may do well to relax our guard so that "entirely reasonable" laws imperiled by strict scrutiny can survive. This point is by no means new. Our concern with content-based regulation arises from the fear that the government will skew the public's debate of ideas—so when "that risk is inconsequential, . . . strict scrutiny is unwarranted." To do its intended work, of course, the category of content-based regulation triggering strict scrutiny must sweep more broadly than the actual harm; that category exists to create a buffer zone guaranteeing that the government cannot favor or disfavor certain viewpoints. But that buffer zone need not extend forever. We can administer our content-regulation doctrine with a dose of common sense, so as to leave standing laws that in no way implicate its intended function.

The absence of any sensible basis for these and other distinctions dooms the Town's ordinance under even the intermediate scrutiny that the Court typically applies to "time, place, or manner" speech regulations. The Town of Gilbert's defense of its sign ordinance—most notably, the law's distinctions between directional signs and others—does not pass strict scrutiny, or intermediate scrutiny, or even the laugh test. Accordingly, there is no need to decide in this case whether strict scrutiny applies to every sign ordinance in every town across this country containing a subject-matter exemption.

I suspect this Court and others will regret the majority's insistence today on answering that question in the affirmative. As the years go by, courts will discover that thousands of towns have such ordinances, many of them "entirely reasonable." And as the challenges to them mount, courts will have to invalidate one after the other. (This Court may soon find itself a veritable Supreme Board of Sign Review.) And courts will strike down those democratically enacted local laws even though no one—certainly not the majority—has ever explained why the vindication of First Amendment values requires that result. Because I see no reason why such an easy case calls for us to cast a constitutional pall on reasonable regulations quite unlike the law before us, I concur only in the judgment.

b. How Is It Determined Whether a Law Is Content-based? (casebook, p. 1222)

In *Republican Party of Minnesota v. White* (casebook, p. 1213), the Court declared unconstitutional state laws restricting speech of candidates running for elected judicial office. But in *Williams-Yulee v. Florida State Bar* (2015), the Court upheld a state law prohibiting candidates for elected judicial office from personally soliciting funds. In reading these decisions, it is important to consider whether these cases can be reconciled and if not, which is the better view.

WILLIAMS-YULEE v. FLORIDA BAR
135 S. Ct. 1656 (2015)

Chief JUSTICE ROBERTS delivered the opinion of the Court, except as to Part II.

Our Founders vested authority to appoint federal judges in the President, with the advice and consent of the Senate, and entrusted those judges to hold their offices during good behavior. The Constitution permits States to make a different choice, and most of them have done so. In 39 States, voters elect trial or appellate judges at the polls. In an effort to preserve public confidence in the integrity of their judiciaries, many of those States prohibit judges and judicial candidates from personally soliciting funds for their campaigns. We must decide whether the First Amendment permits such restrictions on speech.

We hold that it does. Judges are not politicians, even when they come to the bench by way of the ballot. And a State's decision to elect its judiciary does not compel it to treat judicial candidates like campaigners for political office. A State may assure its people that judges will apply the law without fear or favor — and without having personally asked anyone for money. We affirm the judgment of the Florida Supreme Court.

I

In the early 1970s, four Florida Supreme Court justices resigned from office following corruption scandals. Florida voters responded by amending their Constitution again. Under the system now in place, appellate judges are appointed by the Governor from a list of candidates proposed by a nominating committee — a process known as "merit selection." Then, every six years, voters decide whether to retain incumbent appellate judges for another term. Trial judges are still elected by popular vote, unless the local jurisdiction opts instead for merit selection.

Amid the corruption scandals of the 1970s, the first sentence of Canon 1 reads, "An independent and honorable judiciary is indispensable to justice in our society." Canon 1 instructs judges to observe "high standards of conduct" so that "the integrity and independence of the judiciary may be preserved." Canon 2 directs that a judge "shall act at all times in a manner that promotes public confidence in the integrity and impartiality of the judiciary." Other provisions prohibit judges from lending the prestige of their offices to private interests, engaging in certain business transactions, and personally participating in soliciting funds for nonprofit organizations.

Canon 7C(1) governs fundraising in judicial elections. The Canon, which is based on a provision in the American Bar Association's Model Code of Judicial Conduct, provides: "A candidate, including an incumbent judge, for a judicial office that is filled by public election between competing candidates shall not personally solicit campaign funds, or solicit attorneys for publicly stated support, but may establish committees of responsible persons to secure and manage the expenditure of funds for the candidate's campaign and to obtain public statements of support for his or her candidacy. Such committees are not prohibited from soliciting campaign contributions and public support from any person or corporation authorized by law."

Like Florida, most other States prohibit judicial candidates from soliciting campaign funds personally, but allow them to raise money through committees. According to the American Bar Association, 30 of the 39 States that elect trial or appellate judges have adopted restrictions similar to Canon 7C(1).

Lanell Williams–Yulee, who refers to herself as Yulee, has practiced law in Florida since 1991. In September 2009, she decided to run for a seat on the county court for Hillsborough County, a jurisdiction of about 1.3 million people that includes the city of Tampa. Shortly after filing paperwork to enter the race, Yulee drafted a letter announcing her candidacy. The letter described her experience and desire to "bring fresh ideas and positive solutions to the Judicial bench." The letter then stated: "An early contribution of $25, $50, $100, $250, or $500, made payable to 'Lanell Williams–Yulee Campaign for County Judge,' will help raise the initial funds needed to launch the campaign and get our message out to the public. I ask for your support [i]n meeting the primary election fund raiser goals. Thank you in advance for your support."

Yulee signed the letter and mailed it to local voters. She also posted the letter on her campaign Web site.

Yulee's bid for the bench did not unfold as she had hoped. She lost the primary to the incumbent judge. Then the Florida Bar filed a complaint against her. That Rule requires judicial candidates to comply with applicable provisions of Florida's Code of Judicial Conduct, including the ban on personal solicitation of campaign funds in Canon 7C(1).

Yulee admitted that she had signed and sent the fundraising letter. But she argued that the Bar could not discipline her for that conduct because the First Amendment protects a judicial candidate's right to solicit campaign funds in an election.[*]

II

The parties agree that Canon 7C(1) restricts Yulee's speech on the basis of its content by prohibiting her from soliciting contributions to her election campaign. The parties disagree, however, about the level of scrutiny that should govern our review.

We have applied exacting scrutiny to laws restricting the solicitation of contributions to charity, upholding the speech limitations only if they are narrowly tailored to serve a compelling interest. As we have explained, noncommercial solicitation "is characteristically intertwined with informative and perhaps persuasive speech." Applying a lesser standard of scrutiny to such speech would threaten "the exercise of rights so vital to the maintenance of democratic institutions."

The principles underlying these charitable solicitation cases apply with even greater force here. Before asking for money in her fundraising letter, Yulee explained her fitness for the bench and expressed her vision for the judiciary. Her stated purpose for the solicitation was to get her "message out to the public." As we have long recognized, speech about public issues and the qualifications of candidates for elected office commands the highest level of First Amendment protection. Indeed, in our only prior case concerning speech restrictions on a candidate for judicial office, this Court and both parties assumed that strict scrutiny applied. *Republican Party of Minn. v. White* (2002).

In sum, we hold today what we assumed in *White*: A State may restrict the speech of a judicial candidate only if the restriction is narrowly tailored to serve a compelling interest.

III

The Florida Bar faces a demanding task in defending Canon 7C(1) against Yulee's First Amendment challenge. We have emphasized that "it is the rare case" in which a State demonstrates that a speech restriction is narrowly tailored to serve a compelling interest. But those cases do arise. Here, Canon 7C(1) advances the State's compelling interest in preserving public confidence in the integrity of the judiciary, and it does so through means narrowly tailored to avoid unnecessarily abridging speech. This is therefore one of the rare cases in which a speech restriction withstands strict scrutiny.

The Florida Supreme Court adopted Canon 7C(1) to promote the State's interests in "protecting the integrity of the judiciary" and "maintaining the public's confidence in an impartial judiciary." The way the Canon advances those interests is intuitive: Judges, charged with exercising strict neutrality and independence, cannot supplicate campaign donors without diminishing public confidence in judicial integrity. This principle dates back at least eight centuries to Magna Carta, which proclaimed, "To no one will we sell, to no one will we refuse or delay, right or justice." Simply put, Florida and most other States have concluded that the public may lack confidence in a judge's ability to administer justice without fear or favor if he comes to office by asking for favors.

The principal dissent observes that bans on judicial candidate solicitation lack a lengthy historical pedigree. We do not dispute that fact, but it has no relevance here. As the precedent cited by the principal dissent demonstrates, a history and tradition of regulation are important factors in determining whether to recognize "new categories of unprotected speech." But nobody argues that solicitation of campaign funds by judicial candidates is a category of unprotected speech. As explained above, the First Amendment fully applies to Yulee's speech. The question is instead whether that Amendment permits the particular regulation of speech at issue here.

The parties devote considerable attention to our cases analyzing campaign finance restrictions in political elections. But a State's interest in preserving public confidence in the integrity of its judiciary extends beyond its interest in preventing the appearance of corruption in legislative and executive elections. As we explained in *White*, States may regulate judicial elections differently than they regulate political elections, because the role of judges differs from the role of politicians. Politicians are expected to be appropriately responsive to the preferences of their supporters. Indeed, such "responsiveness is key to the very concept of self-governance through elected officials." The same is not true of judges. In deciding cases, a judge is not to follow the preferences of his supporters, or provide any special consideration to his campaign donors. A judge instead must "observe the utmost fairness," striving to be "perfectly and completely independent, with nothing to influence or controul him but God and his conscience." Address of John Marshall, in Proceedings and Debates of the Virginia State Convention of 1829–1830.

The concept of public confidence in judicial integrity does not easily reduce to precise definition, nor does it lend itself to proof by documentary record. But no one denies that it is genuine and compelling. In short, it is the regrettable but unavoidable appearance that judges who personally ask for money may diminish their integrity that prompted the Supreme Court of Florida and most other States to sever the direct link between judicial candidates and campaign contributors. Moreover, personal solicitation by a judicial candidate "inevitably places the solicited individuals in a position to fear retaliation if they fail to financially support that candidate." Potential litigants then fear that "the integrity of the judicial system has been compromised, forcing them to search for an attorney in part based upon the criteria of which attorneys have made the obligatory contributions." A State's decision to elect its judges does not require it to tolerate these risks. The Florida Bar's interest is compelling.

Yulee acknowledges the State's compelling interest in judicial integrity. She argues, however, that the Canon's failure to restrict other speech equally damaging to judicial integrity and its appearance undercuts the Bar's position. In particular, she notes that Canon 7C(1) allows a judge's campaign committee to solicit money, which arguably reduces public confidence in the integrity of the judiciary just as much as a judge's personal solicitation. Yulee also points out that Florida permits judicial candidates to write thank you notes to campaign donors, which ensures that candidates know who contributes and who does not.

It is always somewhat counterintuitive to argue that a law violates the First Amendment by abridging *too little* speech. We have recognized, however, that underinclusiveness can raise "doubts about whether the government is in fact pursuing the interest it invokes, rather than disfavoring a particular speaker or viewpoint."

Although a law's underinclusivity raises a red flag, the First Amendment imposes no freestanding "underinclusiveness limitation." A State need not address all aspects of a problem in one fell swoop; policymakers may focus on their most pressing concerns. We have accordingly upheld laws — even under strict scrutiny — that conceivably could have restricted even greater amounts of speech in service of their stated interests.

Viewed in light of these principles, Canon 7C(1) raises no fatal underinclusivity concerns. The solicitation ban aims squarely at the conduct most likely to undermine public confidence in the integrity of the judiciary: personal requests for money by judges and judicial candidates. The Canon applies evenhandedly to all judges and judicial candidates, regardless of their viewpoint or chosen means of solicitation. And unlike some laws that we have found impermissibly underinclusive, Canon 7C(1) is not riddled with exceptions. Indeed, the Canon contains zero exceptions to its ban on personal solicitation.

Yulee relies heavily on the provision of Canon 7C(1) that allows solicitation by a candidate's campaign committee. But Florida, along with most other States, has reasonably concluded that solicitation by the candidate personally creates a categorically different and more severe risk of undermining public confidence than does solicitation by a campaign committee. The identity of the solicitor matters, as anyone who has encountered a Girl Scout selling cookies outside a grocery store can attest. When the judicial candidate himself asks for money, the stakes are higher for all involved. The candidate has personally invested his time and effort in the fundraising appeal; he has placed his name and reputation behind the request. The solicited individual knows that, and also knows that the solicitor might be in a position to singlehandedly make decisions of great weight: The same person who signed the fundraising letter might one day sign the judgment. This dynamic inevitably creates pressure for the recipient to comply, and it does so in a way that solicitation by a third party does not. Just as inevitably, the personal involvement of the candidate in the solicitation creates the public appearance that the candidate will remember who says yes, and who says no.

In short, personal solicitation by judicial candidates implicates a different problem than solicitation by campaign committees. However similar the two solicitations may be in substance, a State may conclude that they present markedly different appearances to the public. Florida's choice to allow solicitation by campaign committees does not undermine its decision to ban solicitation by judges.

Likewise, allowing judicial candidates to write thank you notes to campaign donors does not detract from the State's interest in preserving public confidence in the integrity of the judiciary. Yulee argues that permitting thank you notes heightens the likelihood of actual bias by ensuring that judicial candidates know who supported their campaigns, and ensuring that the supporter knows that the candidate knows. Maybe so. But the State's compelling interest is implicated most directly by the candidate's personal solicitation itself. A failure to ban thank you notes for contributions not solicited by the candidate does not undercut the Bar's rationale.

Taken to its logical conclusion, the position advanced by Yulee and the principal dissent is that Florida may ban the solicitation of funds by judicial candidates only if the State bans *all* solicitation of funds in judicial elections. The First Amendment does not put a State to that all-or-nothing choice. We will not punish Florida for leaving open more, rather than fewer, avenues of expression, especially when there is no indication that the selective restriction of speech reflects a pretextual motive.

After arguing that Canon 7C(1) violates the First Amendment because it restricts too little speech, Yulee argues that the Canon violates the First Amendment because it restricts too much. In her view, the Canon is not narrowly tailored to advance the State's compelling interest through the least restrictive means.

But in reality, Canon 7C(1) leaves judicial candidates free to discuss any issue with any person at any time. Candidates can write letters, give speeches, and put up billboards. They can contact potential supporters in person, on the phone, or online. They can promote their campaigns on radio, television, or other media. They cannot say, "Please give me money." They can, however, direct their campaign committees to do so. Whatever else may be said of the Canon, it is surely not a "wildly disproportionate restriction upon speech."

Finally, Yulee contends that Florida can accomplish its compelling interest through the less restrictive means of recusal rules and campaign contribution limits. We disagree. A rule requiring judges to recuse themselves from every case in which a lawyer or litigant made a campaign contribution would disable many jurisdictions. And a flood of postelection recusal motions could "erode public confidence in judicial impartiality" and thereby exacerbate the very appearance problem the State is trying to solve. Moreover, the rule that Yulee envisions could create a perverse incentive for litigants to make campaign contributions to judges solely as a means to trigger their later recusal—a form of peremptory strike against a judge that would enable transparent forum shopping.

In sum, because Canon 7C(1) is narrowly tailored to serve a compelling government interest, the First Amendment poses no obstacle to its enforcement in this case. As a result of our decision, Florida may continue to prohibit judicial candidates from personally soliciting campaign funds, while allowing them to raise money through committees and to otherwise communicate their electoral messages in practically any way.

* * *

The desirability of judicial elections is a question that has sparked disagreement for more than 200 years. Hamilton believed that appointing judges to positions with life tenure constituted "the best expedient which can be devised in any government to secure a steady, upright, and impartial administration of the laws." Jefferson thought that making judges "dependent on none but themselves" ran counter to the principle of "a government founded on the public will." The federal courts reflect the view of Hamilton; most States have sided with Jefferson. Both methods have given our Nation jurists of wisdom and rectitude who have devoted themselves to maintaining "the public's respect . . . and a reserve of public goodwill, without becoming subservient to public opinion."

It is not our place to resolve this enduring debate. Our limited task is to apply the Constitution to the question presented in this case. Judicial candidates have a First Amendment right to speak in support of their campaigns. States have a compelling interest in preserving public confidence in their judiciaries. When the State adopts a narrowly tailored restriction like the one at issue here, those principles do not conflict. A State's decision to elect judges does not compel it to compromise public confidence in their integrity.

Justice GINSBURG with whom Justice BREYER joins as to Part II, concurring in part and concurring in the judgment.

I

I join the Court's opinion save for Part II. As explained in my dissenting opinion in *Republican Party of Minnesota v. White* (2002), I would not apply exacting scrutiny to a State's endeavor sensibly to "differentiate elections for political offices . . . , from elections designed to select those whose office it is to administer justice without respect to persons."

II

I write separately to reiterate the substantial latitude, in my view, States should possess to enact campaign-finance rules geared to judicial elections. "Judges," the Court rightly recognizes, "are not politicians," so "States may regulate judicial elections differently than they regulate political elections." And because "the role of judges differs from the role of politicians," *ibid.*, this Court's "precedents applying the First Amendment to political elections [should] have little bearing" on elections to judicial office.

The Court's recent campaign-finance decisions, trained on political actors, should not hold sway for judicial elections. States may therefore impose different campaign-finance rules for judicial elections than for political elections. Experience illustrates why States may wish to do so. When the political campaign-finance apparatus is applied to judicial elections, the distinction of judges from politicians dims. Donors, who gain audience and influence through contributions to political campaigns, anticipate that investment in campaigns for judicial office will yield similar returns. Elected judges understand this dynamic.

In recent years, moreover, issue-oriented organizations and political action committees have spent millions of dollars opposing the reelection of judges whose decisions do not tow a party line or are alleged to be out of step with public opinion. Following the Iowa Supreme Court's 2009 invalidation of the State's same-sex marriage ban, for example, national organizations poured money into a successful campaign to remove three justices from that Court. Attack advertisements funded by issue or politically driven organizations portrayed the justices as political actors; they lambasted the Iowa Supreme Court for "usurp[ing] the will of voters."

Similarly portraying judges as belonging to another political branch, huge amounts have been spent on advertisements opposing retention of judges because they rendered unpopular decisions in favor of criminal defendants.

Disproportionate spending to influence court judgments threatens both the appearance and actuality of judicial independence. Numerous studies report that the money pressure groups spend on judicial elections "can affect judicial decision-making across a broad range of cases."

How does the electorate perceive outsized spending on judicial elections? Multiple surveys over the past 13 years indicate that voters overwhelmingly believe direct contributions to judges' campaigns have at least "some influence" on judicial decisionmaking. Disquieting as well, in response to a recent poll, 87% of voters stated that advertisements purchased by interest groups during judicial elections can have either "some" or "a great deal of influence" on an elected "judge's later decisions."

"A State's decision to elect its judges does not require it to tolerate these risks." States should not be put to the polar choices of either equating judicial elections to political elections, or else abandoning public participation in the selection of judges altogether. Instead, States should have leeway to "balance the constitutional interests in judicial integrity and free expression within the unique setting of an elected judiciary."

Justice SCALIA, with whom Justice THOMAS joins, dissenting.

An ethics canon adopted by the Florida Supreme Court bans a candidate in a judicial election from asking anyone, under any circumstances, for a contribution to his campaign. Faithful application of our precedents would have made short work of this wildly disproportionate restriction upon speech. Intent upon upholding the Canon, however, the Court flattens one settled First Amendment principle after another.

I

The first axiom of the First Amendment is this: As a general rule, the state has no power to ban speech on the basis of its content. One need not equate judges with politicians to see that this principle does not grow weaker merely because the censored speech is a judicial candidate's request for a campaign contribution. Our cases hold that speech enjoys the full protection of the First Amendment unless a widespread and longstanding tradition ratifies its regulation. No such tradition looms here.

One likewise need not equate judges with politicians to see that the electoral setting calls for all the more vigilance in ensuring observance of the First Amendment. When a candidate asks someone for a campaign contribution, he tends (as the principal opinion acknowledges) also to talk about his qualifications for office and his views on public issues. This expression lies at the heart of what the First Amendment is meant to protect. In addition, banning candidates from asking for money personally "favors some candidates over others — incumbent judges (who benefit from their current status) over non-judicial candidates, the well-to-do (who may not need to raise any money at all) over lower-income candidates, and the well-connected (who have an army of potential fundraisers) over outsiders." This danger of legislated (or judicially imposed) favoritism is the very reason the First Amendment exists.

Because Canon 7C(1) restricts fully protected speech on the basis of content, it presumptively violates the First Amendment. We may uphold it only if the State meets its burden of showing that the Canon survives strict scrutiny — that is to say, only if it shows that the Canon is narrowly tailored to serve a compelling interest. I do not for a moment question the Court's conclusion that States have different compelling interests when regulating judicial elections than when regulating political ones. Unlike a legislator, a judge must be impartial — without bias for or against any party or attorney who comes before him. I accept for the sake of argument that States have a compelling interest in ensuring that its judges are *seen* to be impartial. I will likewise assume that a judicial candidate's request to a litigant or attorney presents a danger of coercion that a political candidate's request to a constituent does not.

But Canon 7C(1) does not narrowly target concerns about impartiality or its appearance; it applies even when the person asked for a financial contribution has no chance of ever appearing in the candidate's court. And Florida does not invoke concerns about coercion, presumably because the Canon bans solicitations regardless of whether their object is a lawyer, litigant, or other person vulnerable to judicial pressure. So Canon 7C(1) fails exacting scrutiny and infringes the First Amendment. This case should have been just that straightforward.

II

The Court concludes that Florida may prohibit personal solicitations by judicial candidates as a means of preserving "public confidence in the integrity of the judiciary." It purports to reach this destination by applying strict scrutiny, but it would be more accurate to say that it does so by applying the appearance of strict scrutiny.

In stark contrast to *White,* the Court today relies on Florida's invocation of an ill-defined interest in "public confidence in judicial integrity." The Court at first suggests that "judicial integrity" involves the "ability to administer justice without fear or favor." As its opinion unfolds, however, today's concept of judicial integrity turns out to be "a mere thing of wax in the hands of the judiciary, which they may twist, and shape into any form they please." 12 The Works of Thomas Jefferson 137 (P. Ford ed. 1905). When the Court explains how solicitation undermines confidence in judicial integrity, integrity starts to sound like saintliness. It involves independence from any " '*possible* temptation' " that " '*might* lead' " the judge, "even unknowingly," to favor one party. *Ante,* at 1667 (emphasis added). When the Court turns to distinguishing in-person solicitation from solicitation by proxy, the any-possible-temptation standard no longer helps and thus drops out. The critical factors instead become the "pressure" a listener feels during a solicitation and the "appearance that the candidate will remember who says yes, and who says no." But when it comes time to explain Florida's decision to allow candidates to write thank-you notes, the "appearance that the candidate . . . remember[s] who says yes" gets nary a mention. And when the Court confronts Florida's decision to prohibit mass-mailed solicitations, concern about pressure fades away. More outrageous still, the Court at times molds the interest in the perception that judges have integrity into an interest in the perception that judges do not solicit — for example when it says, "all personal solicitations by judicial candidates create a public appearance that undermines confidence in the integrity of the judiciary; banning all personal solicitations by judicial candidates is narrowly tailored to address that concern." This is not strict scrutiny; it is sleight of hand.

Neither the Court nor the State identifies the slightest evidence that banning requests for contributions will substantially improve public trust in judges. Nor does common sense make this happy forecast obvious. The concept of judicial integrity "dates back at least eight centuries," and judicial elections in America date back more than two centuries — but rules against personal solicitations date back only to 1972. The peaceful coexistence of judicial elections and personal solicitations for most of our history calls into doubt any claim that allowing personal solicitations would imperil public faith in judges. Many States allow judicial candidates to ask for contributions even today, but nobody suggests that public confidence in judges fares worse in these jurisdictions than elsewhere. And in any event, if candidates' appeals for money are " 'characteristically intertwined' " with discussion of qualifications and views on public issues, how can the Court be so sure that the public will regard them as improprieties rather than as legitimate instances of campaigning? In the final analysis, Florida comes nowhere near making the convincing demonstration required by our cases that the speech restriction in this case substantially advances its objective.

This Court has not been shy to enforce the First Amendment in recent Terms — even in cases that do not involve election speech. It has accorded robust protection to depictions of animal torture, sale of violent video games to children, and lies about having won military medals. Who would have thought that the same Court would today exert such heroic efforts to save so plain an abridgement of the freedom of speech? It is no great mystery what is going on here. The judges of this Court, like the judges of the Supreme Court of Florida who promulgated Canon 7C(1), evidently consider the preservation of public respect for the courts a policy objective of the highest order. So it is — but so too are preventing animal torture, protecting the innocence of children, and honoring valiant soldiers. The Court did not relax the Constitution's guarantee of freedom of speech when legislatures pursued those goals; it should not relax the guarantee when the Supreme Court of Florida pursues this one. The First Amendment is not abridged for the benefit of the Brotherhood of the Robe.

Justice KENNEDY, dissenting.

This separate dissent is written to underscore the irony in the Court's having concluded that the very First Amendment protections judges must enforce should be lessened when a judicial candidate's own speech is at issue. It is written to underscore, too, the irony in the Court's having weakened the rigors of the First Amendment in a case concerning elections, a paradigmatic forum for speech and a process intended to protect freedom in so many other manifestations.

First Amendment protections are both personal and structural. Free speech begins with the right of each person to think and then to express his or her own ideas. Protecting this personal sphere of intellect and conscience, in turn, creates structural safeguards for many of the processes that define a free society. The individual speech here is political speech.

The process is a fair election. These realms ought to be the last place, not the first, for the Court to allow unprecedented content-based restrictions on speech. The Court's decision in this case imperils the content neutrality essential both for individual speech and the election process.

With all due respect for the Court, it seems fair and necessary to say its decision rests on two premises, neither one correct. One premise is that in certain elections — here an election to choose the best qualified judge — the public lacks the necessary judgment to make an informed choice. Instead, the State must protect voters by altering the usual dynamics of free speech. The other premise is that since judges should be accorded special respect and dignity, their election can be subject to certain content-based rules that would be unacceptable in other elections. In my respectful view neither premise can justify the speech restriction at issue here. Although States have a compelling interest in seeking to ensure the appearance and the reality of an impartial judiciary, it does not follow that the State may alter basic First Amendment principles in pursuing that goal.

Whether an election is the best way to choose a judge is itself the subject of fair debate. But once the people of a State choose to have elections, the First Amendment protects the candidate's right to speak and the public's ensuing right to open and robust debate. One advantage of judicial elections is the opportunity offered for the public to become more knowledgeable about their courts and their law. This might stimulate discourse over the requisite and highest ethical standards for the judiciary, including whether the people should elect a judge who personally solicits campaign funds. Yet now that teaching process is hindered by state censorship. By allowing the State's speech restriction, the Court undermines the educational process that free speech in elections should facilitate.

This law comes nowhere close to being narrowly tailored. And by saying that it survives that vital First Amendment requirement, the Court now writes what is literally a casebook guide to eviscerating strict scrutiny any time the Court encounters speech it dislikes.

Justice ALITO, dissenting.

The Florida rule before us regulates speech that is part of the process of selecting those who wield the power of the State. Such speech lies at the heart of the protection provided by the First Amendment. The Florida rule regulates that speech based on content and must therefore satisfy strict scrutiny. This means that it must be narrowly tailored to further a compelling state interest. Florida has a compelling interest in making sure that its courts decide cases impartially and in accordance with the law and that its citizens have no good reason to lack confidence that its courts are performing their proper role. But the Florida rule is not narrowly tailored to serve that interest.

Indeed, this rule is about as narrowly tailored as a burlap bag. It applies to all solicitations made in the name of a candidate for judicial office—including, as was the case here, a mass mailing. It even applies to an ad in a newspaper. It applies to requests for contributions in any amount, and it applies even if the person solicited is not a lawyer, has never had any interest at stake in any case in the court in question, and has no prospect of ever having any interest at stake in any litigation in that court. If this rule can be characterized as narrowly tailored, then narrow tailoring has no meaning, and strict scrutiny, which is essential to the protection of free speech, is seriously impaired.

When petitioner sent out a form letter requesting campaign contributions, she was well within her First Amendment rights. The Florida Supreme Court violated the Constitution when it imposed a financial penalty and stained her record with a finding that she had engaged in unethical conduct.

c. Problems in Applying the Distinction Between Content-Based and Content-Neutral Laws (casebook, p. 1222)

In *Pleasant Grove v. Summum* (casebook, p. 1230), the Court held that the First Amendment's limits on government regulation of speech do not apply when the government itself is the speaker. The Court followed this in *Walker v. Texas Division, Sons of Confederate Veterans.*

WALKER v. THOMPSON
135 S. Ct. 2239 (2015)

Justice BREYER delivered the opinion of the Court.

Texas offers automobile owners a choice between ordinary and specialty license plates. Those who want the State to issue a particular specialty plate may propose a plate design, comprising a slogan, a graphic, or (most commonly) both. If the Texas Department of Motor Vehicles Board approves the design, the State will make it available for display on vehicles registered in Texas.

In this case, the Texas Division of the Sons of Confederate Veterans proposed a specialty license plate design featuring a Confederate battle flag. The Board rejected the proposal. We must decide whether that rejection violated the Constitution's free speech guarantees. We conclude that it did not.

I

Texas law requires all motor vehicles operating on the State's roads to display valid license plates. And Texas makes available several kinds of plates. Drivers may choose to display the State's general-issue license plates. In the alternative, drivers may choose from an assortment of specialty license plates. § 504.008(b) (West 2013). Each of these plates contains the word "Texas," a license plate number, and one of a selection of designs prepared by the State. Finally, Texas law provides for personalized plates (also known as vanity plates). Pursuant to the personalization program, a vehicle owner may request a particular alphanumeric pattern for use as a plate number, such as "BOB" or "TEXPL8."

Here we are concerned only with the second category of plates, namely specialty license plates, not with the personalization program. Texas offers vehicle owners a variety of specialty plates, generally for an annual fee. [T]he Board "may create new specialty license plates on its own initiative or on receipt of an application from a" nonprofit entity seeking to sponsor a specialty plate. A nonprofit must include in its application "a draft design of the specialty license plate." And Texas law vests in the Board authority to approve or to disapprove an application. The relevant statute says that the Board "may refuse to create a new specialty license plate" for a number of reasons, for example "if the design might be offensive to any member of the public . . . or for any other reason established by rule." Specialty plates that the Board has sanctioned through this process include plates featuring the words "The Gator Nation," together with the Florida Gators logo, and plates featuring the logo of Rotary International and the words "SERVICE ABOVE SELF."

In 2009, the Sons of Confederate Veterans, Texas Division (a nonprofit entity), applied to sponsor a specialty license plate through this last-mentioned process. SCV's application included a draft plate design. At the bottom of the proposed plate were the words "SONS OF CONFEDERATE VETERANS." At the side was the organization's logo, a square Confederate battle flag framed by the words "Sons of Confederate Veterans 1896." A faint Confederate battle flag appeared in the background on the lower portion of the plate. Additionally, in the middle of the plate was the license plate number, and at the top was the State's name and silhouette. The Board's predecessor denied this application.

In 2010, SCV renewed its application before the Board. The Board invited public comment on its website and at an open meeting. After considering the responses, including a number of letters sent by elected officials who opposed the proposal, the Board voted unanimously against issuing the plate. The Board explained that it had found "it necessary to deny th[e] plate design application, specifically the confederate flag portion of the design, because public comments ha[d] shown that many members of the general public find the design offensive, and because such comments are reasonable." The Board added "that a significant portion of the public associate the confederate flag with organizations advocating expressions of hate directed toward people or groups that is demeaning to those people or groups."

In 2012, SCV and two of its officers (collectively SCV) brought this lawsuit against the chairman and members of the Board (collectively Board). SCV argued that the Board's decision violated the Free Speech Clause of the First Amendment, and it sought an injunction requiring the Board to approve the proposed plate design.

II

When government speaks, it is not barred by the Free Speech Clause from determining the content of what it says. *Pleasant Grove City v. Summum* (2009). That freedom in part reflects the fact that it is the democratic electoral process that first and foremost provides a check on government speech. Thus, government statements (and government actions and programs that take the form of speech) do not normally trigger the First Amendment rules designed to protect the marketplace of ideas. Instead, the Free Speech Clause helps produce informed opinions among members of the public, who are then able to influence the choices of a government that, through words and deeds, will reflect its electoral mandate.

Were the Free Speech Clause interpreted otherwise, government would not work. How could a city government create a successful recycling program if officials, when writing householders asking them to recycle cans and bottles, had to include in the letter a long plea from the local trash disposal enterprise demanding the contrary? How could a state government effectively develop programs designed to encourage and provide vaccinations, if officials also had to voice the perspective of those who oppose this type of immunization? "[I]t is not easy to imagine how government could function if it lacked th[e] freedom" to select the messages it wishes to convey.

We have therefore refused "[t]o hold that the Government unconstitutionally discriminates on the basis of viewpoint when it chooses to fund a program dedicated to advance certain permissible goals, because the program in advancing those goals necessarily discourages alternative goals." We have pointed out that a contrary holding "would render numerous Government programs constitutionally suspect." And we have made clear that "the government can speak for itself."

That is not to say that a government's ability to express itself is without restriction. Constitutional and statutory provisions outside of the Free Speech Clause may limit government speech. And the Free Speech Clause itself may constrain the government's speech if, for example, the government seeks to compel private persons to convey the government's speech. But, as a general matter, when the government speaks it is entitled to promote a program, to espouse a policy, or to take a position. In doing so, it represents its citizens and it carries out its duties on their behalf.

III

In our view, specialty license plates issued pursuant to Texas's statutory scheme convey government speech. Our reasoning rests primarily on our analysis in *Summum,* a recent case that presented a similar problem. We conclude here, as we did there, that our precedents regarding government speech (and not our precedents regarding forums for private speech) provide the appropriate framework through which to approach the case.

In *Summum,* we considered a religious organization's request to erect in a 2.5–acre city park a monument setting forth the organization's religious tenets. In the park were 15 other permanent displays. At least 11 of these — including a wishing well, a September 11 monument, a historic granary, the city's first fire station, and a Ten Commandments monument — had been donated to the city by private entities. The religious organization argued that the Free Speech Clause required the city to display the organization's proposed monument because, by accepting a broad range of permanent exhibitions at the park, the city had created a forum for private speech in the form of monuments.

This Court rejected the organization's argument. We held that the city had not "provid[ed] a forum for private speech" with respect to monuments. Rather, the city, even when "accepting a privately donated monument and placing it on city property," had "engage[d] in expressive conduct." The speech at issue, this Court decided, was "best viewed as a form of government speech" and "therefore [was] not subject to scrutiny under the Free Speech Clause."

Our analysis in *Summum* leads us to the conclusion that here, too, government speech is at issue. First, the history of license plates shows that, insofar as license plates have conveyed more than state names and vehicle identification numbers, they long have communicated messages from the Second, Texas license plate designs "are often closely identified in the public mind with the [State]." Each Texas license plate is a government article serving the governmental purposes of vehicle registration and identification. The governmental nature of the plates is clear from their faces: The State places the name "TEXAS" in large letters at the top of every plate. Moreover, the State requires Texas vehicle owners to display license plates, and every Texas license plate is issued by the State. Texas also owns the designs on its license plates, including the designs that Texas adopts on the basis of proposals made by private individuals and organizations.

Texas license plates are, essentially, government IDs. And issuers of ID "typically do not permit" the placement on their IDs of "message[s] with which they do not wish to be associated." Consequently, "persons who observe" designs on IDs "routinely — and reasonably — interpret them as conveying some message on the [issuer's] behalf."

Third, Texas maintains direct control over the messages conveyed on its specialty plates. Texas law provides that the State "has sole control over the design, typeface, color, and alphanumeric pattern for all license plates." The Board must approve every specialty plate design proposal before the design can appear on a Texas plate. This final approval authority allows Texas to choose how to present itself and its constituency. Thus, Texas offers plates celebrating the many educational institutions attended by its citizens.

These considerations, taken together, convince us that the specialty plates here in question are similar enough to the monuments in *Summum* to call for the same result.

SCV believes that Texas's specialty license plate designs are not government speech, at least with respect to the designs (comprising slogans and graphics) that were initially proposed by private parties. According to SCV, the State does not engage in expressive activity through such slogans and graphics, but rather provides a forum for private speech by making license plates available to display the private parties' designs. We cannot agree.

We have previously used what we have called "forum analysis" to evaluate government restrictions on purely private speech that occurs on government property. But forum analysis is misplaced here. Because the

State is speaking on its own behalf, the First Amendment strictures that attend the various types of government-established forums do not apply.

The fact that private parties take part in the design and propagation of a message does not extinguish the governmental nature of the message or transform the government's role into that of a mere forum-provider. In *Summum,* private entities "financed and donated monuments that the government accept[ed] and display[ed] to the public." Here, similarly, private parties propose designs that Texas may accept and display on its license plates. In this case, as in *Summum,* the "government entity may exercise [its] freedom to express its views" even "when it receives assistance from private sources for the purpose of delivering a government-controlled message." And in this case, as in *Summum,* forum analysis is inapposite.

IV

Our determination that Texas's specialty license plate designs are government speech does not mean that the designs do not also implicate the free speech rights of private persons. We have acknowledged that drivers who display a State's selected license plate designs convey the messages communicated through those designs. See *Wooley v. Maynard* (1977) (observing that a vehicle "is readily associated with its operator" and that drivers displaying license plates "use their private property as a 'mobile billboard' for the State's ideological message"). And we have recognized that the First Amendment stringently limits a State's authority to compel a private party to express a view with which the private party disagrees. But here, compelled private speech is not at issue. And just as Texas cannot require SCV to convey "the State's ideological message," SCV cannot force Texas to include a Confederate battle flag on its specialty license plates.

For the reasons stated, we hold that Texas's specialty license plate designs constitute government speech and that Texas was consequently entitled to refuse to issue plates featuring SCV's proposed design.

Justice ALITO, with whom THE CHIEF JUSTICE, JUSTICE SCALIA, and JUSTICE KENNEDY join, dissenting.

The Court's decision passes off private speech as government speech and, in doing so, establishes a precedent that threatens private speech that government finds displeasing. Under our First Amendment cases, the distinction between government speech and private speech is critical. The First Amendment "does not regulate government speech," and therefore when government speaks, it is free "to select the views that it wants to express." By contrast, "[i]n the realm of private speech or expression, government regulation may not favor one speaker over another."

Unfortunately, the Court's decision categorizes private speech as government speech and thus strips it of all First Amendment protection. The Court holds that all the privately created messages on the many specialty plates issued by the State of Texas convey a government message rather than the message of the motorist displaying the plate. Can this possibly be correct?

Here is a test. Suppose you sat by the side of a Texas highway and studied the license plates on the vehicles passing by. You would see, in addition to the standard Texas plates, an impressive array of specialty plates. (There are now more than 350 varieties.) You would likely observe plates that honor numerous colleges and universities. You might see plates bearing the name of a high school, a fraternity or sorority, the Masons, the Knights of Columbus, the Daughters of the American Revolution, a realty company, a favorite soft drink, a favorite burger restaurant, and a favorite NASCAR driver.

As you sat there watching these plates speed by, would you really think that the sentiments reflected in these specialty plates are the views of the State of Texas and not those of the owners of the cars? If a car with a plate that says "Rather Be Golfing" passed by at 8:30 am on a Monday morning, would you think: "This is the official policy of the State—better to golf than to work?" If you did your viewing at the start of the college football season and you saw Texas plates with the names of the University of Texas's out-of-state competitors in upcoming games—Notre Dame, Oklahoma State, the University of Oklahoma, Kansas State, Iowa State—would you assume that the State of Texas was officially (and perhaps treasonously) rooting for the Longhorns' opponents? And when a car zipped by with a plate that reads "NASCAR—24 Jeff Gordon," would you think that Gordon (born in California, raised in Indiana, resides in North Carolina)[1] is the official favorite of the State government?

The Court says that all of these messages are government speech. It is essential that government be able to express its own viewpoint, the Court reminds us, because otherwise, how would it promote its programs, like recycling and vaccinations? So when Texas issues a "Rather Be Golfing" plate, but not a "Rather Be Playing Tennis" or "Rather Be Bowling" plate, it is furthering a state policy to promote golf but not tennis or bowling. And when Texas allows motorists to obtain a Notre Dame license plate but not a University of Southern California plate, it is taking sides in that long-time rivalry.

This capacious understanding of government speech takes a large and painful bite out of the First Amendment. Specialty plates may seem innocuous. They make motorists happy, and they put money in a State's coffers. But the precedent this case sets is dangerous. While all license plates unquestionably contain *some* government speech (*e.g.,* the name of the State and the numbers and/or letters identifying the vehicle), the State of Texas has converted the remaining space on its specialty plates into little mobile billboards on which motorists can display their own messages. And what Texas did here was to reject one of the messages that members of a private group wanted to post on some of these little billboards because the State thought that many of its citizens would find the message offensive. That is blatant viewpoint discrimination.

If the State can do this with its little mobile billboards, could it do the same with big, stationary billboards? Suppose that a State erected electronic billboards along its highways. Suppose that the State posted some government messages on these billboards and then, to raise money, allowed private entities and individuals to purchase the right to post their own messages. And suppose that the State allowed only those messages that it liked or found not too controversial. Would that be constitutional?

What if a state college or university did the same thing with a similar billboard or a campus bulletin board or dorm list serve? What if it allowed private messages that are consistent with prevailing views on campus but banned those that disturbed some students or faculty? Can there be any doubt that these examples of viewpoint discrimination would violate the First Amendment? I hope not, but the future uses of today's precedent remain to be seen.

The Court believes that messages on privately created plates are government speech because motorists want a seal of state approval for their messages and therefore prefer plates over bumper stickers. This is dangerous reasoning. There is a big difference between government speech (that is, speech by the government in furtherance of its programs) and governmental blessing (or condemnation) of private speech. Many private speakers in a forum would welcome a sign of government approval. But in the realm of private speech, government regulation may not favor one viewpoint over another.

What Texas has done by selling space on its license plates is to create what we have called a limited public forum. It has allowed state property (*i.e.,* motor vehicle license plates) to be used by private speakers according to rules that the State prescribes. Under the First Amendment, however, those rules cannot discriminate on the basis of viewpoint. But that is exactly what Texas did here. The Board rejected Texas SCV's design, "specifically the confederate flag portion of the design, because public comments have shown that many members of the general public find the design offensive, and because such comments are reasonable." These statements indisputably demonstrate that the Board denied Texas SCV's design because of its viewpoint.

The Board's decision cannot be saved by its suggestion that the plate, if allowed, "could distract or disturb some drivers to the point of being unreasonably dangerous." This rationale cannot withstand strict scrutiny. Other States allow specialty plates with the Confederate Battle Flag, and Texas has not pointed to evidence that these plates have led to incidents of road rage or accidents. Texas does not ban bumper stickers bearing the image of the Confederate battle flag. Nor does it ban any of the many other bumper stickers that convey political messages and other messages that are capable of exciting the ire of those who loathe the ideas they express.

Messages that are proposed by private parties and placed on Texas specialty plates are private speech, not government speech. Texas cannot forbid private speech based on its viewpoint. That is what it did here. Because the Court approves this violation of the First Amendment, I respectfully dissent.

4. What Is an Infringement of Speech?

Unconstitutional Conditions (casebook, p. 1290)

The government cannot condition its funds (or any benefit) on a person's having to give up a constitutional right. But the Court has been quite inconsistent as to when conditions on government money are an unconstitutional condition. In the following case, the Court declared conditions unconstitutional. It is worth considering whether the decision adds clarity to this area of law.

UNITED STATES AGENCY FOR INTERNATIONAL
DEVELOPMENT v. ALLIANCE FOR OPEN SOCIETY
INTERNATIONAL
133 S. Ct. 2321 (2013)

Chief Justice ROBERTS delivered the opinion of the Court.

The United States Leadership Against HIV/AIDS, Tuberculosis, and Malaria Act of 2003 (Leadership Act) outlined a comprehensive strategy to combat the spread of HIV/AIDS around the world. As part of that strategy, Congress authorized the appropriation of billions of dollars to fund efforts by nongovernmental organizations to assist in the fight. The Act imposes two related conditions on that funding: First, no funds made available by the Act "may be used to promote or advocate the legalization or practice of prostitution or sex trafficking." And second, no funds may be used by an organization "that does not have a policy explicitly opposing prostitution and sex trafficking." This case concerns the second of these conditions, referred to as the Policy Requirement. The question is whether that funding condition violates a recipient's First Amendment rights.

I

Congress passed the Leadership Act in 2003 after finding that HIV/AIDS had "assumed pandemic proportions, spreading from the most severely affected regions, sub-Saharan Africa and the Caribbean, to all corners of the world, and leaving an unprecedented path of death and devastation." According to congressional findings, more than 65 million people had been infected by HIV and more than 25 million had lost their lives, making HIV/AIDS the fourth highest cause of death worldwide.

The United States has enlisted the assistance of nongovernmental organizations to help achieve the many goals of the program. Such organizations "with experience in health care and HIV/AIDS counseling," Congress found, "have proven effective in combating the HIV/AIDS pandemic and can be a resource in . . . provid[ing] treatment and care for individuals infected with HIV/AIDS." Since 2003, Congress has authorized the appropriation of billions of dollars for funding these organizations' fight against HIV/AIDS around the world.

Those funds, however, come with two conditions: First, no funds made available to carry out the Leadership Act "may be used to promote or advocate the legalization or practice of prostitution or sex trafficking." Second, no funds made available may "provide assistance to any group or organization that does not have a policy explicitly opposing prostitution and sex trafficking, except . . . to the Global Fund to Fight AIDS, Tuberculosis and Malaria, the World Health Organization, the International AIDS Vaccine Initiative or to any United Nations agency." It is this second condition—the Policy Requirement—that is at issue here.

II

Respondents are a group of domestic organizations engaged in combating HIV/AIDS overseas. In addition to substantial private funding, they receive billions annually in financial assistance from the United States, including under the Leadership Act. Their work includes programs aimed at limiting injection drug use in Uzbekistan, Tajikistan, and Kyrgyzstan, preventing mother-to-child HIV transmission in Kenya, and promoting safer sex practices in India. Respondents fear that adopting a policy explicitly opposing prostitution may alienate certain host governments, and may diminish the effectiveness of some of their programs by making it more difficult to work with prostitutes in the fight against HIV/AIDS. They are also concerned that the Policy Requirement may require them to censor their privately funded discussions in publications, at conferences, and in other forums about how best to prevent the spread of HIV/AIDS among prostitutes.

In 2005, respondents Alliance for Open Society International and Pathfinder International commenced this litigation, seeking a declaratory judgment that the Government's implementation of the Policy Requirement violated their First Amendment rights.

III

The Policy Requirement mandates that recipients of Leadership Act funds explicitly agree with the Government's policy to oppose prostitution and sex trafficking. It is, however, a basic First Amendment principle that "freedom of speech prohibits the government from telling people what they must say." "At the heart of the First Amendment lies the principle that each person should decide for himself or herself the ideas and beliefs deserving of expression, consideration, and adherence." Were it enacted as a direct regulation of speech, the Policy Requirement would plainly violate the First Amendment. The question is whether the Government may nonetheless impose that requirement as a condition on the receipt of federal funds.

The Spending Clause of the Federal Constitution grants Congress the power "[t]o lay and collect Taxes, Duties, Imposts and Excises, to pay the Debts and provide for the common Defence and general Welfare of the United States." Art. I, § 8, cl. 1. The Clause provides Congress broad discretion to tax and spend for the "general Welfare," including by funding particular state or private programs or activities. That power includes the authority to impose limits on the use of such funds to ensure they are used in the manner Congress intends. *Rust v. Sullivan* (1991).

As a general matter, if a party objects to a condition on the receipt of federal funding, its recourse is to decline the funds. This remains true when the objection is that a condition may affect the recipient's exercise of its First Amendment rights.

At the same time, however, we have held that the Government " 'may not deny a benefit to a person on a basis that infringes his constitutionally protected . . . freedom of speech even if he has no entitlement to that benefit.' " In some cases, a funding condition can result in an unconstitutional burden on First Amendment rights.

The dissent thinks that can only be true when the condition is not relevant to the objectives of the program (although it has its doubts about that), or when the condition is actually coercive, in the sense of an offer that cannot be refused. Our precedents, however, are not so limited. In the present context, the relevant distinction that has emerged from our cases is between conditions that define the limits of the government spending program—those that specify the activities Congress wants to subsidize—and conditions that seek to leverage funding to regulate speech outside the contours of the program itself. The line is hardly clear, in part because the definition of a particular program can always be manipulated to subsume the challenged condition. We have held, however, that "Congress cannot recast a condition on funding as a mere definition of its program in every case, lest the First Amendment be reduced to a simple semantic exercise."

A comparison of two cases helps illustrate the distinction: In *Regan v. Taxation With Representation of Washington*, the Court upheld a requirement that nonprofit organizations seeking tax-exempt status under 26 U.S.C. § 501(c)(3) not engage in substantial efforts to influence legislation. The tax-exempt status, we explained, "ha[d] much the same effect as a cash grant to the organization." And by limiting § 501(c)(3) status to organizations that did not attempt to influence legislation, Congress had merely "chose[n] not to subsidize lobbying."

In *FCC v. League of Women Voters of California*, by contrast, the Court struck down a condition on federal financial assistance to noncommercial broadcast television and radio stations that prohibited all editorializing, including with private funds. Even a station receiving only one percent of its overall budget from the Federal Government, the Court explained, was "barred absolutely from all editorializing." Unlike the situation in *Regan*, the law provided no way for a station to limit its use of federal funds to noneditorializing activities, while using private funds "to make known its views on matters of public importance." The prohibition thus went beyond ensuring that federal funds not be used to subsidize "public broadcasting station editorials," and instead leveraged the federal funding to regulate the stations' speech outside the scope of the program.

Our decision in *Rust v. Sullivan* elaborated on the approach reflected in *Regan* and *League of Women Voters*. In *Rust*, we considered Title X of the Public Health Service Act, a Spending Clause program that issued grants to nonprofit health-care organizations "to assist in the establishment and operation of voluntary family planning projects [to] offer a broad range of acceptable and effective family planning methods and services." The organizations received funds from a variety of sources other than the Federal Government for a variety of purposes. The Act, however, prohibited the Title X federal funds from being "used in programs where abortion is a method of family planning." To enforce this provision, HHS regulations barred Title X projects from advocating abortion as a method of family planning, and required grantees to ensure that their Title X projects were " 'physically and financially separate' " from their other projects that engaged in the prohibited activities. A group of Title X funding recipients brought suit, claiming the regulations imposed an unconstitutional condition on their First Amendment rights. We rejected their claim.

We explained that Congress can, without offending the Constitution, selectively fund certain programs to address an issue of public concern, without funding alternative ways of addressing the same problem. In Title X, Congress had defined the federal program to encourage only particular family planning methods. The challenged regulations were simply "designed to ensure that the limits of the federal program are observed," and "that public funds [are] spent for the purposes for which they were authorized."

As noted, the distinction drawn in these cases—between conditions that define the federal program and those that reach outside it—is not always self-evident. Here, however, we are confident that the Policy Requirement falls on the unconstitutional side of the line.

To begin, it is important to recall that the Leadership Act has two conditions relevant here. The first—unchallenged in this litigation—prohibits Leadership Act funds from being used "to promote or advocate the legalization or practice of prostitution or sex trafficking." The Government concedes that § 7631(e) by itself ensures that federal funds will not be used for the prohibited purposes.

The Policy Requirement therefore must be doing something more—and it is. The dissent views the Requirement as simply a selection criterion by which the Government identifies organizations "who believe in its ideas to carry them to fruition." As an initial matter, whatever purpose the Policy Requirement serves in selecting funding recipients, its effects go beyond selection. The Policy Requirement is an ongoing condition on recipients' speech and activities, a ground for terminating a grant after selection is complete. In any event, as the Government acknowledges, it is not simply seeking organizations that oppose prostitution. Rather, it explains, "Congress has expressed its purpose 'to eradicate' prostitution and sex trafficking, and it wants recipients to adopt a similar stance." This case is not about the Government's ability to enlist the assistance of those with whom it already agrees. It is about compelling a grant recipient to adopt a particular belief as a condition of funding.

By demanding that funding recipients adopt—as their own—the Government's view on an issue of public concern, the condition by its very nature affects "protected conduct outside the scope of the federally funded program." A recipient cannot avow the belief dictated by the Policy Requirement when spending Leadership Act funds, and then turn around and assert a contrary belief, or claim neutrality, when participating in activities on its own time and dime. By requiring recipients to profess a specific belief, the Policy Requirement goes beyond defining the limits of the federally funded program to defining the recipient.

The Policy Requirement compels as a condition of federal funding the affirmation of a belief that by its nature cannot be confined within the scope of the Government program. In so doing, it violates the First Amendment and cannot be sustained.

Justice SCALIA, with whom Justice THOMAS joins, dissenting.

The Leadership Act provides that "any group or organization that does not have a policy explicitly opposing prostitution and sex trafficking" may not receive funds appropriated under the Act. This Policy Requirement is nothing more than a means of selecting suitable agents to implement the Government's chosen strategy to eradicate HIV/AIDS. That is perfectly permissible under the Constitution.

The First Amendment does not mandate a viewpoint-neutral government. Government must choose between rival ideas and adopt some as its own: competition over cartels, solar energy over coal, weapon development over disarmament, and so forth. Moreover, the government may enlist the assistance of those who believe in its ideas to carry them to fruition; and it need not enlist for that purpose those who oppose or do not support the ideas. That seems to me a matter of the most common common sense. For example: One of the purposes of America's foreign-aid programs is the fostering of good will towards this country. If the organization Hamas—reputed to have an efficient system for delivering welfare—were excluded from a program for the distribution of U.S. food assistance, no one could reasonably object. And that would remain true if Hamas were an organization of United States citizens entitled to the protection of the Constitution. So long as the unfunded organization remains free to engage in its activities (including anti-American propaganda) "without federal assistance," refusing to make use of its assistance for an enterprise to which it is opposed does not abridge its speech. And the same is true when the rejected organization is not affirmatively opposed to, but merely unsupportive of, the object of the federal program, which appears to be the case here. (Respondents do not promote prostitution, but neither do they wish to oppose it.) A federal program to encourage healthy eating habits need not be administered by the American Gourmet Society, which has nothing against healthy food but does not insist upon it.

The argument is that this commonsense principle will enable the government to discriminate against, and injure, points of view to which it is opposed. Of course the Constitution does not prohibit government spending that discriminates against, and injures, points of view to which the government is opposed; every government program which takes a position on a controversial issue does that. Anti-smoking programs injure cigar aficionados, programs encouraging sexual abstinence injure free-love advocates, etc. The constitutional prohibition at issue here is not a prohibition against discriminating against or injuring opposing points of view, but the First Amendment's prohibition against the coercing of speech. I am frankly dubious that a condition for eligibility to participate in a minor federal program such as this one runs afoul of that prohibition even when the condition is irrelevant to the goals of the program. Not every disadvantage is a coercion.

Ideological-commitment requirements such as the one here are quite rare; but making the choice between competing applicants on relevant ideological grounds is undoubtedly quite common. As far as the Constitution is concerned, it is quite impossible to distinguish between the two. If the government cannot demand a relevant ideological commitment as a condition of application, neither can it distinguish between applicants on a relevant ideological ground. And that is the real evil of today's opinion. One can expect, in the future, frequent challenges to the denial of government funding for relevant ideological reasons.

The Court's opinion contains stirring quotations from cases like *West Virginia State Bd. of Ed. v. Barnette* (1943), and *Turner Broadcasting System, Inc. v. FCC* (1994). They serve only to distract attention from the elephant in the room: that the Government is not forcing *anyone* to say *anything*. What Congress has done here—requiring an ideological commitment relevant to the Government task at hand—is approved by the Constitution itself. Americans need not support the Constitution; they may be Communists or anarchists. But "[t]he Senators and Representatives

. . . , and the Members of the several State Legislatures, and all executive and judicial Officers, both of the United States and of the several States, shall be bound by Oath or Affirmation, to support [the] Constitution." U.S. Const., Art.VI, cl. 3. The Framers saw the wisdom of imposing affirmative ideological commitments prerequisite to assisting in the government's work. And so should we.

C. Types of Unprotected and Less Protected Speech

7. Conduct That Communicates

c. When May the Government Regulate Conduct That Communicates?

iii. Spending Money as Political Speech (casebook, p. 1500)

Buckley v. Valeo (casebook, p. 1501) drew a distinction between government regulation of contributions in elections as opposed to government regulation of expenditures. In *McCutcheon v. Federal Election Commission*, the Court considered whether the government may impose aggregate limits on campaign contributions in federal elections.

McCUTCHEON v. FEDERAL ELECTION COMMISSION
134 S. Ct. 1434 (2014)

Chief Justice ROBERTS announced the judgment of the Court and delivered an opinion, in which Justice SCALIA, Justice KENNEDY, and Justice ALITO join.

There is no right more basic in our democracy than the right to participate in electing our political leaders. Citizens can exercise that right in a variety of ways: They can run for office themselves, vote, urge others to vote for a particular candidate, volunteer to work on a campaign, and contribute to a candidate's campaign. This case is about the last of those options.

The right to participate in democracy through political contributions is protected by the First Amendment, but that right is not absolute. Our cases have held that Congress may regulate campaign contributions to protect against corruption or the appearance of corruption. At the same time, we have made clear that Congress may not regulate contributions simply to reduce the amount of money in politics, or to restrict the political participation of some in order to enhance the relative influence of others.

Many people might find those latter objectives attractive: They would be delighted to see fewer television commercials touting a candidate's accomplishments or disparaging an opponent's character. Money in politics may at times seem repugnant to some, but so too does much of what the First Amendment vigorously protects. If the First Amendment protects flag burning, funeral protests, and Nazi parades-despite the profound offense such spectacles cause-it surely protects political campaign speech despite popular opposition. Indeed, as we have emphasized, the First Amendment "has its fullest and most urgent application precisely to the conduct of campaigns for political office."

In a series of cases over the past 40 years, we have spelled out how to draw the constitutional line between the permissible goal of avoiding corruption in the political process and the impermissible desire simply to limit political speech. We have said [that government regulation may not target the general gratitude a candidate may feel toward those who support him or his allies, or the political access such support may afford. "Ingratiation and access . . . are not corruption." *Citizens United v. Federal Election Commission* (2010). They embody a central feature of democracy-that constituents support candidates who share their beliefs and interests, and candidates who are elected can be expected to be responsive to those concerns.

Any regulation must instead target what we have called "quid pro quo" corruption or its appearance. That Latin phrase captures the notion of a direct exchange of an official act for money. "The hallmark of corruption is the financial quid pro quo: dollars for political favors." Campaign finance restrictions that pursue other objectives, we have explained, impermissibly inject the Government "into the debate over who should govern." And those who govern should be the last people to help decide who should govern.

The statute at issue in this case imposes two types of limits on campaign contributions. The first, called base limits, restricts how much money a donor may contribute to a particular candidate or committee. The second, called aggregate limits, restricts how much money a donor may contribute in total to all candidates or committees.

This case does not involve any challenge to the base limits, which we have previously upheld as serving the permissible objective of combatting corruption. The Government contends that the aggregate limits also serve that objective, by preventing circumvention of the base limits.

We conclude, however, that the aggregate limits do little, if anything, to address that concern, while seriously restricting participation in the democratic process. The aggregate limits are therefore invalid under the First Amendment.

I

For the 2013-2014 election cycle, the base limits in the Federal Election Campaign Act of 1971 (FECA), as amended by the Bipartisan Campaign Reform Act of 2002 (BCRA), permit an individual to contribute up to $2,600 per election to a candidate ($5,200 total for the primary and general elections); $32,400 per year to a national party committee; $10,000 per year to a state or local party committee; and $5,000 per year to a political action committee, or "PAC." A national committee, state or local party committee, or multicandidate PAC may in turn contribute up to $5,000 per election to a candidate.

The base limits apply with equal force to contributions that are "in any way earmarked or otherwise directed through an intermediary or conduit" to a candidate. If, for example, a donor gives money to a party committee but directs the party committee to pass the contribution along to a particular candidate, then the transaction is treated as a contribution from the original donor to the specified candidate.

For the 2013-2014 election cycle, the aggregate limits in BCRA permit an individual to contribute a total of $48,600 to federal candidates and a total of $74,600 to other political committees. Of that $74,600, only $48,600 may be contributed to state or local party committees and PACs, as opposed to national party committees. All told, an individual may contribute up to $123,200 to candidate and noncandidate committees during each two-year election cycle.

The base limits thus restrict how much money a donor may contribute to any particular candidate or committee; the aggregate limits have the effect of restricting how many candidates or committees the donor may support, to the extent permitted by the base lim

In the 2011-2012 election cycle, appellant Shaun McCutcheon contributed a total of $33,088 to 16 different federal candidates, in compliance with the base limits applicable to each. He alleges that he wished to contribute $1,776 to each of 12 additional candidates but was prevented from doing so by the aggregate limit on contributions to candidates. McCutcheon also contributed a total of $27,328 to several noncandidate political committees, in compliance with the base limits applicable to each. He alleges that he wished to contribute to various other political committees, including $25,000 to each of the three Republican national party committees, but was prevented from doing so by the aggregate limit on contributions to political committees. McCutcheon further alleges that he plans to make similar contributions in the future. In the 2013-2014 election cycle, he again wishes to contribute at least $60,000 to various candidates and $75,000 to non-candidate political committees.

Appellant Republican National Committee is a national political party committee charged with the general management of the Republican Party. The RNC wishes to receive the contributions that McCutcheon and similarly situated individuals would like to make—contributions otherwise permissible under the base limits for national party committees but foreclosed by the aggregate limit on contributions to political committees.

II

The parties and amici curiae spend significant energy debating whether the line that *Buckley* [*v. Valeo* (1976)] drew between contributions and expenditures should remain the law. Notwithstanding the robust debate, we see no need in this case to revisit *Buckley*'s distinction between contributions and expenditures and the corollary distinction in the applicable standards of review. *Buckley* held that the Government's interest in preventing quid pro quo corruption or its appearance was "sufficiently important"; we have elsewhere stated that the same interest may properly be labeled "compelling," so that the interest would satisfy even strict scrutiny. Moreover, regardless whether we apply strict scrutiny or *Buckley*'s "closely drawn" test, we must assess the fit between the stated governmental objective and the means selected to achieve that objective. Or to put it another way, if a law that restricts political speech does not "avoid unnecessary abridgement" of First Amendment rights, *Buckley*, 424 U.S., at 25, it cannot survive "rigorous" review.

Because we find a substantial mismatch between the Government's stated objective and the means selected to achieve it, the aggregate limits fail even under the "closely drawn" test. We therefore need not parse the differences between the two standards in this case.

Buckley treated the constitutionality of the $25,000 aggregate limit as contingent upon that limit's ability to prevent circumvention of the $1,000 base limit, describing the aggregate limit as "no more than a corollary" of the base limit. The Court determined that circumvention could occur when an individual legally contributes "massive amounts of money to a particular candidate through the use of unearmarked contributions" to entities that are themselves likely to contribute to the candidate. For that reason, the Court upheld the $25,000 aggregate limit.

Although *Buckley* provides some guidance, we think that its ultimate conclusion about the constitutionality of the aggregate limit in place under FECA does not control here. *Buckley* spent a total of three sentences analyzing that limit; in fact, the opinion pointed out that the constitutionality of the aggregate limit "ha[d] not been separately addressed at length by the parties." We are now asked to address appellants' direct challenge to the aggregate limits in place under BCRA. BCRA is a different statutory regime, and the aggregate limits it imposes operate against a distinct legal backdrop.

Most notably, statutory safeguards against circumvention have been considerably strengthened since *Buckley* was decided, through both statutory additions and the introduction of a comprehensive regulatory scheme. With more targeted anticircumvention measures in place today, the indiscriminate aggregate limits under BCRA appear particularly heavy-handed.

Given the foregoing, this case cannot be resolved merely by pointing to three sentences in *Buckley* that were written without the benefit of full briefing or argument on the issue.

III

The First Amendment "is designed and intended to remove governmental restraints from the arena of public discussion, putting the decision as to what views shall be voiced largely into the hands of each of us, ... in the belief that no other approach would comport with the premise of individual dignity and choice upon which our political system rests." As relevant here, the First Amendment safeguards an individual's right to participate in the public debate through political expression and political association. When an individual contributes money to a candidate, he exercises both of those rights: The contribution "serves as a general expression of support for the candidate and his views" and "serves to affiliate a person with a candidate."

An aggregate limit on how many candidates and committees an individual may support through contributions is not a "modest restraint" at all. The Government may no more restrict how many candidates or causes a donor may support than it may tell a newspaper how many candidates it may endorse.

To put it in the simplest terms, the aggregate limits prohibit an individual from fully contributing to the primary and general election campaigns of ten or more candidates, even if all contributions fall within the base limits Congress views as adequate to protect against corruption. The individual may give up to $5,200 each to nine candidates, but the aggregate limits constitute an outright ban on further contributions to any other candidate (beyond the additional $1,800 that may be spent before reaching the $48,600 aggregate limit). At that point, the limits deny the individual all ability to exercise his expressive and associational rights by contributing to someone who will advocate for his policy preferences. A donor must limit the number of candidates he supports, and may have to choose which of several policy concerns he will advance-clear First Amendment harms that the dissent never acknowledges.

It is no answer to say that the individual can simply contribute less money to more people. To require one person to contribute at lower levels than others because he wants to support more candidates or causes is to impose a special burden on broader participation in the democratic process. And as we have recently admonished, the Government may not penalize an individual for "robustly exercis[ing]" his First Amendment rights.

The First Amendment burden is especially great for individuals who do not have ready access to alternative avenues for supporting their preferred politicians and policies. In the context of base contribution limits, *Buckley* observed that a supporter could vindicate his associational interests by personally volunteering his time and energy on behalf of a candidate. Such personal volunteering is not a realistic alternative for those who wish to support a wide variety of candidates or causes. Other effective methods of supporting preferred candidates or causes without contributing money are reserved for a select few, such as entertainers capable of raising hundreds of thousands of dollars in a single evening.

IV

With the significant First Amendment costs for individual citizens in mind, we turn to the governmental interests asserted in this case. This Court has identified only one legitimate governmental interest for restricting campaign finances: preventing corruption or the appearance of corruption. We have consistently rejected attempts to suppress campaign speech based on other legislative objectives. No matter how desirable it may seem, it is not an acceptable governmental objective to "level the playing field," or to "level electoral opportunities," or to "equaliz[e] the financial resources of candidates." The First Amendment prohibits such legislative attempts to "fine-tun[e]" the electoral process, no matter how well intentioned.

Moreover, while preventing corruption or its appearance is a legitimate objective, Congress may target only a specific type of corruption — "quid pro quo" corruption. As *Buckley* explained, Congress may permissibly seek to rein in "large contributions [that] are given to secure a political quid pro quo from current and potential office holders." In addition to "actual quid pro quo arrangements," Congress may permissibly limit "the appearance of corruption stemming from public awareness of the opportunities for abuse inherent in a regime of large individual financial contributions" to particular candidates.

Spending large sums of money in connection with elections, but not in connection with an effort to control the exercise of an officeholder's official duties, does not give rise to such quid pro quo corruption. Nor does the possibility that an individual who spends large sums may garner "influence over or access to" elected officials or political parties.

The dissent advocates a broader conception of corruption, and would apply the label to any individual contributions above limits deemed necessary to protect "collective speech." Thus, under the dissent's view, it is perfectly fine to contribute $5,200 to nine candidates but somehow corrupt to give the same amount to a tenth.

The line between quid pro quo corruption and general influence may seem vague at times, but the distinction must be respected in order to safeguard basic First Amendment rights. In addition, "[i]n drawing that line, the First Amendment requires us to err on the side of protecting political speech rather than suppressing it."

The dissent laments that our opinion leaves only remnants of FECA and BCRA that are inadequate to combat corruption. Such rhetoric ignores the fact that we leave the base limits undisturbed. Those base limits remain the primary means of regulating campaign contributions-the obvious explanation for why the aggregate limits received a scant few sentences of attention in *Buckley*.

"When the Government restricts speech, the Government bears the burden of proving the constitutionality of its actions." Here, the Government seeks to carry that burden by arguing that the aggregate limits further the permissible objective of preventing quid pro quo corruption.

The difficulty is that once the aggregate limits kick in, they ban all contributions of any amount. But Congress's selection of a $5,200 base limit indicates its belief that contributions of that amount or less do not create a cognizable risk of corruption. If there is no corruption concern in giving nine candidates up to $5,200 each, it is difficult to understand how a tenth candidate can be regarded as corruptible if given $1,801, and all others corruptible if given a dime. And if there is no risk that additional candidates will be corrupted by donations of up to $5,200, then the Government must defend the aggregate limits by demonstrating that they prevent circumvention of the base limits.

The problem is that they do not serve that function in any meaningful way. In light of the various statutes and regulations currently in effect, Buckley's fear that an individual might "contribute massive amounts of money to a particular candidate through the use of unearmarked contributions" to entities likely to support the candidate, is far too speculative. And—importantly—we "have never accepted mere conjecture as adequate to carry a First Amendment burden."

Quite apart from the foregoing, the aggregate limits violate the First Amendment because they are not "closely drawn to avoid unnecessary abridgment of associational freedoms." In the First Amendment context, fit matters. Even when the Court is not applying strict scrutiny, we still require "a fit that is not necessarily perfect, but reasonable; that represents not necessarily the single best disposition but one whose scope is 'in proportion to the interest served,' . . . that employs not necessarily the least restrictive means but . . . a means narrowly tailored to achieve the desired objective." Here, because the statute is poorly tailored to the Government's interest in preventing circumvention of the base limits, it impermissibly restricts participation in the political process.

The Government argues that the aggregate limits are justified because they prevent an individual from giving to too many initial recipients who might subsequently recontribute a donation. After all, only recontributed funds can conceivably give rise to circumvention of the base limits. Yet all indications are that many types of recipients have scant interest in regifting donations they receive.

Experience suggests that the vast majority of contributions made in excess of the aggregate limits are likely to be retained and spent by their recipients rather than rerouted to candidates. In the 2012 election cycle, federal candidates, political parties, and PACs spent a total of $7 billion, according to the FEC. In particular, each national political party's spending ran in the hundreds of millions of dollars. The National Republican Senatorial Committee (NRSC), National Republican Congressional Committee (NRCC), Democratic Senatorial Campaign Committee (DSCC), and Democratic Congressional Campaign Committee (DCCC), however, spent less than $1 million each on direct candidate contributions and less than $10 million each on coordinated expenditures. Including both coordinated expenditures and direct candidate contributions, the NRSC and DSCC spent just 7% of their total funds on contributions to candidates and the NRCC and DCCC spent just 3%.

Likewise, as explained previously, state parties rarely contribute to candidates in other States. In the 2012 election cycle, the Republican and Democratic state party committees in all 50 States (and the District of Columbia) contributed a paltry $17,750 to House and Senate candidates in other States. The state party committees spent over half a billion dollars over the same time period, of which the $17,750 in contributions to other States' candidates constituted just 0.003%.

As with national and state party committees, candidates contribute only a small fraction of their campaign funds to other candidates. Authorized candidate committees may support other candidates up to a $2,000 base limit. In the 2012 election, House candidates spent a total of $1.1 billion. Candidate-to-candidate contributions among House candidates totaled $3.65 million, making up just 0.3% of candidates' overall spending. The most that any one individual candidate received from all other candidates was around $100,000. The fact is that candidates who receive campaign contributions spend most of the money on themselves, rather than passing along donations to other candidates. In this arena at least, charity begins at home.

Based on what we can discern from experience, the indiscriminate ban on all contributions above the aggregate limits is disproportionate to the Government's interest in preventing circumvention. The Government has not given us any reason to believe that parties or candidates would dramatically shift their priorities if the aggregate limits were lifted. Absent such a showing, we cannot conclude that the sweeping aggregate limits are appropriately tailored to guard against any contributions that might implicate the Government's anticircumvention interest.

A final point: It is worth keeping in mind that the base limits themselves are a prophylactic measure. As we have explained, "restrictions on direct contributions are preventative, because few if any contributions to candidates will involve quid pro quo arrangements." The aggregate limits are then layered on top, ostensibly to prevent circumvention of the base limits. This "prophylaxis-upon-prophylaxis approach" requires that we be particularly diligent in scrutinizing the law's fit.

Importantly, there are multiple alternatives available to Congress that would serve the Government's anticircumvention interest, while avoiding "unnecessary abridgment" of First Amendment rights.

The most obvious might involve targeted restrictions on transfers among candidates and political committees. There are currently no such limits on transfers among party committees and from candidates to party committees. Doing so would impose a lesser burden on First Amendment rights, as compared to aggregate limits that flatly ban contributions beyond certain levels.

One possible option for restricting transfers would be to require contributions above the current aggregate limits to be deposited into segregated, nontransferable accounts and spent only by their recipients. Such a solution would address the same circumvention possibilities as the current aggregate limits, while not completely barring contributions beyond the aggregate levels. In addition (or as an alternative), if Congress believes that circumvention is especially likely to occur through creation of a joint fundraising committee, it could require that funds received through those committees be spent by their recipients (or perhaps it could simply limit the size of joint fundraising committees). Such alternatives to the aggregate limits properly refocus the inquiry on the delinquent actor: the recipient of a contribution within the base limits, who then routes the money in a manner that undermines those limits.

Other alternatives might focus on earmarking. Many of the scenarios that the Government and the dissent hypothesize involve at least implicit agreements to circumvent the base limits — agreements that are already prohibited by the earmarking rules. The FEC might strengthen those rules further by, for example, defining how many candidates a PAC must support in order to ensure that "a substantial portion" of a donor's contribution is not rerouted to a certain candidate. Congress might also consider a modified version of the aggregate limits, such as one that prohibits donors who have contributed the current maximum sums from further contributing to political committees that have indicated they will support candidates to whom the donor has already contributed.

We do not mean to opine on the validity of any particular proposal. The point is that there are numerous alternative approaches available to Congress to prevent circumvention of the base limits.

Finally, disclosure of contributions minimizes the potential for abuse of the campaign finance system. Disclosure requirements are in part "justified based on a governmental interest in 'provid[ing] the electorate with information' about the sources of election-related spending." They may also "deter actual corruption and avoid the appearance of corruption by exposing large contributions and expenditures to the light of publicity." Disclosure requirements burden speech, but—unlike the aggregate limits—they do not impose a ceiling on speech. With modern technology, disclosure now offers a particularly effective means of arming the voting public with information.

For the past 40 years, our campaign finance jurisprudence has focused on the need to preserve authority for the Government to combat corruption, without at the same time compromising the political responsiveness at the heart of the democratic process, or allowing the Government to favor some participants in that process over others.

The Government has a strong interest, no less critical to our democratic system, in combatting corruption and its appearance. We have, however, held that this interest must be limited to a specific kind of corruption—quid pro quo corruption—in order to ensure that the Government's efforts do not have the effect of restricting the First Amendment right of citizens to choose who shall govern them. For the reasons set forth, we conclude that the aggregate limits on contributions do not further the only governmental interest this Court accepted as legitimate in Buckley. They instead intrude without justification on a citizen's ability to exercise "the most fundamental First Amendment activities."

Justice THOMAS, concurring in the judgment.

I adhere to the view that this Court's decision in *Buckley v. Valeo* (1976) denigrates core First Amendment speech and should be overruled. Political speech is " 'the primary object of First Amendment protection' " and "the lifeblood of a self-governing people." Contributions to political campaigns, no less than direct expenditures, "generate essential political speech" by fostering discussion of public issues and candidate qualifications. *Buckley* itself recognized that both contribution and expenditure limits "operate in an area of the most fundamental First Amendment activities" and "implicate fundamental First Amendment interests." But instead of treating political giving and political spending alike, *Buckley* distinguished the two, embracing a bifurcated standard of review under which contribution limits receive less rigorous scrutiny.

As I have explained before, "[t]he analytic foundation of *Buckley* . . . was tenuous from the very beginning and has only continued to erode in the intervening years." To justify a lesser standard of review for contribution limits, *Buckley* relied on the premise that contributions are different in kind from direct expenditures. None of the Court's bases for that premise withstands careful review. The linchpin of the Court's analysis was its assertion that "[w]hile contributions may result in political expression if spent by a candidate or an association to present views to the voters, the transformation of contributions into political debate involves speech by someone other than the contributor." But that " 'speech by proxy' " rationale quickly breaks down, given that "[e]ven in the case of a direct expenditure, there is usually some go-between that facilitates the dissemination of the spender's message—for instance, an advertising agency or a television station." Moreover, we have since rejected the " 'proxy speech' " approach as affording insufficient First Amendment protection to "the voices of those of modest means as opposed to those sufficiently wealthy to be able to buy expensive media ads with their own resources."

The remaining justifications *Buckley* provided are also flawed. For example, *Buckley* claimed that contribution limits entail only a "marginal" speech restriction because "[a] contribution serves as a general expression of support for the candidate and his views, but does not communicate the underlying basis for the support." But this Court has never required a speaker to explain the reasons for his position in order to obtain full First Amendment protection. Instead, we have consistently held that speech is protected even "when the underlying basis for a position is not given."

Equally unpersuasive is *Buckley*'s suggestion that contribution limits warrant less stringent review because "[t]he quantity of communication by the contributor does not increase perceptibly with the size of his contribution," and "[a]t most, the size of the contribution provides a very rough index of the intensity of the contributor's support for the candidate." Contributions do increase the quantity of communication by "amplifying the voice of the candidate" and "help[ing] to ensure the dissemination of the messages that the contributor wishes to convey." They also serve as a quantifiable metric of the intensity of a particular contributor's support, as demonstrated by the frequent practice of giving different amounts to different candidates. *Buckley* simply failed to recognize that "we have accorded full First Amendment protection to expressions of intensity."

In sum, what remains of *Buckley* is a rule without a rationale. Contributions and expenditures are simply "two sides of the same First Amendment coin," and our efforts to distinguish the two have produced mere "word games" rather than any cognizable principle of constitutional law. For that reason, I would overrule *Buckley* and subject the aggregate limits in BCRA to strict scrutiny, which they would surely fail.

This case represents yet another missed opportunity to right the course of our campaign finance jurisprudence by restoring a standard that is faithful to the First Amendment. Until we undertake that reexamination, we remain in a "halfway house" of our own design. For these reasons, I concur only in the judgment.

Justice BREYER, with whom Justice GINSBURG, Justice SOTOMAYOR, and Justice KAGAN join dissenting.

Nearly 40 years ago in *Buckley v. Valeo* (1976), this Court considered the constitutionality of laws that imposed limits upon the overall amount a single person can contribute to all federal candidates, political parties, and committees taken together. The Court held that those limits did not violate the Constitution.

The *Buckley* Court focused upon the same problem that concerns the Court today, and it wrote:

The overall $25,000 ceiling does impose an ultimate restriction upon the number of candidates and committees with which an individual may associate himself by means of financial support. But this quite modest restraint upon protected political activity serves to prevent evasion of the $1,000 contribution limitation by a person who might otherwise contribute massive amounts of money to a particular candidate through the use of unearmarked contributions to political committees likely to contribute to that candidate, or huge contributions to the candidate's political party. The limited, additional restriction on associational freedom imposed by the overall ceiling is thus no more than a corollary of the basic individual contribution limitation that we have found to be constitutionally valid

Today a majority of the Court overrules this holding. It is wrong to do so. Its conclusion rests upon its own, not a record-based, view of the facts. Its legal analysis is faulty: It misconstrues the nature of the competing constitutional interests at stake. It understates the importance of protecting the political integrity of our governmental institutions. It creates a loophole that will allow a single individual to contribute millions of dollars to a political party or to a candidate's campaign. Taken together with *Citizens United v. Federal Election Comm'n* (2010), today's decision eviscerates our Nation's campaign finance laws, leaving a remnant incapable of dealing with the grave problems of democratic legitimacy that those laws were intended to resolve.

I

The plurality concludes that the aggregate contribution limits " 'unnecessar[ily] abridg[e]' " First Amendment rights. The plurality's conclusion rests upon three separate but related claims. Each is fatally flawed. First, the plurality says that given the base limits on contributions to candidates and political committees, aggregate limits do not further any independent governmental objective worthy of protection.

Second, the plurality assesses the instrumental objective of the aggregate limits, namely, safeguarding the base limits. It finds that they "do not serve that function in any meaningful way." That is because, even without the aggregate limits, the possibilities for circumventing the base limits are "implausible" and "divorced from reality."

Third, the plurality says the aggregate limits are not a " 'reasonable' " policy tool. Rather, they are "poorly tailored to the Government's interest in preventing circumvention of the base limits."

II

The plurality's first claim—that large aggregate contributions do not "give rise" to "corruption"—is plausible only because the plurality defines "corruption" too narrowly. The plurality describes the constitutionally permissible objective of campaign finance regulation as follows: "Congress may target only a specific type of corruption—" 'quid pro quo' corruption." It then defines quid pro quo corruption to mean no more than "a direct exchange of an official act for money"—an act akin to bribery. It adds specifically that corruption does not include efforts to "garner 'influence over or access to' elected officials or political parties." Moreover, the Government's efforts to prevent the "appearance of corruption" are "equally confined to the appearance of quid pro quo corruption," as narrowly defined.

This critically important definition of "corruption" is inconsistent with the Court's prior case law (with the possible exception of *Citizens United*). And it misunderstands the constitutional importance of the interests at stake. In fact, constitutional interests—indeed, First Amendment interests—lie on both sides of the legal equation.

In reality, as the history of campaign finance reform shows and as our earlier cases on the subject have recognized, the anticorruption interest that drives Congress to regulate campaign contributions is a far broader, more important interest than the plurality acknowledges. It is an interest in maintaining the integrity of our public governmental institutions. And it is an interest rooted in the Constitution and in the First Amendment itself.

Consider at least one reason why the First Amendment protects political speech. Speech does not exist in a vacuum. Rather, political communication seeks to secure government action. A politically oriented "marketplace of ideas" seeks to form a public opinion that can and will influence elected representatives.

What has this to do with corruption? It has everything to do with corruption. Corruption breaks the constitutionally necessary "chain of communication" between the people and their representatives. It derails the essential speech-to-government-action tie. Where enough money calls the tune, the general public will not be heard. Insofar as corruption cuts the link between political thought and political action, a free marketplace of political ideas loses its point. That is one reason why the Court has stressed the constitutional importance of Congress' concern that a few large donations not drown out the voices of the many.

That is also why the Court has used the phrase "subversion of the political process" to describe circumstances in which "[e]lected officials are influenced to act contrary to their obligations of office by the prospect of financial gain to themselves or infusions of money into their campaigns."

The "appearance of corruption" can make matters worse. It can lead the public to believe that its efforts to communicate with its representatives or to help sway public opinion have little purpose. And a cynical public can lose interest in political participation altogether.

The upshot is that the interests the Court has long described as preventing "corruption" or the "appearance of corruption" are more than ordinary factors to be weighed against the constitutional right to political speech. Rather, they are interests rooted in the First Amendment itself. They are rooted in the constitutional effort to create a democracy responsive to the people — a government where laws reflect the very thoughts, views, ideas, and sentiments, the expression of which the First Amendment protects.

Since the kinds of corruption that can destroy the link between public opinion and governmental action extend well beyond those the plurality describes, the plurality's notion of corruption is flatly inconsistent with the basic constitutional rationale I have just described. Thus, it should surprise no one that this Court's case law (*Citizens United* excepted) insists upon a considerably broader definition.

III

The plurality invalidates the aggregate contribution limits for a second reason. It believes they are no longer needed to prevent contributors from circumventing federal limits on direct contributions to individuals, political parties, and political action committees.

The plurality is wrong. Here, as in *Buckley*, in the absence of limits on aggregate political contributions, donors can and likely will find ways to channel millions of dollars to parties and to individual candidates, producing precisely the kind of "corruption" or "appearance of corruption" that previously led the Court to hold aggregate limits constitutional. Those opportunities for circumvention will also produce the type of corruption that concerns the plurality today. The methods for using today's opinion to evade the law's individual contribution limits are complex, but they are well known, or will become well known, to party fundraisers.

IV

The plurality concludes that even if circumvention were a threat, the aggregate limits are "poorly tailored" to address it. The plurality, however, does not show, or try to show, that these hypothetical alternatives could effectively replace aggregate contribution limits. Indeed, it does not even "opine on the validity of any particular proposal," — presumably because these proposals themselves could be subject to constitutional challenges. For the most part, the alternatives the plurality mentions were similarly available at the time of *Buckley*. Their hypothetical presence did not prevent the Court from upholding aggregate limits in 1976. How can their continued hypothetical presence lead the plurality now to conclude that aggregate limits are "poorly tailored" How can their continued hypothetical presence lead the Court to overrule *Buckley* now?

In sum, the explanation of why aggregate limits are needed is complicated, as is the explanation of why other methods will not work. But the conclusion is simple: There is no "substantial mismatch" between Congress' legitimate objective and the "means selected to achieve it." The Court, as in *Buckley*, should hold that aggregate contribution limits are constitutional.

V

The District Court in this case, holding that *Buckley* foreclosed McCutcheon's constitutional challenge to the aggregate limits, granted the Government's motion to dismiss the complaint prior to a full evidentiary hearing. If the plurality now believes the District Court was wrong, then why does it not return the case for the further evidentiary development which has not yet taken place?

In the past, when evaluating the constitutionality of campaign finance restrictions, we have typically relied upon an evidentiary record amassed below to determine whether the law served a compelling governmental objective. If we are to overturn an act of Congress here, we should do so on the basis of a similar record.

Determining whether anticorruption objectives justify a particular set of contribution limits requires answering empirically based questions, and applying significant discretion and judgment. To what extent will unrestricted giving lead to corruption or its appearance? What forms will any such corruption take? To what extent will a lack of regulation undermine public confidence in the democratic system? To what extent can regulation restore it?

These kinds of questions, while not easily answered, are questions that Congress is far better suited to resolve than are judges. Thus, while court review of contribution limits has been and should be "rigorous," we have also recognized that "deference to legislative choice is warranted." And that deference has taken account of facts and circumstances set forth in an evidentiary record.

For another thing, a comparison of the plurality's opinion with this dissent reveals important differences of opinion on fact-related matters. We disagree, for example, on the possibilities for circumvention of the base limits in the absence of aggregate limits. We disagree about how effectively the plurality's "alternatives" could prevent evasion. An evidentiary proceeding would permit the parties to explore these matters, and it would permit the courts to reach a more accurate judgment. The plurality rationalizes its haste to forgo an evidentiary record by noting that "the parties have treated the question as a purely legal one." But without a doubt, the legal question—whether the aggregate limits are closely drawn to further a compelling governmental interest—turns on factual questions about whether corruption, in the absence of such limits, is a realistic threat to our democracy. The plurality itself spends pages citing figures about campaign spending to defend its "legal" conclusion. The problem with such reasoning is that this Court's expertise does not lie in marshaling facts in the primary instance. That is why in the past, when answering similar questions about the constitutionality of restrictions on campaign contributions, we have relied on an extensive evidentiary record produced below to inform our decision.

Without further development of the record, however, I fail to see how the plurality can now find grounds for overturning *Buckley*. The result, as I said at the outset, is a decision that substitutes judges' understandings of how the political process works for the understanding of Congress; that fails to recognize the difference between influence resting upon public opinion and influence bought by money alone; that overturns key precedent; that creates huge loopholes in the law; and that undermines, perhaps devastates, what remains of campaign finance reform.

D. What Places Are Available for Speech?

1. Government Properties and Speech

c. Public Forums

ii. Time, Place, and Manner Restrictions (casebook, p. 1553)

In *Hill v. Colorado* (casebook, p. 1554), the Supreme Court upheld a state law that created buffer zones around health care facilities. The majority and the dissent sharply disagreed as to whether the law was content neutral. In *McCullen v. Coakley*, the Court considered a different buffer zone and distinguished *Hill v. Colorado*. Although the Court was unanimous in striking down the law, there still sharp disagreement among the justices as to whether the law was content neutral.

McCULLEN v. COAKLEY
134 S. Ct. 2518 (2014)

Chief Justice ROBERTS delivered the opinion of the Court.

A Massachusetts statute makes it a crime to knowingly stand on a "public way or sidewalk" within 35 feet of an entrance or driveway to any place, other than a hospital, where abortions are performed. Petitioners are individuals who approach and talk to women outside such facilities, attempting to dissuade them from having abortions. The statute prevents petitioners from doing so near the facilities' entrances. The question presented is whether the statute violates the First Amendment.

I

In 2000, the Massachusetts Legislature enacted the Massachusetts Reproductive Health Care Facilities Act. The law was designed to address clashes between abortion opponents and advocates of abortion rights that were occurring outside clinics where abortions were performed. The Act established a defined area with an 18-foot radius around the entrances and driveways of such facilities. Anyone could enter that area, but once within it, no one (other than certain exempt individuals) could knowingly approach within six feet of another person—unless that person consented—"for the purpose of passing a leaflet or handbill to, displaying a sign to, or engaging in oral protest, education, or counseling with such other person." A separate provision subjected to criminal punishment anyone who "knowingly obstructs, detains, hinders, impedes or blocks another person's entry to or exit from a reproductive health care facility." The statute was modeled on a similar Colorado law that this Court had upheld in *Hill v. Colorado* (2000).

By 2007, some Massachusetts legislators and law enforcement officials had come to regard the 2000 statute as inadequate. At legislative hearings, multiple witnesses recounted apparent violations of the law. Massachusetts Attorney General Martha Coakley, for example, testified that protestors violated the statute "on a routine basis." To illustrate this claim, she played a video depicting protestors approaching patients and clinic staff within the buffer zones, ostensibly without the latter individuals' consent. Clinic employees and volunteers also testified that protestors congregated near the doors and in the driveways of the clinics, with the result that prospective patients occasionally retreated from the clinics rather than try to make their way to the clinic entrances or parking lots.

To address these concerns, the Massachusetts Legislature amended the statute in 2007, replacing the six-foot no-approach zones (within the 18-foot area) with a 35-foot fixed buffer zone from which individuals are categorically excluded. The statute now provides:

> No person shall knowingly enter or remain on a public way or sidewalk adjacent to a reproductive health care facility within a radius of 35 feet of any portion of an entrance, exit or driveway of a reproductive health care facility or within the area within a rectangle created by extending the outside boundaries of any entrance, exit or driveway of a reproductive health care facility in straight lines to the point where such lines intersect the sideline of the street in front of such entrance, exit or driveway

A "reproductive health care facility," in turn, is defined as "a place, other than within or upon the grounds of a hospital, where abortions are offered or performed." The 35-foot buffer zone applies only "during a facility's business hours," and the area must be "clearly marked and posted." In practice, facilities typically mark the zones with painted arcs and posted signs on adjacent sidewalks and streets.

The Act exempts four classes of individuals: (1) "persons entering or leaving such facility"; (2) "employees or agents of such facility acting within the scope of their employment"; (3) "law enforcement, ambulance, firefighting, construction, utilities, public works and other municipal agents acting within the scope of their employment"; and (4) "persons using the public sidewalk or street right-of-way adjacent to such facility solely for the purpose of reaching a destination other than such facility."

Some of the individuals who stand outside Massachusetts abortion clinics are fairly described as protestors, who express their moral or religious opposition to abortion through signs and chants or, in some cases, more aggressive methods such as face-to-face confrontation. Petitioners take a different tack. They attempt to engage women approaching the clinics in what they call "sidewalk counseling," which involves offering information about alternatives to abortion and help pursuing those options. In unrefuted testimony, petitioners say they have collectively persuaded hundreds of women to forgo abortions. The buffer zones have displaced petitioners from their previous positions outside the clinics.

II

By its very terms, the Massachusetts Act regulates access to "public way[s]" and "sidewalk[s]." Such areas occupy a "special position in terms of First Amendment protection" because of their historic role as sites for discussion and debate. These places—which we have labeled "traditional public fora"—"have immemorially been held in trust for the use of the public and, time out of mind, have been used for purposes of assembly, communicating thoughts between citizens, and discussing public questions."

It is no accident that public streets and sidewalks have developed as venues for the exchange of ideas. Even today, they remain one of the few places where a speaker can be confident that he is not simply preaching to the choir. With respect to other means of communication, an individual confronted with an uncomfortable message can always turn the page, change the channel, or leave the Web site. Not so on public streets and sidewalks. There, a listener often encounters speech he might otherwise tune out. In light of the First Amendment's purpose "to preserve an uninhibited marketplace of ideas in which truth will ultimately prevail," this aspect of traditional public fora is a virtue, not a vice.

In short, traditional public fora are areas that have historically been open to the public for speech activities. Thus, even though the Act says nothing about speech on its face, there is no doubt—and respondents do not dispute—that it restricts access to traditional public fora and is therefore subject to First Amendment scrutiny.

Consistent with the traditionally open character of public streets and sidewalks, we have held that the government's ability to restrict speech in such locations is "very limited." In particular, the guiding First

Amendment principle that the "government has no power to restrict expression because of its message, its ideas, its subject matter, or its content" applies with full force in a traditional public forum. As a general rule, in such a forum the government may not "selectively . . . shield the public from some kinds of speech on the ground that they are more offensive than others."

We have, however, afforded the government somewhat wider leeway to regulate features of speech unrelated to its content. "[E]ven in a public forum the government may impose reasonable restrictions on the time, place, or manner of protected speech, provided the restrictions are justified without reference to the content of the regulated speech, that they are narrowly tailored to serve a significant governmental interest, and that they leave open ample alternative channels for communication of the information."

While the parties agree that this test supplies the proper framework for assessing the constitutionality of the Massachusetts Act, they disagree about whether the Act satisfies the test's three requirements.

III

Petitioners contend that the Act is not content neutral for two independent reasons: First, they argue that it discriminates against abortion-related speech because it establishes buffer zones only at clinics that perform abortions. Second, petitioners contend that the Act, by exempting clinic employees and agents, favors one viewpoint about abortion over the other. If either of these arguments is correct, then the Act must satisfy strict scrutiny — that is, it must be the least restrictive means of achieving a compelling state interest.

A

The Act applies only at a "reproductive health care facility," defined as "a place, other than within or upon the grounds of a hospital, where abortions are offered or performed." Given this definition, petitioners argue, "virtually all speech affected by the Act is speech concerning abortion," thus rendering the Act content based.

We disagree. To begin, the Act does not draw content-based distinctions on its face. The Act would be content based if it required "enforcement authorities" to "examine the content of the message that is conveyed to determine whether" a violation has occurred. But it does not. Whether petitioners violate the Act "depends" not "on what they say," but simply on where they say it. Indeed, petitioners can violate the Act merely by standing in a buffer zone, without displaying a sign or uttering a word.

It is true, of course, that by limiting the buffer zones to abortion clinics, the Act has the "inevitable effect" of restricting abortion-related speech more than speech on other subjects. But a facially neutral law does not become content based simply because it may disproportionately affect speech on certain topics. On the contrary, "[a] regulation that serves purposes unrelated to the content of expression is deemed neutral, even if it has an incidental effect on some speakers or messages but not others." The question in such a case is whether the law is "justified without reference to the content of the regulated speech."

The Massachusetts Act is. Its stated purpose is to "increase forthwith public safety at reproductive health care facilities." Respondents have articulated similar purposes before this Court — namely, "public safety, patient access to healthcare, and the unobstructed use of public sidewalks and roadways." We have previously deemed the foregoing concerns to be content neutral.

B

Petitioners also argue that the Act is content based because it exempts four classes of individuals. This exemption, petitioners say, favors one side in the abortion debate and thus constitutes viewpoint discrimination-an "egregious form of content discrimination," In particular, petitioners argue that the exemption allows clinic employees and agents — including the volunteers who "escort" patients arriving at the Boston clinic — to speak inside the buffer zones.

It is of course true that "an exemption from an otherwise permissible regulation of speech may represent a governmental attempt to give one side of a debatable public question an advantage in expressing its views to the people." At least on the record before us, however, the statutory exemption for clinic employees and agents acting within the scope of their employment does not appear to be such an attempt.

There is nothing inherently suspect about providing some kind of exemption to allow individuals who work at the clinics to enter or remain within the buffer zones. In particular, the exemption cannot be regarded as simply a carve-out for the clinic escorts; it also covers employees such as the maintenance worker shoveling a snowy sidewalk or the security guard patrolling a clinic entrance. Given the need for an exemption for clinic employees, the "scope of their employment" qualification simply ensures that the exemption is limited to its purpose of allowing the employees to do their jobs.

It would be a very different question if it turned out that a clinic authorized escorts to speak about abortion inside the buffer zones. In that case, the escorts would not seem to be violating the Act because the speech would be within the scope of their employment. The Act's exemption for clinic employees would then facilitate speech on only one side of the abortion debate—a clear form of viewpoint discrimination that would support an as-applied challenge to the buffer zone at that clinic. But the record before us contains insufficient evidence to show that the exemption operates in this way at any of the clinics, perhaps because the clinics do not want to doom the Act by allowing their employees to speak about abortion within the buffer zones.

We thus conclude that the Act is neither content nor view point based and therefore need not be analyzed under strict scrutiny.

IV

Even though the Act is content neutral, it still must be "narrowly tailored to serve a significant governmental interest." The tailoring requirement does not simply guard against an impermissible desire to censor. The government may attempt to suppress speech not only because it disagrees with the message being expressed, but also for mere convenience. Where certain speech is associated with particular problems, silencing the speech is sometimes the path of least resistance. But by demanding a close fit between ends and means, the tailoring requirement prevents the government from too readily "sacrific[ing] speech for efficiency."

For a content-neutral time, place, or manner regulation to be narrowly tailored, it must not "burden substantially more speech than is necessary to further the government's legitimate interests." Such a regulation, unlike a content-based restriction of speech, "need not be the least restrictive or least intrusive means of" serving the government's interests. But the government still "may not regulate expression in such a manner that a substantial portion of the burden on speech does not serve to advance its goals."

A

As noted, respondents claim that the Act promotes "public safety, patient access to healthcare, and the unobstructed use of public sidewalks and roadways." Petitioners do not dispute the significance of these interests.

At the same time, the buffer zones impose serious burdens on petitioners' speech. At each of the three Planned Parenthood clinics where petitioners attempt to counsel patients, the zones carve out a significant portion of the adjacent public sidewalks, pushing petitioners well back from the clinics' entrances and driveways. The zones thereby compromise petitioners' ability to initiate the close, personal conversations that they view as essential to "sidewalk counseling."

These burdens on petitioners' speech have clearly taken their toll. Although McCullen claims that she has persuaded about 80 women not to terminate their pregnancies since the 2007 amendment, she also says that she reaches "far fewer people" than she did before the amendment. Zarrella reports an even more precipitous decline in her success rate: She estimated having about 100 successful interactions over the years before the 2007 amendment, but not a single one since.

The buffer zones have also made it substantially more difficult for petitioners to distribute literature to arriving patients. In the context of petition campaigns, we have observed that "one-on-one communication" is "the most effective, fundamental, and perhaps economical avenue of political discourse."

Respondents also emphasize that the Act does not prevent petitioners from engaging in various forms of "protest" — such as chanting slogans and displaying signs — outside the buffer zones. That misses the point. Petitioners are not protestors. They seek not merely to express their opposition to abortion, but to inform women of various alternatives and to provide help in pursuing them. Petitioners believe that they can accomplish this objective only through personal, caring, consensual conversations. And for good reason: It is easier to ignore a strained voice or a waving hand than a direct greeting or an outstretched arm. If all that the women can see and hear are vociferous opponents of abortion, then the buffer zones have effectively stifled petitioners' message.

B

The buffer zones burden substantially more speech than necessary to achieve the Commonwealth's asserted interests. At the outset, we note that the Act is truly exceptional: Respondents and their *amici* identify no other State with a law that creates fixed buffer zones around abortion clinics. That of course does not mean that the law is invalid. It does, however, raise concern that the Commonwealth has too readily forgone options that could serve its interests just as well, without substantially burdening the kind of speech in which petitioners wish to engage.

That is the case here. The Commonwealth's interests include ensuring public safety outside abortion clinics, preventing harassment and intimidation of patients and clinic staff, and combating deliberate obstruction of clinic entrances. The Act itself contains a separate provision, subsection (e)—unchallenged by petitioners—that prohibits much of this conduct. That provision subjects to criminal punishment "[a]ny person who knowingly obstructs, detains, hinders, impedes or blocks another person's entry to or exit from a reproductive health care facility." If Massachusetts determines that broader prohibitions along the same lines are necessary, it could enact legislation similar to the federal Freedom of Access to Clinic Entrances Act of 1994 (FACE Act), which subjects to both criminal and civil penalties anyone who "by force or threat of force or by physical obstruction, intentionally injures, intimidates or interferes with or attempts to injure, intimidate or interfere with any person because that person is or has been, or in order to intimidate such person or any other person or any class of persons from, obtaining or providing reproductive health services." Some dozen other States have done so. If the Commonwealth is particularly concerned about harassment, it could also consider an ordinance such as the one adopted in New York City that not only prohibits obstructing access to a clinic, but also makes it a crime "to follow and harass another person within 15 feet of the premises of a reproductive health care facility."

All of the foregoing measures are, of course, in addition to available generic criminal statutes forbidding assault, breach of the peace, trespass, vandalism, and the like.

The point is not that Massachusetts must enact all or even any of the proposed measures discussed above. The point is instead that the Commonwealth has available to it a variety of approaches that appear capable of serving its interests, without excluding individuals from areas historically open for speech and debate.

Respondents have but one reply: "We have tried other approaches, but they do not work." Respondents emphasize the history in Massachusetts of obstruction at abortion clinics, and the Commonwealth's allegedly failed attempts to combat such obstruction with injunctions and individual prosecutions.

We cannot accept that contention. Although respondents claim that Massachusetts "tried other laws already on the books," they identify not a single prosecution brought under those laws within at least the last 17 years. And while they also claim that the Commonwealth "tried injunctions," the last injunctions they cite date to the 1990s. In short, the Commonwealth has not shown that it seriously undertook to address the problem with less intrusive tools readily available to it. Nor has it shown that it considered different methods that other jurisdictions have found effective.

Given the vital First Amendment interests at stake, it is not enough for Massachusetts simply to say that other approaches have not worked.

Petitioners wish to converse with their fellow citizens about an important subject on the public streets and sidewalks-sites that have hosted discussions about the issues of the day throughout history. Respondents assert undeniably significant interests in maintaining public safety on those same streets and sidewalks, as well as in preserving access to adjacent healthcare facilities. But here the Commonwealth has pursued those interests by the extreme step of closing a substantial portion of a traditional public forum to all speakers. It has done so without seriously addressing the problem through alternatives that leave the forum open for its time-honored purposes. The Commonwealth may not do that consistent with the First Amendment.

Justice SCALIA, with whom Justice KENNEDY and Justice THOMAS join, concurring in the judgment.

Today's opinion carries forward this Court's practice of giving abortion-rights advocates a pass when it comes to suppressing the free-speech rights of their opponents. There is an entirely separate, abridged edition of the First Amendment applicable to speech against abortion. See, *e.g.*, *Hill v. Colorado* (2000); *Madsen v. Women's Health Center, Inc.* 1994).

The second half of the Court's analysis today, invalidating the law at issue because of inadequate "tailoring," is certainly attractive to those of us who oppose an abortion-speech edition of the First Amendment. But think again. This is an opinion that has Something for Everyone, and the more significant portion continues the onward march of abortion-speech-only jurisprudence. That is the first half of the Court's analysis, which concludes that a statute of this sort is not content based and hence not subject to so-called strict scrutiny. The Court reaches out to decide that question unnecessarily — or at least unnecessarily insofar as legal analysis is concerned.

I disagree with the Court's dicta (Part III) and hence see no reason to opine on its holding (Part IV).

I. THE COURT'S CONTENT-NEUTRALITY DISCUSSION IS UNNECESSARY

The gratuitous portion of today's opinion is Part III, which concludes — in seven pages of the purest dicta — that subsection (b) of the Massachusetts Reproductive Health Care Facilities Act is not specifically directed at speech opposing (or even concerning) abortion and hence need not meet the strict-scrutiny standard applicable to content-based speech regulations. Inasmuch as Part IV holds that the Act is unconstitutional because it does not survive the lesser level of scrutiny associated with content-neutral "time, place, and manner" regulations, there is no principled reason for the majority to decide whether the statute is subject to strict scrutiny.

II. THE STATUTE IS CONTENT BASED AND FAILS STRICT SCRUTINY

Having eagerly volunteered to take on the level-of-scrutiny question, the Court provides the wrong answer. Petitioners argue for two reasons that subsection (b) articulates a content-based speech restriction—and that we must therefore evaluate it through the lens of strict scrutiny.

A.   APPLICATION TO ABORTION CLINICS ONLY

First, petitioners maintain that the Act targets abortion-related—for practical purposes, abortion-opposing—speech because it applies outside abortion clinics only (rather than outside other buildings as well).

It blinks reality to say, as the majority does, that a blanket prohibition on the use of streets and sidewalks where speech on only one politically controversial topic is likely to occur—and where that speech can most effectively be communicated—is not content based. Would the Court exempt from strict scrutiny a law banning access to the streets and sidewalks surrounding the site of the Republican National Convention? Or those used annually to commemorate the 1965 Selma-to-Montgomery civil rights marches? Or those outside the Internal Revenue Service? Surely not.

The majority says, correctly enough, that a facially neutral speech restriction escapes strict scrutiny, even when it "may disproportionately affect speech on certain topics," so long as it is "justified without reference to the content of the regulated speech." But the cases in which the Court has previously found that standard satisfied—in particular, both of which the majority cites—are a far cry from what confronts us here.

Renton upheld a zoning ordinance prohibiting adult motion-picture theaters within 1,000 feet of residential neighborhoods, churches, parks, and schools. The ordinance was content neutral, the Court held, because its purpose was not to suppress pornographic speech *qua* speech but, rather, to mitigate the "secondary effects" of adult theaters—including by "prevent[ing] crime, protect[ing] the city's retail trade, [and] maintain[ing] property values." *Ward*, in turn, involved a New York City regulation requiring the use of the city's own sound equipment and technician for events at a bandshell in Central Park. The Court held the regulation content neutral because its "principal justification [was] the city's desire to control noise levels," a justification that " 'ha[d] nothing to do with [the] content' " of respondent's rock concerts or of music more generally. The regulation "ha[d] no material impact on any performer's ability to exercise complete artistic control over sound quality."

Compare these cases' reasons for concluding that the regulations in question were "justified without reference to the content of the regulated speech" with the feeble reasons for the majority's adoption of that conclusion in the present case. The majority points only to the statute's stated purpose of increasing "public safety" at abortion clinics, and to the additional aims articulated by respondents before this Court — namely, protecting "patient access to healthcare . . . and the unobstructed use of public sidewalks and roadways." Really? Does a statute become "justified without reference to the content of the regulated speech" simply because the statute itself and those defending it in court *say* that it is? Every objective indication shows that the provision's primary purpose is to restrict speech that opposes abortion.

I begin, as suggested above, with the fact that the Act burdens only the public spaces outside abortion clinics. One might have expected the majority to defend the statute's peculiar targeting by arguing that those locations regularly face the safety and access problems that it says the Act was designed to solve. But the majority does not make that argument because it would be untrue. As the Court belatedly discovers in Part IV of its opinion, although the statute applies to all abortion clinics in Massachusetts, only one is known to have been beset by the problems that the statute supposedly addresses. The Court uses this striking fact (a smoking gun, so to speak) as a basis for concluding that the law is insufficiently "tailored" to safety and access concerns (Part IV) rather than as a basis for concluding that it is not *directed* to those concerns at all, but to the suppression of antiabortion speech. That is rather like invoking the eight missed human targets of a shooter who has killed one victim to prove, not that he is guilty of attempted mass murder, but that *he has bad aim*.

Whether the statute "restrict[s] more speech than necessary" in light of the problems that it allegedly addresses, is, to be sure, relevant to the tailoring component of the First Amendment analysis (the shooter doubtless did have bad aim), but it is also relevant — powerfully relevant — to whether the law is really directed to safety and access concerns or rather to the suppression of a particular type of speech. Showing that a law that suppresses speech on a specific subject is so far-reaching that it applies even when the asserted non-speech-related problems are not present is persuasive evidence that the law is content based. In its zeal to treat abortion-related speech as a special category, the majority distorts not only the First Amendment but also the ordinary logic of probative inferences.

B. EXEMPTION FOR ABORTION-CLINIC EMPLOYEES OR AGENTS

Petitioners contend that the Act targets speech opposing abortion (and thus constitutes a presumptively invalid viewpoint-discriminatory restriction) for another reason as well: It exempts "employees or agents" of an abortion clinic "acting within the scope of their employment."

It goes without saying that "[g]ranting waivers to favored speakers (or . . . denying them to disfavored speakers) would of course be unconstitutional." Is there any serious doubt that *abortion-clinic employees or agents* "acting within the scope of their employment" near clinic entrances may—indeed, often will—speak in favor of abortion ("You are doing the right thing")? Or speak in opposition to the message of abortion opponents—saying, for example, that "this is a safe facility" to rebut the statement that it is not? The Court's contrary assumption is simply incredible.

Going from bad to worse, the majority's opinion contends that "the record before us contains insufficient evidence to show" that abortion-facility escorts have actually spoken in favor of abortion (or, presumably, hindered antiabortion speech) while acting within the scope of their employment. Here is a brave new First Amendment test: Speech restrictions favoring one viewpoint over another are not content based unless it can be shown that the favored viewpoint has actually been expressed. A city ordinance closing a park adjoining the Republican National Convention to all speakers except those whose remarks have been approved by the Republican National Committee is thus not subject to strict scrutiny unless it can be shown that someone has given committee-endorsed remarks. For this Court to suggest such a test is astonishing.

C. CONCLUSION

In sum, the Act should be reviewed under the strict-scrutiny standard applicable to content-based legislation. That standard requires that a regulation represent "the least restrictive means" of furthering "a compelling Government interest."

The obvious purpose of the challenged portion of the Massachusetts Reproductive Health Care Facilities Act is to "protect" prospective clients of abortion clinics from having to hear abortion-opposing speech on public streets and sidewalks. The provision is thus unconstitutional root and branch and cannot be saved, as the majority suggests, by limiting its application to the single facility that has experienced the safety and access problems to which it is quite obviously not addressed. I concur only in the judgment that the statute is unconstitutional under the First Amendment.

Justice ALITO, concurring in the judgment.

I agree that the Massachusetts statute at issue in this case violates the First Amendment. As the Court recognizes, if the Massachusetts law discriminates on the basis of viewpoint, it is unconstitutional, and I believe the law clearly discriminates on this ground.

The Massachusetts statute generally prohibits any person from entering a buffer zone around an abortion clinic during the clinic's business hours, but the law contains an exemption for "employees or agents of such facility acting within the scope of their employment. Thus, during business hours, individuals who wish to counsel against abortion or to criticize the particular clinic may not do so within the buffer zone. If they engage in such conduct, they commit a crime. By contrast, employees and agents of the clinic may enter the zone and engage in any conduct that falls within the scope of their employment. A clinic may direct or authorize an employee or agent, while within the zone, to express favorable views about abortion or the clinic, and if the employee exercises that authority, the employee's conduct is perfectly lawful. In short, petitioners and other critics of a clinic are silenced, while the clinic may authorize its employees to express speech in support of the clinic and its work.

Consider this entirely realistic situation. A woman enters a buffer zone and heads haltingly toward the entrance. A sidewalk counselor, such as petitioners, enters the buffer zone, approaches the woman and says, "If you have doubts about an abortion, let me try to answer any questions you may have. The clinic will not give you good information." At the same time, a clinic employee, as instructed by the management, approaches the same woman and says, "Come inside and we will give you honest answers to all your questions." The sidewalk counselor and the clinic employee expressed opposing viewpoints, but only the first violated the statute.

Or suppose that the issue is not abortion but the safety of a particular facility. Suppose that there was a recent report of a botched abortion at the clinic. A nonemployee may not enter the buffer zone to warn about the clinic's health record, but an employee may enter and tell prospective clients that the clinic is safe.

It is clear on the face of the Massachusetts law that it discriminates based on viewpoint. Speech in favor of the clinic and its work by employees and agents is permitted; speech criticizing the clinic and its work is a crime. This is blatant viewpoint discrimination.

D.   What Places Are Available for Speech?

3.   Speech in Authoritarian Environments

d.   The Speech Rights of Government Employees (casebook, p. 1609)

In *Garcetti v. Ceballos* (casebook, p. 1610), the Court held that there is no First Amendment protection for the speech of government employees on the job in the scope of their duties. In *Lane v. Franks*, 134 S. Ct. 2369 (2014), the Court said that *Garcetti v. Ceballos* does not apply to a situation where a government employee testifies truthfully pursuant to a subpoena.

Edward Lane worked for the community college system in Alabama. He conducted an audit of the program's expenses and discovered that Suzanne Schmitz, an Alabama State Representative on his payroll, had not been reporting for work. Lane eventually terminated Schmitz's employment. Shortly thereafter, federal authorities indicted Schmitz on charges of mail fraud and theft concerning a program receiving federal funds.

Lane testified before the grand jury and twice at trial under subpoena regarding the events that led to his terminating Schmitz. Schmitz was convicted and sentenced to 30 months in prison. Steve Franks then terminated Lane. Lane sued claiming a violation of his First Amendment rights.

Justice Sotomayor, writing for a unanimous Court, found that Lane's speech is protected by the First Amendment. The Court said that it is citizen speech on a matter of public concern, as opposed to the speech of a government employee on the job. Sworn testimony in judicial proceedings is a quintessential example of citizen speech. The Court said that under *Garcetti*, the speech must be within the duties of the employee and not just concern them. The Court said that the speech involved a matter of public concern and on balance protecting truthful testimony is desirable.

E.   *Freedom of Association*

2.   Compelled Association (casebook, p. 1622)

In *Abood v. Detroit Board of Education* (1977) (casebook, p. 1622), the Supreme Court held that no one can be forced to join a public employee union. But non-members can be required to pay for their share of the collective bargaining activities of the union because they benefit from them. *Abood* said, though, that non-union members do not have to pay for the political activities of the union.

In *Harris v. Quinn*, 134 S. Ct. 2618 (2014), a majority of the Court questioned *Abood* and refused to do what the majority considered extending it. Illinois law allows Medicaid recipients who would normally need institutional care to hire a "personal assistant" to provide homecare services. Customers control most aspects of the employment relationship, including the hiring, firing, training, supervising, and disciplining of personal assistants; they also define the personal assistant's duties by proposing a "Service Plan."

Other than compensating personal assistants, the State's involvement in employment matters is minimal. But state law deems the personal assistants to be state employees so that they can join a labor union and engage in collective bargaining. Personal assistants who did not want to join the union or pay the agency fees, their share of the collective bargaining costs of the union, brought a challenge saying that it violated their First Amendment rights to compel them to do so.

The Court in a 5-4 decision held that it violated the First Amendment rights of personal assistants to compel them to pay for the collective bargaining activities of the union. Justice Alito, writing for the Court, said that *Abood* is "questionable." The concern in *Abood* was that non-union members could be "free riders," benefiting from the union's collective bargaining activities, but not paying for their share of the costs of them. The Court said, though, that "preventing nonmembers from free-riding on the union's efforts" is a rationale "generally insufficient to overcome First Amendment objections." The Court said that *Abood* is an anomaly and should not be extended.

The Court said that personal assistants are different from "full-fledged" public employees. Unlike full-fledged public employees, personal assistants are almost entirely answerable to the customers and not to the State, do not enjoy most of the rights and benefits that inure to state employees, and are not indemnified by the State for claims against them arising from actions taken during the course of their employment.

The Court said that since *Abood* did not apply, traditional First Amendment principles were to be applied. The Court found that the government failed to meet strict scrutiny in requiring the personal assistants to pay agency fees, their share of the collective bargaining activities of the union.

Justice Kagan wrote for the four dissenters and defended *Abood* and its application to this situation. She stressed the enormous reliance on *Abood* in the public sector workplace for over 45 years. She defended the need to require non-union members to pay for their fair share of the costs of collective bargaining. She rejected a distinction among types of public employees.

Chapter 10

First Amendment: Religion

B. The Free Exercise Clause

2. The Current Test

c. Cases Rejecting Exemptions Based on the Free Exercise Clause

Statutory Protection of Religious Freedom (casebook, p. 1701)

The Religious Freedom Restoration Act (RFRA) (described on p. 1701) was intended to restore religious freedom to what it had been before *Employment Division v. Smith*. In *Burwell v. Hobby Lobby*, the Court considered a challenge by secular, for-profit, closely held corporations to aspects of the contraceptive mandate under regulations adopted pursuant to the Patient Protection and Affordable Care Act. The Court's decision, entirely in the context of RFRA, considered such questions as to whether secular corporations can exercise religious beliefs, what is a substantial burdening of religion, and what is sufficiently narrowly tailored to meet the strict scrutiny imposed by RFRA.

BURWELL v. HOBBY LOBBY
134 S. Ct. ___ (2014)

Justice ALITO delivered the opinion of the Court.

We must decide in these cases whether the Religious Freedom Restoration Act of 1993 (RFRA), permits the United States Department of Health and Human Services (HHS) to demand that three closely held corporations provide health-insurance coverage for methods of contraception that violate the sincerely held religious beliefs of the companies' owners. We hold that the regulations that impose this obligation violate

RFRA, which prohibits the Federal Government from taking any action that substantially burdens the exercise of religion unless that action constitutes the least restrictive means of serving a compelling government interest.

In holding that the HHS mandate is unlawful, we reject HHS's argument that the owners of the companies forfeited all RFRA protection when they decided to organize their businesses as corporations rather than sole proprietorships or general partnerships. The plain terms of RFRA make it perfectly clear that Congress did not discriminate in this way against men and women who wish to run their businesses as for-profit corporations in the manner required by their religious beliefs.

Since RFRA applies in these cases, we must decide whether the challenged HHS regulations substantially burden the exercise of religion, and we hold that they do. The owners of the businesses have religious objections to abortion, and according to their religious beliefs the four contraceptive methods at issue are abortifacients. If the owners comply with the HHS mandate, they believe they will be facilitating abortions, and if they do not comply, they will pay a very heavy price — as much as $1.3 million per day, or about $475 million per year, in the case of one of the companies. If these consequences do not amount to a substantial burden, it is hard to see what would.

Under RFRA, a Government action that imposes a substantial burden on religious exercise must serve a compelling government interest, and we assume that the HHS regulations satisfy this requirement. But in order for the HHS mandate to be sustained, it must also constitute the least restrictive means of serving that interest, and the mandate plainly fails that test. There are other ways in which Congress or HHS could equally ensure that every woman has cost-free access to the particular contraceptives at issue here and, indeed, to all FDA-approved contraceptives.

In fact, HHS has already devised and implemented a system that seeks to respect the religious liberty of religious nonprofit corporations while ensuring that the employees of these entities have precisely the same access to all FDA-approved contraceptives as employees of companies whose owners have no religious objections to providing such coverage. The employees of these religious nonprofit corporations still have access to insurance coverage without cost sharing for all FDA-approved contraceptives; and according to HHS, this system imposes no net economic burden on the insurance companies that are required to provide or secure the coverage.

Although HHS has made this system available to religious nonprofits that have religious objections to the contraceptive mandate, HHS has provided no reason why the same system cannot be made available when the owners of for-profit corporations have similar religious objections. We therefore conclude that this system constitutes an alternative that achieves all of the Government's aims while providing greater respect for religious liberty. And under RFRA, that conclusion means that enforcement of the HHS contraceptive mandate against the objecting parties in these cases is unlawful.

As this description of our reasoning shows, our holding is very specific. We do not hold, as the principal dissent alleges, that for-profit corporations and other commercial enterprises can "opt out of any law (saving only tax laws) they judge incompatible with their sincerely held religious beliefs." Nor do we hold, as the dissent implies, that such corporations have free rein to take steps that impose "disadvantages . . . on others" or that require "the general public [to] pick up the tab." And we certainly do not hold or suggest that "RFRA demands accommodation of a for-profit corporation's religious beliefs no matter the impact that accommodation may have on . . . thousands of women employed by Hobby Lobby." The effect of the HHS-created accommodation on the women employed by Hobby Lobby and the other companies involved in these cases would be precisely zero. Under that accommodation, these women would still be entitled to all FDA-approved contraceptives without cost sharing.

I

A

Congress enacted RFRA in 1993 in order to provide very broad protection for religious liberty. RFRA's enactment came three years after this Court's decision in *Employment Div., Dept. of Human Resources of Ore. v. Smith* (1990), which largely repudiated the method of analyzing free-exercise claims that had been used in cases like *Sherbert v. Verner* (1963), and *Wisconsin v. Yoder* (1972). In determining whether challenged government actions violated the Free Exercise Clause of the First Amendment, those decisions used a balancing test that took into account whether the challenged action imposed a substantial burden on the practice of religion, and if it did, whether it was needed to serve a compelling government interest.

In *Smith*, however, the Court rejected "the balancing test set forth in *Sherbert*." The Court therefore held that, under the First Amendment, "neutral, generally applicable laws may be applied to religious practices even when not supported by a compelling governmental interest."

Congress responded to *Smith* by enacting RFRA. "[L]aws [that are] 'neutral' toward religion," Congress found, "may burden religious exercise as surely as laws intended to interfere with religious exercise." In order to ensure broad protection for religious liberty, RFRA provides that "Government shall not substantially burden a person's exercise of religion even if the burden results from a rule of general applicability." If the Government substantially burdens a person's exercise of religion, under the Act that person is entitled to an exemption from the rule unless the Government "demonstrates that application of the burden to the person — (1) is in furtherance of a compelling governmental interest; and (2) is the least restrictive means of furthering that compelling governmental interest."

B

At issue in these cases are HHS regulations promulgated under the Patient Protection and Affordable Care Act of 2010 (ACA) ACA generally requires employers with 50 or more full-time employees to offer "a group health plan or group health insurance coverage" that provides "minimum essential coverage." Any covered employer that does not provide such coverage must pay a substantial price. Specifically, if a covered employer provides group health insurance but its plan fails to comply with ACA's group-health-plan requirements, the employer may be required to pay $100 per day for each affected "individual." And if the employer decides to stop providing health insurance altogether and at least one full-time employee enrolls in a health plan and qualifies for a subsidy on one of the government-run ACA exchanges, the employer must pay $2,000 per year for each of its full-time employees.

Unless an exception applies, ACA requires an employer's group health plan or group-health-insurance coverage to furnish "preventive care and screenings" for women without "any cost sharing requirements." Congress itself, however, did not specify what types of preventive care must be covered. Instead, Congress authorized the Health Resources and Services Administration (HRSA), a component of HHS, to make that important and sensitive decision.

In August 2011, the HRSA promulgated the Women's Preventive Services Guidelines. The Guidelines provide that nonexempt employers are generally required to provide "coverage, without cost sharing" for "[a]ll Food and Drug Administration [(FDA)] approved contraceptive methods, sterilization procedures, and patient education and counseling." Although many of the required, FDA-approved methods of contraception work by preventing the fertilization of an egg, four of those methods (those specifically at issue in these cases) may have the effect of preventing an already fertilized egg from developing any further by inhibiting its attachment to the uterus.

HHS also authorized the HRSA to establish exemptions from the contraceptive mandate for "religious employers." That category encompasses "churches, their integrated auxiliaries, and conventions or associations of churches," as well as "the exclusively religious activities of any religious order." In its Guidelines, HRSA exempted these organizations from the requirement to cover contraceptive services.

In addition, HHS has effectively exempted certain religious nonprofit organizations, described under HHS regulations as "eligible organizations," from the contraceptive mandate. An "eligible organization" means a nonprofit organization that "holds itself out as a religious organization" and "opposes providing coverage for some or all of any contraceptive services required to be covered . . . on account of religious objections." To qualify for this accommodation, an employer must certify that it is such an organization. When a group-health-insurance issuer receives notice that one of its clients has invoked this provision, the issuer must then exclude contraceptive coverage from the employer's plan and provide separate payments for contraceptive services for plan participants without imposing any cost-sharing requirements on the eligible organization, its insurance plan, or its employee beneficiaries. Although this procedure requires the issuer to bear the cost of these services, HHS has determined that this obligation will not impose any net expense on issuers because its cost will be less than or equal to the cost savings resulting from the services.

In addition to these exemptions for religious organizations, ACA exempts a great many employers from most of its coverage requirements. All told, the contraceptive mandate "presently does not apply to tens of millions of people." This is attributable, in large part, to grandfathered health plans: Over one-third of the 149 million nonelderly people in America with employer-sponsored health plans were enrolled in grandfathered plans in 2013

II

A

Norman and Elizabeth Hahn and their three sons are devout members of the Mennonite Church, a Christian denomination. The Mennonite Church opposes abortion and believes that "[t]he fetus in its earliest stages . . . shares humanity with those who conceived it."

As explained in Conestoga's board-adopted "Statement on the Sanctity of Human Life," the Hahns believe that "human life begins at conception."

The Hahns have accordingly excluded from the group-health-insurance plan they offer to their employees certain contraceptive methods that they consider to be abortifacients. These include two forms of emergency contraception commonly called "morning after" pills and two types of intra-uterine devices.

B

David and Barbara Green and their three children are Christians who own and operate two family businesses. Forty-five years ago, David Green started an arts-and-crafts store that has grown into a nationwide chain called Hobby Lobby. There are now 500 Hobby Lobby stores, and the company has more than 13,000 employees. Hobby Lobby is organized as a for-profit corporation under Oklahoma law.

One of David's sons started an affiliated business, Mardel, which operates 35 Christian bookstores and employs close to 400 people. Mardel is also organized as a for-profit corporation under Oklahoma law.

Though these two businesses have expanded over the years, they remain closely held, and David, Barbara, and their children retain exclusive control of both companies. Hobby Lobby's statement of purpose commits the Greens to "[h]onoring the Lord in all [they] do by operating the company in a manner consistent with Biblical principles."

Like the Hahns, the Greens believe that life begins at conception and that it would violate their religion to facilitate access to contraceptive drugs or devices that operate after that point. They specifically object to the same four contraceptive methods as the Hahns and, like the Hahns, they have no objection to the other 16 FDA-approved methods of birth control.

III

A

RFRA prohibits the "Government [from] substantially burden[ing] *a person's* exercise of religion even if the burden results from a rule of general applicability" unless the Government "demonstrates that application of the burden to *the person* —(1) is in furtherance of a compelling governmental interest; and (2) is the least restrictive means of furthering that compelling governmental interest." The first question that we must address is whether this provision applies to regulations that govern the activities of for-profit corporations like Hobby Lobby, Conestoga, and Mardel.

HHS would put these merchants to a difficult choice: either give up the right to seek judicial protection of their religious liberty or forgo the benefits, available to their competitors, of operating as corporations. As we have seen, RFRA was designed to provide very broad protection for religious liberty. By enacting RFRA, Congress went far beyond what this Court has held is constitutionally required. Is there any reason to think that the Congress that enacted such sweeping protection put small-business owners to the choice that HHS suggests? An examination of RFRA's text, to which we turn in the next part of this opinion, reveals that Congress did no such thing.

As we will show, Congress provided protection for people like the Hahns and Greens by employing a familiar legal fiction: It included corporations within RFRA's definition of "persons." But it is important to keep in mind that the purpose of this fiction is to provide protection for human beings. For example, extending Fourth Amendment protection to corporations protects the privacy interests of employees and others associated with the company. Protecting corporations from government seizure of their property without just compensation protects all those who have a stake in the corporations' financial well-being. And protecting the free-exercise rights of corporations like Hobby Lobby, Conestoga, and Mardel protects the religious liberty of the humans who own and control those companies. Corporations, "separate and apart from" the human beings who own, run, and are employed by them, cannot do anything at all.

B

As we noted above, RFRA applies to "a person's" exercise of religion and RFRA itself does not define the term "person." We therefore look to the Dictionary Act, which we must consult "[i]n determining the meaning of any Act of Congress, unless the context indicates otherwise." Under the Dictionary Act, "the wor[d] 'person' . . . include[s] corporations, companies, associations, firms, partnerships, societies, and joint stock companies, as well as individuals." We see nothing in RFRA that suggests a congressional intent to depart from the Dictionary Act definition, and HHS makes little effort to argue otherwise.

The principal argument advanced by HHS and the principal dissent regarding RFRA protection for Hobby Lobby, Conestoga, and Mardel focuses not on the statutory term "person," but on the phrase "exercise of religion." According to HHS and the dissent, these corporations are not protected by RFRA because they cannot exercise religion. Neither HHS nor the dissent, however, provides any persuasive explanation for this conclusion.

Is it because of the corporate form? The corporate form alone cannot provide the explanation because, as we have pointed out, HHS concedes that nonprofit corporations can be protected by RFRA. The dissent suggests that nonprofit corporations are special because furthering their religious "autonomy . . . often furthers individual religious freedom as well."). But this principle applies equally to for-profit corporations: Furthering their religious freedom also "furthers individual religious freedom." In these cases, for example, allowing Hobby Lobby, Conestoga, and Mardel to assert RFRA claims protects the religious liberty of the Greens and the Hahns.

If the corporate form is not enough, what about the profit-making objective? Some lower court judges have suggested that RFRA does not protect for-profit corporations because the purpose of such corporations is simply to make money. While it is certainly true that a central objective of for-profit corporations is to make money, modern corporate law does not require for-profit corporations to pursue profit at the expense of everything else, and many do not do so. For-profit corporations, with ownership approval, support a wide variety of charitable causes, and it is not at all uncommon for such corporations to further humanitarian and other altruistic objectives.

Finally, HHS contends that Congress could not have wanted RFRA to apply to for-profit corporations because it is difficult as a practical matter to ascertain the sincere "beliefs" of a corporation. HHS goes so far as to raise the specter of "divisive, polarizing proxy battles over the religious identity of large, publicly traded corporations such as IBM or General Electric."

These cases, however, do not involve publicly traded corporations, and it seems unlikely that the sort of corporate giants to which HHS refers will often assert RFRA claims. HHS has not pointed to any example of a publicly traded corporation asserting RFRA rights, and numerous practical restraints would likely prevent that from occurring. For example, the idea that unrelated shareholders — including institutional investors with their own set of stakeholders — would agree to run a corporation under the same religious beliefs seems improbable. In any event, we have no occasion in these cases to consider RFRA's applicability to such companies. The companies in the cases before us are closely held corporations, each owned and controlled by members of a single family, and no one has disputed the sincerity of their religious beliefs.

For all these reasons, we hold that a federal regulation's restriction on the activities of a for-profit closely held corporation must comply with RFRA.

IV

Because RFRA applies in these cases, we must next ask whether the HHS contraceptive mandate "substantially burden[s]" the exercise of religion. We have little trouble concluding that it does.

As we have noted, the Hahns and Greens have a sincere religious belief that life begins at conception. They therefore object on religious grounds to providing health insurance that covers methods of birth control that, as HHS acknowledges, may result in the destruction of an embryo. By requiring the Hahns and Greens and their companies to arrange for such coverage, the HHS mandate demands that they engage in conduct that seriously violates their religious beliefs.

If the Hahns and Greens and their companies do not yield to this demand, the economic consequences will be severe. If the companies continue to offer group health plans that do not cover the contraceptives at issue, they will be taxed $100 per day for each affected individual. For Hobby Lobby, the bill could amount to $1.3 million per day or about $475 million per year; for Conestoga, the assessment could be $90,000 per day or $33 million per year; and for Mardel, it could be $40,000 per day or about $15 million per year. These sums are surely substantial.

It is true that the plaintiffs could avoid these assessments by dropping insurance coverage altogether and thus forcing their employees to obtain health insurance on one of the exchanges established under ACA. But if at least one of their full-time employees were to qualify for a subsidy on one of the government-run exchanges, this course would also entail substantial economic consequences. The companies could face penalties of $2,000 per employee each year. These penalties would amount to roughly $26 million for Hobby Lobby, $1.8 million for Conestoga, and $800,000 for Mardel.

Although these totals are high, *amici* supporting HHS have suggested that the $2,000 per-employee penalty is actually less than the average cost of providing health insurance, and therefore, they claim, the companies could readily eliminate any substantial burden by forcing their employees to obtain insurance in the government exchanges. We do not generally entertain arguments that were not raised below and are not advanced in this Court by any party, and there are strong reasons to adhere to that practice in these cases. HHS, which presumably could have compiled the relevant statistics, has never made this argument—not in its voluminous briefing or at oral argument in this Court nor, to our knowledge, in any of the numerous cases in which the issue now before us has been litigated around the country. As things now stand, we do not even know what the

Government's position might be with respect to these *amici's* intensely empirical argument. For this same reason, the plaintiffs have never had an opportunity to respond to this novel claim that—contrary to their long-standing practice and that of most large employers—they would be better off discarding their employer insurance plans altogether.

Even if we were to reach this argument, we would find it unpersuasive. As an initial matter, it entirely ignores the fact that the Hahns and Greens and their companies have religious reasons for providing health-insurance coverage for their employees. Putting aside the religious dimension of the decision to provide insurance, moreover, it is far from clear that the net cost to the companies of providing insurance is more than the cost of dropping their insurance plans and paying the ACA penalty.

In taking the position that the HHS mandate does not impose a substantial burden on the exercise of religion, HHS's main argument (echoed by the principal dissent) is basically that the connection between what the objecting parties must do (provide health-insurance coverage for four methods of contraception that may operate after the fertilization of an egg) and the end that they find to be morally wrong (destruction of an embryo) is simply too attenuated. HHS and the dissent note that providing the coverage would not itself result in the destruction of an embryo; that would occur only if an employee chose to take advantage of the coverage and to use one of the four methods at issue.

This argument dodges the question that RFRA presents (whether the HHS mandate imposes a substantial burden on the ability of the objecting parties to conduct business in accordance with *their religious beliefs*) and instead addresses a very different question that the federal courts have no business addressing (whether the religious belief asserted in a RFRA case is reasonable). The Hahns and Greens believe that providing the coverage demanded by the HHS regulations is connected to the destruction of an embryo in a way that is sufficient to make it immoral for them to provide the coverage. This belief implicates a difficult and important question of religion and moral philosophy, namely, the circumstances under which it is wrong for a person to perform an act that is innocent in itself but that has the effect of enabling or facilitating the commission of an immoral act by another. Arrogating the authority to provide a binding national answer to this religious and philosophical question, HHS and the principal dissent in effect tell the plaintiffs that their beliefs are flawed. For good reason, we have repeatedly refused to take such a step.

[I]n these cases, the Hahns and Greens and their companies sincerely believe that providing the insurance coverage demanded by the HHS regulations lies on the forbidden side of the line, and it is not for us to say that their religious beliefs are mistaken or insubstantial. Instead, our "narrow function . . . in this context is to determine" whether the line drawn reflects "an honest conviction," and there is no dispute that it does.

V

Since the HHS contraceptive mandate imposes a substantial burden on the exercise of religion, we must move on and decide whether HHS has shown that the mandate both "(1) is in furtherance of a compelling governmental interest; and (2) is the least restrictive means of furthering that compelling governmental interest."

A

HHS asserts that the contraceptive mandate serves a variety of important interests, but many of these are couched in very broad terms, such as promoting "public health" and "gender equality." RFRA, however, contemplates a "more focused" inquiry: It "requires the Government to demonstrate that the compelling interest test is satisfied through application of the challenged law 'to the person' — the particular claimant whose sincere exercise of religion is being substantially burdened." This requires us to "loo[k] beyond broadly formulated interests" and to "scrutiniz[e] the asserted harm of granting specific exemptions to particular religious claimants" — in other words, to look to the marginal interest in enforcing the contraceptive mandate in these cases.

In addition to asserting these very broadly framed interests, HHS maintains that the mandate serves a compelling interest in ensuring that all women have access to all FDA-approved contraceptives without cost sharing. Under our cases, women (and men) have a constitutional right to obtain contraceptives, see *Griswold v. Connecticut* (1965), and HHS tells us that "[s]tudies have demonstrated that even moderate copayments for preventive services can deter patients from receiving those services."

We find it unnecessary to adjudicate this issue. We will assume that the interest in guaranteeing cost-free access to the four challenged contraceptive methods is compelling within the meaning of RFRA, and we will proceed to consider the final prong of the RFRA test, *i.e.*, whether HHS has shown that the contraceptive mandate is "the least restrictive means of furthering that compelling governmental interest."

B

The least-restrictive-means standard is exceptionally demanding, and it is not satisfied here. HHS has not shown that it lacks other means of achieving its desired goal without imposing a substantial burden on the exercise of religion by the objecting parties in these cases.

The most straightforward way of doing this would be for the Government to assume the cost of providing the four contraceptives at issue to any women who are unable to obtain them under their health-insurance policies due to their employers' religious objections. This would certainly be less restrictive of the plaintiffs' religious liberty, and HHS has not shown, that this is not a viable alternative. HHS has not provided any estimate of the average cost per employee of providing access to these contraceptives, two of which, according to the FDA, are designed primarily for emergency use.

HHS contends that RFRA does not permit us to take this option into account because "RFRA cannot be used to require creation of entirely new programs." But we see nothing in RFRA that supports this argument, and drawing the line between the "creation of an entirely new program" and the modification of an existing program (which RFRA surely allows) would be fraught with problems. HHS's view that RFRA can never require the Government to spend even a small amount reflects a judgment about the importance of religious liberty that was not shared by the Congress that enacted that law.

In the end, however, we need not rely on the option of a new, government-funded program in order to conclude that the HHS regulations fail the least-restrictive-means test. HHS itself has demonstrated that it has at its disposal an approach that is less restrictive than requiring employers to fund contraceptive methods that violate their religious beliefs. As we explained above, HHS has already established an accommodation for nonprofit organizations with religious objections. Under that accommodation, the organization can self-certify that it opposes providing coverage for particular contraceptive services. If the organization makes such a certification, the organization's insurance issuer or third-party administrator must "[e]xpressly exclude contraceptive coverage from the group health insurance coverage provided in connection with the group health plan" and "[p]rovide separate payments for any contraceptive services required to be covered" without imposing "any cost-sharing requirements . . . on the eligible organization, the group health plan, or plan participants or beneficiaries."

We do not decide today whether an approach of this type complies with RFRA for purposes of all religious claims. At a minimum, however, it does not impinge on the plaintiffs' religious belief that providing insurance coverage for the contraceptives at issue here violates their religion, and it serves HHS's stated interests equally well.

The principal dissent identifies no reason why this accommodation would fail to protect the asserted needs of women as effectively as the contraceptive mandate, and there is none. Under the accommodation, the plaintiffs' female employees would continue to receive contraceptive coverage without cost sharing for all FDA-approved contraceptives, and they would continue to "face minimal logistical and administrative obstacles," because their employers' insurers would be responsible for providing information and coverage.

C

HHS and the principal dissent argue that a ruling in favor of the objecting parties in these cases will lead to a flood of religious objections regarding a wide variety of medical procedures and drugs, such as vaccinations and blood transfusions, but HHS has made no effort to substantiate this prediction. HHS points to no evidence that insurance plans in existence prior to the enactment of ACA excluded coverage for such items. Nor has HHS provided evidence that any significant number of employers sought exemption, on religious grounds, from any of ACA's coverage requirements other than the contraceptive mandate.

It is HHS's apparent belief that no insurance-coverage mandate would violate RFRA — no matter how significantly it impinges on the religious liberties of employers — that would lead to intolerable consequences. Under HHS's view, RFRA would permit the Government to require all employers to provide coverage for any medical procedure allowed by law in the jurisdiction in question — for instance, third-trimester abortions or assisted suicide. The owners of many closely held corporations could not in good conscience provide such coverage, and thus HHS would effectively exclude these people from full participation in the economic life of the Nation. RFRA was enacted to prevent such an outcome.

In any event, our decision in these cases is concerned solely with the contraceptive mandate. Our decision should not be understood to hold that an insurance-coverage mandate must necessarily fall if it conflicts with an employer's religious beliefs. Other coverage requirements, such as immunizations, may be supported by different interests (for example, the need to combat the spread of infectious diseases) and may involve different arguments about the least restrictive means of providing them.

The principal dissent raises the possibility that discrimination in hiring, for example on the basis of race, might be cloaked as religious practice to escape legal sanction. Our decision today provides no such shield. The Government has a compelling interest in providing an equal opportunity to participate in the workforce without regard to race, and prohibitions on racial discrimination are precisely tailored to achieve that critical goal.

The contraceptive mandate, as applied to closely held corporations, violates RFRA. Our decision on that statutory question makes it unnecessary to reach the First Amendment claim raised by Conestoga and the Hahns.

Justice KENNEDY, concurring.

It seems to me appropriate, in joining the Court's opinion, to add these few remarks. At the outset it should be said that the Court's opinion does not have the breadth and sweep ascribed to it by the respectful and powerful dissent. The Court and the dissent disagree on the proper interpretation of the Religious Freedom and Restoration Act of 1993 (RFRA), but do agree on the purpose of that statute. It is to ensure that interests in religious freedom are protected.

In our constitutional tradition, freedom means that all persons have the right to believe or strive to believe in a divine creator and a divine law. For those who choose this course, free exercise is essential in preserving their own dignity and in striving for a self-definition shaped by their religious precepts. Free exercise in this sense implicates more than just freedom of belief. It means, too, the right to express those beliefs and to establish one's religious (or nonreligious) self-definition in the political, civic, and economic life of our larger community. But in a complex society and an era of pervasive governmental regulation, defining the proper realm for free exercise can be difficult. In these cases the plaintiffs deem it necessary to exercise their religious beliefs within the context of their own closely held, for-profit corporations. They claim protection under RFRA, the federal statute discussed with care and in detail in the Court's opinion.

It is important to confirm that a premise of the Court's opinion is its assumption that the HHS regulation here at issue furthers a legitimate and compelling interest in the health of female employees.

But the Government has not made the second showing required by RFRA, that the means it uses to regulate is the least restrictive way to further its interest. As the Court's opinion explains, the record in these cases shows that there is an existing, recognized, workable, and already-implemented framework to provide coverage. That framework is one that HHS has itself devised, that the plaintiffs have not criticized with a specific objection that has been considered in detail by the courts in this litigation, and that is less restrictive than the means challenged by the plaintiffs in these cases.

On this record and as explained by the Court, the Government has not met its burden of showing that it cannot accommodate the plaintiffs' similar religious objections under this established framework. RFRA is inconsistent with the insistence of an agency such as HHS on distinguishing between different religious believers — burdening one while accommodating the other — when it may treat both equally by offering both of them the same accommodation.

Justice GINSBURG, with whom Justice SOTOMAYOR joins, and with whom Justice BREYER and Justice KAGAN join as to all but Part III-C-1, dissenting.

In a decision of startling breadth, the Court holds that commercial enterprises, including corporations, along with partnerships and sole proprietorships, can opt out of any law (saving only tax laws) they judge incompatible with their sincerely held religious beliefs. Compelling governmental interests in uniform compliance with the law, and disadvantages that religion-based opt-outs impose on others, hold no sway, the Court decides, at least when there is a "less restrictive alternative." And such an alternative, the Court suggests, there always will be whenever, in lieu of tolling an enterprise claiming a religion-based exemption, the government, *i.e.,* the general public, can pick up the tab.

The Court does not pretend that the First Amendment's Free Exercise Clause demands religion-based accommodations so extreme, for our decisions leave no doubt on that score. Instead, the Court holds that Congress, in the Religious Freedom Restoration Act of 1993 (RFRA), dictated the extraordinary religion-based exemptions today's decision endorses. In the Court's view, RFRA demands accommodation of a for-profit corporation's religious beliefs no matter the impact that accommodation may have on third parties who do not share the corporation owners' religious faith-in these cases, thousands of women employed by Hobby Lobby and Conestoga or dependents of persons those corporations employ. Persuaded that Congress enacted RFRA to serve a far less radical purpose, and mindful of the havoc the Court's judgment can introduce, I dissent.

I

"The ability of women to participate equally in the economic and social life of the Nation has been facilitated by their ability to control their reproductive lives." Congress acted on that understanding when, as part of a nationwide insurance program intended to be comprehensive, it called for coverage of preventive care responsive to women's needs. Carrying out Congress' direction, the Department of Health and Human Services

(HHS), in consultation with public health experts, promulgated regulations requiring group health plans to cover all forms of contraception approved by the Food and Drug Administration (FDA). The genesis of this coverage should enlighten the Court's resolution of these cases.

The Affordable Care Act (ACA), in its initial form, specified three categories of preventive care that health plans must cover at no added cost to the plan participant or beneficiary. The scheme had a large gap, however; it left out preventive services that "many women's health advocates and medical professionals believe are critically important." To correct this oversight, Senator Barbara Mikulski introduced the Women's Health Amendment, which added to the ACA's minimum coverage requirements a new category of preventive services specific to women's health.

Women paid significantly more than men for preventive care, the amendment's proponents noted; in fact, cost barriers operated to block many women from obtaining needed care at all. See, e.g., (statement of Sen. Feinstein) ("Women of childbearing age spend 68 percent more in out-of-pocket health care costs than men."); (statement of Sen. Mikulski) ("copayments are [often] so high that [women] avoid getting [preventive and screening services] in the first place"). And increased access to contraceptive services, the sponsors comprehended, would yield important public health gains. See, e.g., (statement of Sen. Durbin) ("This bill will expand health insurance coverage to the vast majority of [the 17 million women of reproductive age in the United States who are uninsured] . . . . This expanded access will reduce unintended pregnancies.").

The HRSA adopted guidelines recommending coverage of "[a]ll [FDA-]approved contraceptive methods, sterilization procedures, and patient education and counseling for all women with reproductive capacity." Thereafter, HHS, the Department of Labor, and the Department of Treasury promulgated regulations requiring group health plans to include coverage of the contraceptive services recommended in the HRSA guidelines, subject to certain exceptions.

While the Women's Health Amendment succeeded, a countermove proved unavailing. The Senate voted down the so-called "conscience amendment," which would have enabled any employer or insurance provider to deny coverage based on its asserted "religious beliefs or moral convictions."

II

Any First Amendment Free Exercise Clause claim Hobby Lobby or Conestoga might assert is foreclosed by this Court's decision in

Employment Div., Dept. of Human Resources of Ore. v. Smith (1990). Even if *Smith* did not control, the Free Exercise Clause would not require the exemption Hobby Lobby and Conestoga seek. Accommodations to religious beliefs or observances, the Court has clarified, must not significantly impinge on the interests of third parties.

The exemption sought by Hobby Lobby and Conestoga would override significant interests of the corporations' employees and covered dependents. It would deny legions of women who do not hold their employers' beliefs access to contraceptive coverage that the ACA would otherwise secure. In sum, with respect to free exercise claims no less than free speech claims, "[y]our right to swing your arms ends just where the other man's nose begins."

III

A

Lacking a tenable claim under the Free Exercise Clause, Hobby Lobby and Conestoga rely on RFRA, a statute instructing that "[g]overnment shall not substantially burden a person's exercise of religion even if the burden results from a rule of general applicability" unless the government shows that application of the burden is "the least restrictive means" to further a "compelling governmental interest." In RFRA, Congress "adopt[ed] a statutory rule comparable to the constitutional rule rejected in *Smith*."

RFRA's purpose is specific and written into the statute itself. The Act was crafted to "restore the compelling interest test as set forth in *Sherbert v. Verner* (1963) and *Wisconsin v. Yoder* (1972) and to guarantee its application in all cases where free exercise of religion is substantially burdened."

B

Despite these authoritative indications, the Court sees RFRA as a bold initiative departing from, rather than restoring, pre-*Smith* jurisprudence. The Congress that passed RFRA correctly read this Court's pre-*Smith* case law as including within the "compelling interest test" a "least restrictive means" requirement.

Our decision in *City of Boerne*, it is true, states that the least restrictive means requirement "was not used in the pre-*Smith* jurisprudence RFRA purported to codify." As just indicated, however, that statement does not accurately convey the Court's pre-*Smith* jurisprudence.

C

With RFRA's restorative purpose in mind, I turn to the Act's application to the instant lawsuits. That task, in view of the positions taken by the Court, requires consideration of several questions, each potentially dispositive of Hobby Lobby's and Conestoga's claims: Do for-profit corporations rank among "person[s]" who "exercise . . . religion"? Assuming that they do, does the contraceptive coverage requirement "substantially burden" their religious exercise? If so, is the requirement "in furtherance of a compelling government interest"? And last, does the requirement represent the least restrictive means for furthering that interest?

Misguided by its errant premise that RFRA moved beyond the pre-*Smith* case law, the Court falters at each step of its analysis.

1

RFRA's compelling interest test, as noted, applies to government actions that "substantially burden *a person's exercise of religion.*" Whether a corporation qualifies as a "person" capable of exercising religion is an inquiry one cannot answer without reference to the "full body" of pre-*Smith* "free-exercise caselaw." There is in that case law no support for the notion that free exercise rights pertain to for-profit corporations. Until this litigation, no decision of this Court recognized a for-profit corporation's qualification for a religious exemption from a generally applicable law, whether under the Free Exercise Clause or RFRA. The absence of such precedent is just what one would expect, for the exercise of religion is characteristic of natural persons, not artificial legal entities.

The First Amendment's free exercise protections, the Court has indeed recognized, shelter churches and other nonprofit religion-based organizations. Indeed, until today, religious exemptions had never been extended to any entity operating in "the commercial, profit-making world."

The reason why is hardly obscure. Religious organizations exist to foster the interests of persons subscribing to the same religious faith. Not so of for-profit corporations. Workers who sustain the operations of those corporations commonly are not drawn from one religious community. Indeed, by law, no religion-based criterion can restrict the work force of for-profit corporations. The distinction between a community made up of believers in the same religion and one embracing persons of diverse beliefs, clear as it is, constantly escapes the Court's attention. One can only wonder why the Court shuts this key difference from sight.

The Court's determination that RFRA extends to for-profit corporations is bound to have untoward effects. Although the Court attempts to cabin its language to closely held corporations, its logic extends to corporations of any size, public or private. Little doubt that RFRA claims will proliferate, for the Court's expansive notion of corporate personhood—combined with its other errors in construing RFRA—invites for-profit entities to seek religion-based exemptions from regulations they deem offensive to their faith.

2

Even if Hobby Lobby and Conestoga were deemed RFRA "person[s]," to gain an exemption, they must demonstrate that the contraceptive coverage requirement "substantially burden[s] [their] exercise of religion." Congress no doubt meant the modifier "substantially" to carry weight. In the original draft of RFRA, the word "burden" appeared unmodified. The word "substantially" was inserted pursuant to a clarifying amendment offered by Senators Kennedy and Hatch.

The Court barely pauses to inquire whether any burden imposed by the contraceptive coverage requirement is substantial. Instead, it rests on the Greens' and Hahns' "belie[f] that providing the coverage demanded by the HHS regulations is connected to the destruction of an embryo in a way that is sufficient to make it immoral for them to provide the coverage." I agree with the Court that the Green and Hahn families' religious convictions regarding contraception are sincerely held. But those beliefs, however deeply held, do not suffice to sustain a RFRA claim. RFRA, properly understood, distinguishes between "factual allegations that [plaintiffs'] beliefs are sincere and of a religious nature," which a court must accept as true, and the "legal conclusion . . . that [plaintiffs'] religious exercise is substantially burdened," an inquiry the court must undertake.

Undertaking the inquiry that the Court forgoes, I would conclude that the connection between the families' religious objections and the contraceptive coverage requirement is too attenuated to rank as substantial. The requirement carries no command that Hobby Lobby or Conestoga purchase or provide the contraceptives they find objectionable. Instead, it calls on the companies covered by the requirement to direct money into undifferentiated funds that finance a wide variety of benefits under comprehensive health plans. Those plans, in order to comply with the ACA, must offer contraceptive coverage without cost sharing, just as they must cover an array of other preventive services.

Importantly, the decisions whether to claim benefits under the plans are made not by Hobby Lobby or Conestoga, but by the covered employees and dependents, in consultation with their health care providers. Should an employee of Hobby Lobby or Conestoga share the religious beliefs of the Greens and Hahns, she is of course under no compulsion to use the contraceptives in question. But "[n]o individual decision by an employee and her physician—be it to use contraception, treat an infection, or have a hip replaced—is in any meaningful sense [her employer's] decision or action." It is doubtful that Congress, when it specified that burdens must be "substantia[l]," had in mind a linkage thus interrupted by independent decisionmakers (the woman and her health counselor) standing between the challenged government action and the religious exercise claimed to be infringed. Any decision to use contraceptives made by a woman covered under Hobby Lobby's or Conestoga's plan will not be propelled by the Government, it will be the woman's autonomous choice, informed by the physician she consults.

3

Even if one were to conclude that Hobby Lobby and Conestoga meet the substantial burden requirement, the Government has shown that the contraceptive coverage for which the ACA provides furthers compelling interests in public health and women's well being. Those interests are concrete, specific, and demonstrated by a wealth of empirical evidence.

That Hobby Lobby and Conestoga resist coverage for only 4 of the 20 FDA-approved contraceptives does not lessen these compelling interests. Notably, the corporations exclude intrauterine devices (IUDs), devices significantly more effective, and significantly more expensive than other contraceptive methods. Moreover, the Court's reasoning appears to permit commercial enterprises like Hobby Lobby and Conestoga to exclude from their group health plans all forms of contraceptives.

Perhaps the gravity of the interests at stake has led the Court to assume, for purposes of its RFRA analysis, that the compelling interest criterion is met in these cases. It bears note in this regard that the cost of an IUD is nearly equivalent to a month's full-time pay for workers earning the minimum wage; that almost one-third of women would change their contraceptive method if costs were not a factor; and that only one-fourth of women who request an IUD actually have one inserted after finding out how expensive it would be.

4

After assuming the existence of compelling government interests, the Court holds that the contraceptive coverage requirement fails to satisfy

RFRA's least restrictive means test. But the Government has shown that there is no less restrictive, equally effective means that would both (1) satisfy the challengers' religious objections to providing insurance coverage for certain contraceptives (which they believe cause abortions); and (2) carry out the objective of the ACA's contraceptive coverage requirement, to ensure that women employees receive, at no cost to them, the preventive care needed to safeguard their health and well being. A "least restrictive means" cannot require employees to relinquish benefits accorded them by federal law in order to ensure that their commercial employers can adhere unreservedly to their religious tenets.

Then let the government pay (rather than the employees who do not share their employer's faith), the Court suggests. "The most straightforward [alternative]," the Court asserts, "would be for the Government to assume the cost of providing . . . contraceptives . . . to any women who are unable to obtain them under their health-insurance policies due to their employers' religious objections." The ACA, however, requires coverage of preventive services through the existing employer-based system of health insurance "so that [employees] face minimal logistical and administrative obstacles." Impeding women's receipt of benefits "by requiring them to take steps to learn about, and to sign up for, a new [government funded and administered] health benefit" was scarcely what Congress contemplated.

And where is the stopping point to the "let the government pay" alternative? Suppose an employer's sincerely held religious belief is offended by health coverage of vaccines, or paying the minimum wage, or according women equal pay for substantially similar work? Does it rank as a less restrictive alternative to require the government to provide the money or benefit to which the employer has a religion-based objection?

Because the Court cannot easily answer that question, it proposes something else: Extension to commercial enterprises of the accommodation already afforded to nonprofit religion-based organizations. Ultimately, the Court hedges on its proposal to align for-profit enterprises with nonprofit religion-based organizations. "We do not decide today whether [the] approach [the opinion advances] complies with RFRA for purposes of all religious claims."

In sum, in view of what Congress sought to accomplish, *i.e.,* comprehensive preventive care for women furnished through employer-based health plans, none of the proffered alternatives would satisfactorily serve the compelling interests to which Congress responded.

IV

Would the exemption the Court holds RFRA demands for employers with religiously grounded objections to the use of certain contraceptives extend to employers with religiously grounded objections to blood transfusions (Jehovah's Witnesses); antidepressants (Scientologists); medications derived from pigs, including anesthesia, intravenous fluids, and pills coated with gelatin (certain Muslims, Jews, and Hindus); and vaccinations (Christian Scientists, among others)?

The Court, however, sees nothing to worry about. Today's cases, the Court concludes, are "concerned solely with the contraceptive mandate. Our decision should not be understood to hold that an insurance-coverage mandate must necessarily fall if it conflicts with an employer's religious beliefs. Other coverage requirements, such as immunizations, may be supported by different interests (for example, the need to combat the spread of infectious diseases) and may involve different arguments about the least restrictive means of providing them." But the Court has assumed, for RFRA purposes, that the interest in women's health and well being is compelling and has come up with no means adequate to serve that interest, the one motivating Congress to adopt the Women's Health Amendment.

There is an overriding interest, I believe, in keeping the courts "out of the business of evaluating the relative merits of differing religious claims," or the sincerity with which an asserted religious belief is held. Indeed, approving some religious claims while deeming others unworthy of accommodation could be "perceived as favoring one religion over another," the very "risk the Establishment Clause was designed to preclude." The Court, I fear, has ventured into a minefield by its immoderate reading of RFRA. I would confine religious exemptions under that Act to organizations formed "for a religious purpose," "engage[d] primarily in carrying out that religious purpose," and not "engaged . . . substantially in the exchange of goods or services for money beyond nominal amounts."

Justice BREYER and Justice KAGAN, dissenting.

We agree with Justice Ginsburg that the plaintiffs' challenge to the contraceptive coverage requirement fails on the merits. We need not and do not decide whether either for-profit corporations or their owners may bring claims under the Religious Freedom Restoration Act of 1993. Accordingly, we join all but Part III-C-1 of Justice Ginsburg's dissenting opinion.

C.   The Establishment Clause

5.   When Can Religion Be a Part of Government Activities?

b.   Religion as a Part of Government Activities: Legislative Chaplains (casebook, p. 1773)

In *Marsh v. Chambers* (casebook, p. 1773), the Court upheld the constitutionality of a minister delivering "non-sectarian prayers" before a state legislature's sessions. In *Town of Greece v. Galloway*, the Court considered whether it matters that a town invited almost exclusively Christian clergy over approximately a 10-year period and they often delivered explicitly Christian prayers.

TOWN OF GREECE v. GALLOWAY
134 S. Ct. 1811 (2014)

Justice KENNEDY delivered the opinion of the Court, except as to Part II-B.

The Court must decide whether the town of Greece, New York, imposes an impermissible establishment of religion by opening its monthly board meetings with a prayer. It must be concluded, consistent with the Court's opinion in *Marsh v. Chambers*, that no violation of the Constitution has been shown.

I

Greece, a town with a population of 94,000, is in upstate New York. For some years, it began its monthly town board meetings with a moment of silence. In 1999, the newly elected town supervisor, John Auberger, decided to replicate the prayer practice he had found meaningful while serving in the county legislature. Following the roll call and recitation of the Pledge of Allegiance, Auberger would invite a local clergyman to the front of the room to deliver an invocation. After the prayer, Auberger would thank the minister for serving as the board's "chaplain for the month" and present him with a commemorative plaque. The prayer was intended to place town board members in a solemn and deliberative frame of mind, invoke divine guidance in town affairs, and follow a tradition practiced by Congress and dozens of state legislatures.

The town followed an informal method for selecting prayer givers, all of whom were unpaid volunteers. A town employee would call the congregations listed in a local directory until she found a minister available for that month's meeting. The town eventually compiled a list of willing "board chaplains" who had accepted invitations and agreed to return in the future. The town at no point excluded or denied an opportunity to a would-be prayer giver. Its leaders maintained that a minister or layperson of any persuasion, including an atheist, could give the invocation. But nearly all of the congregations in town were Christian; and from 1999 to 2007, all of the participating ministers were too.

Greece neither reviewed the prayers in advance of the meetings nor provided guidance as to their tone or content, in the belief that exercising any degree of control over the prayers would infringe both the free exercise and speech rights of the ministers. The town instead left the guest clergy free to compose their own devotions. The resulting prayers often sounded both civic and religious themes. Typical were invocations that asked the divinity to abide at the meeting and bestow blessings on the community. Some of the ministers spoke in a distinctly Christian idiom; and a minority invoked religious holidays, scripture, or doctrine.

Respondents Susan Galloway and Linda Stephens attended town board meetings to speak about issues of local concern, and they objected that the prayers violated their religious or philosophical views. At one meeting, Galloway admonished board members that she found the prayers "offensive," "intolerable," and an affront to a "diverse community." After respondents complained that Christian themes pervaded the prayers, to the exclusion of citizens who did not share those beliefs, the town invited a Jewish layman and the chairman of the local Baha'i temple to deliver prayers. A Wiccan priestess who had read press reports about the prayer controversy requested, and was granted, an opportunity to give the invocation.

Galloway and Stephens brought suit in the United States District Court for the Western District of New York. They alleged that the town violated the First Amendment's Establishment Clause by preferring Christians over other prayer givers and by sponsoring sectarian prayers, such as those given "in Jesus' name."

II

In *Marsh v. Chambers*, the Court found no First Amendment violation in the Nebraska Legislature's practice of opening its sessions with a prayer delivered by a chaplain paid from state funds. The decision concluded that legislative prayer, while religious in nature, has long been understood as compatible with the Establishment Clause. As practiced by Congress since the framing of the Constitution, legislative prayer lends gravity to public business, reminds lawmakers to transcend petty differences in pursuit of a higher purpose, and expresses a common aspiration to a just and peaceful society. The Court has considered this symbolic expression to be a "tolerable acknowledgement of beliefs widely held," rather than a first, treacherous step towards establishment of a state church.

Marsh is sometimes described as "carving out an exception" to the Court's Establishment Clause jurisprudence, because it sustained legislative prayer without subjecting the practice to "any of the formal 'tests' that have traditionally structured" this inquiry. The Court in *Marsh* found those tests unnecessary because history supported the conclusion that legislative invocations are compatible with the Establishment Clause. The First Congress made it an early item of business to appoint and pay official chaplains, and both the House and Senate have maintained the office virtually uninterrupted since that time.

Marsh must not be understood as permitting a practice that would amount to a constitutional violation if not for its historical foundation. The case teaches instead that the Establishment Clause must be interpreted "by reference to historical practices and understandings." That the First Congress provided for the appointment of chaplains only days after approving language for the First Amendment demonstrates that the Framers considered legislative prayer a benign acknowledgment of religion's role in society. In the 1850's, the judiciary committees in both the House and Senate reevaluated the practice of official chaplaincies after receiving petitions to abolish the office. The committees concluded that the office posed no threat of an establishment because lawmakers were not compelled to attend the daily prayer, no faith was excluded by law, nor any favored, and the cost of the chaplain's salary imposed a vanishingly small burden on taxpayers. *Marsh* stands for the proposition that it is not necessary to define the precise boundary of the Establishment Clause where history shows that the specific practice is permitted. Any test the Court adopts must acknowledge a practice that was accepted by the Framers and has withstood the critical scrutiny of time and political change. A test that would sweep away what has so long been settled would create new controversy and begin anew the very divisions along religious lines that the Establishment Clause seeks to prevent.

The Court's inquiry, then, must be to determine whether the prayer practice in the town of Greece fits within the tradition long followed in Congress and the state legislatures.

A

Respondents maintain that prayer must be nonsectarian, or not identifiable with any one religion; and they fault the town for permitting guest chaplains to deliver prayers that "use overtly Christian terms" or "invoke specifics of Christian theology." A prayer is fitting for the public sphere, in their view, only if it contains "the most general, nonsectarian reference to God," and eschews mention of doctrines associated with any one faith.

An insistence on nonsectarian or ecumenical prayer as a single, fixed standard is not consistent with the tradition of legislative prayer outlined in the Court's cases. The Court found the prayers in *Marsh* consistent with the First Amendment not because they espoused only a generic theism but because our history and tradition have shown that prayer in this limited context could "coexis[t] with the principles of disestablishment and religious freedom." The Congress that drafted the First Amendment would have been accustomed to invocations containing explicitly religious themes of the sort respondents find objectionable. One of the Senate's first chaplains, the Rev. William White, gave prayers in a series that included the Lord's Prayer, the Collect for Ash Wednesday, prayers for peace and grace, a general thanksgiving, St. Chrysostom's Prayer, and a prayer seeking "the grace of our Lord Jesus Christ, &c."

To hold that invocations must be nonsectarian would force the legislatures that sponsor prayers and the courts that are asked to decide these cases to act as supervisors and censors of religious speech, a rule that would involve government in religious matters to a far greater degree than is the case under the town's current practice of neither editing or approving prayers in advance nor criticizing their content after the fact. Our Government is prohibited from prescribing prayers to be recited in our public institutions in order to promote a preferred system of belief or code of moral behavior. It would be but a few steps removed from that prohibition for legislatures to require chaplains to redact the religious content from their message in order to make it acceptable for the public sphere. Government may not mandate a civic religion that stifles any but the most generic reference to the sacred any more than it may prescribe a religious orthodoxy.

Respondents argue, in effect, that legislative prayer may be addressed only to a generic God. The law and the Court could not draw this line for each specific prayer or seek to require ministers to set aside their nuanced and deeply personal beliefs for vague and artificial ones. There is doubt, in any event, that consensus might be reached as to what qualifies as generic or nonsectarian. Honorifics like "Lord of Lords" or "King of Kings" might strike a Christian audience as ecumenical, yet these titles may have no place in the vocabulary of other faith traditions.

In rejecting the suggestion that legislative prayer must be nonsectarian, the Court does not imply that no constraints remain on its content. The relevant constraint derives from its place at the opening of legislative sessions, where it is meant to lend gravity to the occasion and reflect values long part of the Nation's heritage. Prayer that is solemn and respectful in tone, that invites lawmakers to reflect upon shared ideals and common ends before they embark on the fractious business of governing, serves that legitimate function. If the course and practice over time shows that the invocations denigrate nonbelievers or religious minorities, threaten damnation, or preach conversion, many present may consider the prayer to fall short of the desire to elevate the purpose of the occasion and to unite lawmakers in their common effort. That circumstance would present a different case than the one presently before the Court.

The prayers delivered in the town of Greece do not fall outside the tradition this Court has recognized. A number of the prayers did invoke the name of Jesus, the Heavenly Father, or the Holy Spirit, but they also invoked universal themes, as by celebrating the changing of the seasons or calling for a "spirit of cooperation" among town leaders.

Absent a pattern of prayers that over time denigrate, proselytize, or betray an impermissible government purpose, a challenge based solely on the content of a prayer will not likely establish a constitutional violation. *Marsh*, indeed, requires an inquiry into the prayer opportunity as a whole, rather than into the contents of a single prayer.

Finally, the Court disagrees with the view taken by the Court of Appeals that the town of Greece contravened the Establishment Clause by inviting a predominantly Christian set of ministers to lead the prayer. The town made reasonable efforts to identify all of the congregations located within its borders and represented that it would welcome a prayer by any minister or layman who wished to give one. That nearly all of the congregations in town turned out to be Christian does not reflect an aversion or bias on the part of town leaders against minority faiths. So long as the town maintains a policy of nondiscrimination, the Constitution does not require it to search beyond its borders for non-Christian prayer givers in an effort to achieve religious balancing. The quest to promote "a 'diversity' of religious views" would require the town "to make wholly inappropriate judgments about the number of religions [it] should sponsor and the relative frequency with which it should sponsor each," a form of government entanglement with religion that is far more troublesome than the current approach.

B

Respondents further seek to distinguish the town's prayer practice from the tradition upheld in *Marsh* on the ground that it coerces participation by nonadherents. They and some *amici* contend that prayer conducted in the intimate setting of a town board meeting differs in fundamental ways from the invocations delivered in Congress and state legislatures, where the public remains segregated from legislative activity and may not address the body except by occasional invitation. Citizens attend town meetings, on the other hand, to accept awards; speak on matters of local importance; and petition the board for action that may affect their economic interests, such as the granting of permits, business licenses, and zoning variances. Respondents argue that the public may feel subtle pressure to participate in prayers that violate their beliefs in order to please the board members from whom they are about to seek a favorable ruling. In their view the fact that board members in small towns know many of their constituents by name only increases the pressure to conform.

It is an elemental First Amendment principle that government may not coerce its citizens "to support or participate in any religion or its exercise." On the record in this case the Court is not persuaded that the town of Greece, through the act of offering a brief, solemn, and respectful prayer to open its monthly meetings, compelled its citizens to engage in a religious observance. The inquiry remains a fact-sensitive one that considers both the setting in which the prayer arises and the audience to whom it is directed.

The prayer opportunity in this case must be evaluated against the backdrop of historical practice. As a practice that has long endured, legislative prayer has become part of our heritage and tradition, part of our expressive idiom, similar to the Pledge of Allegiance, inaugural prayer, or the recitation of "God save the United States and this honorable Court" at the opening of this Court's sessions. It is presumed that the reasonable observer is acquainted with this tradition and understands that its purposes are to lend gravity to public proceedings and to acknowledge the place religion holds in the lives of many private citizens, not to afford government an opportunity to proselytize or force truant constituents into the pews.

The principal audience for these invocations is not, indeed, the public but lawmakers themselves, who may find that a moment of prayer or quiet reflection sets the mind to a higher purpose and thereby eases the task of governing. For members of town boards and commissions, who often serve part-time and as volunteers, ceremonial prayer may also reflect the values they hold as private citizens. The prayer is an opportunity for them to show who and what they are without denying the right to dissent by those who disagree.

The analysis would be different if town board members directed the public to participate in the prayers, singled out dissidents for opprobrium, or indicated that their decisions might be influenced by a person's acquiescence in the prayer opportunity. No such thing occurred in the town of Greece.

In their declarations in the trial court, respondents stated that the prayers gave them offense and made them feel excluded and disrespected. Offense, however, does not equate to coercion. Adults often encounter speech they find disagreeable; and an Establishment Clause violation is not made out any time a person experiences a sense of affront from the expression of contrary religious views in a legislative forum, especially where, as here, any member of the public is welcome in turn to offer an invocation reflecting his or her own convictions.

Ceremonial prayer is but a recognition that, since this Nation was founded and until the present day, many Americans deem that their own existence must be understood by precepts far beyond the authority of government to alter or define and that willing participation in civic affairs can be consistent with a brief acknowledgment of their belief in a higher power, always with due respect for those who adhere to other beliefs. The prayer in this case has a permissible ceremonial purpose. It is not an unconstitutional establishment of religion.

The town of Greece does not violate the First Amendment by opening its meetings with prayer that comports with our tradition and does not coerce participation by nonadherents.

Justice ALITO, with whom Justice SCALIA joins, concurring.

I write separately to respond to the principal dissent, which really consists of two very different but intertwined opinions. One is quite narrow; the other is sweeping. I will address both. [W]hat we find here is that the principal dissent's objection, in the end, is really quite niggling. According to the principal dissent, the town could have avoided any constitutional problem in either of two ways.

II

A

First, the principal dissent writes, "[i]f the Town Board had let its chaplains know that they should speak in nonsectarian terms, common to diverse religious groups, then no one would have valid grounds for complaint." But any argument that nonsectarian prayer is constitutionally required runs headlong into a long history of contrary congressional practice.

Not only is there no historical support for the proposition that only generic prayer is allowed, but as our country has become more diverse, composing a prayer that is acceptable to all members of the community who hold religious beliefs has become harder and harder. It was one thing to compose a prayer that is acceptable to both Christians and Jews; it is much harder to compose a prayer that is also acceptable to followers of Eastern religions that are now well represented in this country. Many local clergy may find the project daunting, if not impossible, and some may feel that they cannot in good faith deliver such a vague prayer.

In addition, if a town attempts to go beyond simply *recommending* that a guest chaplain deliver a prayer that is broadly acceptable to all members of a particular community (and the groups represented in different communities will vary), the town will inevitably encounter sensitive problems. Must a town screen and, if necessary, edit prayers before they are given? If prescreening is not required, must the town review prayers after they are delivered in order to determine if they were sufficiently generic? And if a guest chaplain crosses the line, what must the town do? Must the chaplain be corrected on the spot? Must the town strike this chaplain (and perhaps his or her house of worship) from the approved list?

B

If a town wants to avoid the problems associated with this first option, the principal dissent argues, it has another choice: It may "invit[e] clergy of many faiths." "When one month a clergy member refers to Jesus, and the next to Allah or Jehovah," the principal dissent explains, "the government does not identify itself with one religion or align itself with that faith's citizens, and the effect of even sectarian prayer is transformed."

If, as the principal dissent appears to concede, such a rotating system would obviate any constitutional problems, then despite all its high rhetoric, the principal dissent's quarrel with the town of Greece really boils down to this: The town's clerical employees did a bad job in compiling the list of potential guest chaplains. For that is really the only difference between what the town did and what the principal dissent is willing to accept. The Greece clerical employee drew up her list using the town directory instead of a directory covering the entire greater Rochester area. If the task of putting together the list had been handled in a more sophisticated way, the employee in charge would have realized that the town's Jewish residents attended synagogues on the Rochester side of the border and would have added one or more synagogues to the list. But the mistake was at worst careless, and it was not done with a discriminatory intent. (I would view this case very differently if the omission of these synagogues were intentional.)

III

While the principal dissent, in the end, would demand no more than a small modification in the procedure that the town of Greece initially followed, much of the rhetoric in that opinion sweeps more broadly. Indeed, the logical thrust of many of its arguments is that prayer is *never* permissible prior to meetings of local government legislative bodies.

The principal dissent claims to accept the Court's decision in *Marsh v. Chambers,* which upheld the constitutionality of the Nebraska Legislature's practice of prayer at the beginning of legislative sessions, but the principal dissent's acceptance of *Marsh* appears to be predicated on the view that the prayer at issue in that case was little more than a formality to which the legislators paid scant attention.

There can be little doubt that the decision in *Marsh* reflected the original understanding of the First Amendment. It is virtually inconceivable that the First Congress, having appointed chaplains whose responsibilities prominently included the delivery of prayers at the beginning of each daily session, thought that this practice was inconsistent with the Establishment Clause. And since this practice was well established and undoubtedly well known, it seems equally clear that the state legislatures that ratified the First Amendment had the same understanding.

V

This brings me to my final point. I am troubled by the message that some readers may take from the principal dissent's rhetoric and its highly imaginative hypotheticals. For example, the principal dissent conjures up the image of a litigant awaiting trial who is asked by the presiding judge to rise for a Christian prayer, of an official at a polling place who conveys the expectation that citizens wishing to vote make the sign of the cross before casting their ballots, and of an immigrant seeking naturalization who is asked to bow her head and recite a Christian prayer. Although I do not suggest that the implication is intentional, I am concerned that at least some readers will take these hypotheticals as a warning that this is where today's decision leads—to a country in which religious minorities are denied the equal benefits of citizenship.

Nothing could be further from the truth. All that the Court does today is to allow a town to follow a practice that we have previously held is permissible for Congress and state legislatures. In seeming to suggest otherwise, the principal dissent goes far astray.

Justice THOMAS, with whom Justice SCALIA joins as to Part II, concurring in part and concurring in the judgment.

I write separately to reiterate my view that the Establishment Clause is "best understood as a federalism provision," and to state my understanding of the proper "coercion" analysis.

I

As I have explained before, the text and history of the [Establishment] Clause "resis[t] incorporation" against the States. If the Establishment Clause is not incorporated, then it has no application here, where only municipal action is at issue.

As an initial matter, the Clause probably prohibits Congress from establishing a national religion. The text of the Clause also suggests that Congress "could not interfere with state establishments, notwithstanding any argument that could be made based on Congress' power under the Necessary and Proper Clause." That choice of language—"Congress shall make no law"—effectively denied Congress any power to regulate state establishments.

II

Even if the Establishment Clause were properly incorporated against the States, the municipal prayers at issue in this case bear no resemblance to the coercive state establishments that existed at the founding. "The coercion that was a hallmark of historical establishments of religion was coercion of religious orthodoxy and of financial support *by force of law and threat of penalty.*"

Thus, to the extent coercion is relevant to the Establishment Clause analysis, it is actual legal coercion that counts-not the "subtle coercive pressures" allegedly felt by respondents in this case. The majority properly concludes that "[o]ffense . . . does not equate to coercion," since "[a]dults often encounter speech they find disagreeable[,] and an Establishment Clause violation is not made out any time a person experiences a sense of affront from the expression of contrary religious views in a legislative forum." I would simply add, in light of the foregoing history of the Establishment Clause, that "[p]eer pressure, unpleasant as it may be, is not coercion" either.

Justice BREYER, dissenting.

In my view, the Court of Appeals' conclusion and its reasoning are convincing. Justice Kagan's dissent is consistent with that view, and I join it. I also here emphasize several factors that I believe underlie the conclusion that, on the particular facts of this case, the town's prayer practice violated the Establishment Clause.

First, Greece is a predominantly Christian town, but it is not exclusively so. A map of the town's houses of worship introduced in the District Court shows many Christian churches within the town's limits. It also shows a Buddhist temple within the town and several Jewish synagogues just outside its borders, in the adjacent city of Rochester, New York. Yet during the more than 120 monthly meetings at which prayers were delivered during the record period (from 1999 to 2010), only four prayers were delivered by non-Christians. And all of these occurred in 2008, shortly after the plaintiffs began complaining about the town's Christian prayer practice and nearly a decade after that practice had commenced.

Second, the town made no significant effort to inform the area's non-Christian houses of worship about the possibility of delivering an opening prayer.

Third, in this context, the fact that nearly all of the prayers given reflected a single denomination takes on significance. That significance would have been the same had all the prayers been Jewish, or Hindu, or Buddhist, or of any other denomination. The significance is that, in a context where religious minorities exist and where more could easily have been done to include their participation, the town chose to do nothing.

Fourth, the fact that the board meeting audience included citizens with business to conduct also contributes to the importance of making more of an effort to include members of other denominations. It does not, however, automatically change the nature of the meeting from one where an opening prayer is permissible under the Establishment Clause to one where it is not.

Fifth, it is not normally government's place to rewrite, to parse, or to critique the language of particular prayers. And it is always possible that members of one religious group will find that prayers of other groups (or perhaps even a moment of silence) are not compatible with their faith. Despite this risk, the Constitution does not forbid opening prayers. But neither does the Constitution forbid efforts to explain to those who give the prayers the nature of the occasion and the audience.

In seeking an answer to that fact-sensitive question, "I see no test-related substitute for the exercise of legal judgment." Having applied my legal judgment to the relevant facts, I conclude, like Justice Kagan, that the town of Greece failed to make reasonable efforts to include prayer givers of minority faiths, with the result that, although it is a community of several faiths, its prayer givers were almost exclusively persons of a single faith. Under these circumstances, I would affirm the judgment of the Court of Appeals that Greece's prayer practice violated the Establishment Clause.

Justice KAGAN, with whom Justice GINSBURG, Justice BREYER, and Justice SOTOMAYOR join, dissenting.

For centuries now, people have come to this country from every corner of the world to share in the blessing of religious freedom. Our Constitution promises that they may worship in their own way, without fear of penalty or danger, and that in itself is a momentous offering. Yet our Constitution makes a commitment still more remarkable — that however those individuals worship, they will count as full and equal American citizens. A Christian, a Jew, a Muslim (and so forth) — each stands in the same relationship with her country, with her state and local communities, and with every level and body of government. So that when each person performs the duties or seeks the benefits of citizenship, she does so not as an adherent to one or another religion, but simply as an American.

I respectfully dissent from the Court's opinion because I think the Town of Greece's prayer practices violate that norm of religious equality-the breathtakingly generous constitutional idea that our public institutions belong no less to the Buddhist or Hindu than to the Methodist or Episcopalian. I do not contend that principle translates here into a bright separationist line. To the contrary, I agree with the Court's decision in *Marsh v. Chambers* (1983), upholding the Nebraska Legislature's tradition of beginning each session with a chaplain's prayer. And I believe that pluralism and inclusion in a town hall can satisfy the constitutional requirement of neutrality; such a forum need not become a religion-free zone. But still, the Town of Greece should lose this case. The practice at issue here differs from the one sustained in *Marsh* because Greece's town meetings involve participation by ordinary citizens, and the invocations given — directly to those citizens — were predominantly sectarian in content. Still more, Greece's Board did nothing to recognize religious diversity: In arranging for clergy members to open each meeting, the Town never sought (except briefly when this suit was filed) to involve, accommodate, or in any way reach out to adherents of non-Christian religions. So month in and month out for over a decade, prayers steeped in only one faith, addressed toward members of the public, commenced meetings to discuss local affairs and distribute government benefits. In my view, that practice does not square with the First Amendment's promise that every citizen, irrespective of her religion, owns an equal share in her government.

I

To begin to see what has gone wrong in the Town of Greece, consider several hypothetical scenarios in which sectarian prayer—taken straight from this case's record—infuses governmental activities. None involves, as this case does, a proceeding that could be characterized as a legislative session, but they are useful to elaborate some general principles. In each instance, assume (as was true in Greece) that the invocation is given pursuant to government policy and is representative of the prayers generally offered in the designated setting:

You are a party in a case going to trial; let's say you have filed suit against the government for violating one of your legal rights. The judge bangs his gavel to call the court to order, asks a minister to come to the front of the room, and instructs the 10 or so individuals present to rise for an opening prayer. The clergyman faces those in attendance and says: "Lord, God of all creation. . . . We acknowledge the saving sacrifice of Jesus Christ on the cross. We draw strength . . . from his resurrection at Easter. Jesus Christ, who took away the sins of the world, destroyed our death, through his dying and in his rising, he has restored our life. Blessed are you, who has raised up the Lord Jesus, you who will raise us, in our turn, and put us by His side. . . . Amen." The judge then asks your lawyer to begin the trial.

It's election day, and you head over to your local polling place to vote. As you and others wait to give your names and receive your ballots, an election official asks everyone there to join him in prayer. He says: "We pray this [day] for the guidance of the Holy Spirit as [we vote] . . . . Let's just say the Our Father together. 'Our Father, who art in Heaven, hallowed be thy name; thy Kingdom come, thy will be done, on earth as it is in Heaven. . . .'" And after he concludes, he makes the sign of the cross, and appears to wait expectantly for you and the other prospective voters to do so too.

You are an immigrant attending a naturalization ceremony to finally become a citizen. The presiding official tells you and your fellow applicants that before administering the oath of allegiance, he would like a minister to pray for you and with you. The pastor steps to the front of the room, asks everyone to bow their heads, and recites: "[F]ather, son, and Holy Spirit—it is with a due sense of reverence and awe that we come before you [today] seeking your blessing . . . . You are . . . a wise God, oh Lord, . . . as evidenced even in the plan of redemption that is fulfilled in Jesus Christ. We ask that you would give freely and abundantly wisdom to one and to all . . . in the name of the Lord and Savior Jesus Christ, who lives with you and the Holy Spirit, one God for ever and ever. Amen."

I would hold that the government officials responsible for the above practices—that is, for prayer repeatedly invoking a single religion's beliefs in these settings—crossed a constitutional line. I have every confidence the Court would agree.

Why? The reason, of course, has nothing to do with Christianity as such. This opinion is full of Christian prayers, because those were the only invocations offered in the Town of Greece. But if my hypotheticals involved the prayer of some other religion, the outcome would be exactly the same. Suppose, for example, that government officials in a predominantly Jewish community asked a rabbi to begin all public functions with a chanting of the Sh'ma and V'ahavta. ("Hear O Israel! The Lord our God, the Lord is One. . . . Bind [these words] as a sign upon your hand; let them be a symbol before your eyes; inscribe them on the doorposts of your house, and on your gates.") Or assume officials in a mostly Muslim town requested a muezzin to commence such functions, over and over again, with a recitation of the Adhan. ("God is greatest, God is greatest. I bear witness that there is no deity but God. I bear witness that Muhammad is the Messenger of God.") In any instance, the question would be why such government-sponsored prayer of a single religion goes beyond the constitutional pale.

One glaring problem is that the government in all these hypotheticals has aligned itself with, and placed its imprimatur on, a particular religious creed. "The clearest command of the Establishment Clause," this Court has held, "is that one religious denomination cannot be officially preferred over another."

By authorizing and overseeing prayers associated with a single religion—to the exclusion of all others—the government officials in my hypothetical cases (whether federal, state, or local does not matter) have violated that foundational principle. They have embarked on a course of religious favoritism anathema to the First Amendment. And making matters still worse: They have done so in a place where individuals come to interact with, and participate in, the institutions and processes of their government. And so a civic function of some kind brings religious differences to the fore: That public proceeding becomes (whether intentionally or not) an instrument for dividing her from adherents to the community's majority religion, and for altering the very nature of her relationship with her government.

That is not the country we are, because that is not what our Constitution permits. Here, when a citizen stands before her government, whether to perform a service or request a benefit, her religious beliefs do not enter into the picture.

II

In both Greece's and the majority's view, everything I have discussed is irrelevant here because this case involves "the tradition of legislative prayer outlined" in *Marsh v. Chambers*. And before I dispute the Town and Court, I want to give them their due: They are right that, under *Marsh*, legislative prayer has a distinctive constitutional warrant by virtue of tradition. As the Court today describes, a long history, stretching back to the first session of Congress (when chaplains began to give prayers in both Chambers). And so I agree with the majority that the issue here is "whether the prayer practice in the Town of Greece fits within the tradition long followed in Congress and the state legislatures."

Where I depart from the majority is in my reply to that question. Instead, the prayers given in Greece, addressed directly to the Town's citizenry, were *more* sectarian, and *less* inclusive, than anything this Court sustained in *Marsh*. For those reasons, the prayer in Greece departs from the legislative tradition that the majority takes as its benchmark.

Marsh upheld prayer addressed to legislators alone, in a proceeding in which citizens had no role — and even then, only when it did not "proselytize or advance" any single religion. It was that legislative prayer practice (not every prayer in a body exercising any legislative function) that the Court found constitutional given its "unambiguous and unbroken history." But that approved practice, as I have shown, is not Greece's. None of the history *Marsh* cited — and none the majority details today — supports calling on citizens to pray, in a manner consonant with only a single religion's beliefs, at a participatory public proceeding, having both legislative and adjudicative components. Or to use the majority's phrase, no "history shows that th[is] specific practice is permitted." And so, contra the majority, Greece's prayers cannot simply ride on the constitutional coattails of the legislative tradition *Marsh* described. The Board's practice must, in its own particulars, meet constitutional requirements.

And the guideposts for addressing that inquiry include the principles of religious neutrality I discussed earlier. The government (whether federal, state, or local) may not favor, or align itself with, any particular creed. And that is nowhere more true than when officials and citizens come face to face in their shared institutions of governance. In performing civic functions and seeking civic benefits, each person of this nation must experience a government that belongs to one and all, irrespective of belief. And for its part, each government must ensure that its participatory processes will not classify those citizens by faith, or make relevant their religious differences.

But Greece could not do what it did: infuse a participatory government body with one (and only one) faith, so that month in and month out, the citizens appearing before it become partly defined by their creed-as those who share, and those who do not, the community's majority religious belief. In this country, when citizens go before the government, they go not as Christians or Muslims or Jews (or what have you), but just as Americans (or here, as Grecians). That is what it means to be an equal citizen, irrespective of religion. And that is what the Town of Greece precluded by so identifying

When the citizens of this country approach their government, they do so only as Americans, not as members of one faith or another. And that means that even in a partly legislative body, they should not confront government-sponsored worship that divides them along religious lines. I believe, for all the reasons I have given, that the Town of Greece betrayed that promise. I therefore respectfully dissent from the Court's decision.

Made in the USA
San Bernardino, CA
16 August 2015